NEW DIRECTIONS IN BLENDED LEARNING – CASE STUDIES AND INTERVENTIONS

UNIVERSITY OF BOLTON

NEW DIRECTIONS IN BLENDED LEARNING – CASE STUDIES AND INTERVENTIONS

Edited by
Dr Mohammed Sadiq,
Professor Russell Gurbutt,
Dr Alicia Danielsson &
Dr Brian Williamson

First published in 2023 by Libri Publishing

Copyright © Libri Publishing

Contributors retain copyright of their chapters.

The right of Mohammed Sadiq, Russell Gurbutt, Alicia Danielsson and Brian Williamson to be identified as the editors of this work has been asserted in accordance with the Copyright, Designs and Patents Act, 1988.

ISBN: 978-1-911450-99-3 (Hardback)
ISBN: 978-1-911450-98-6 (Paperback)

All rights reserved. No part of this publication may be reproduced, stored in any retrieval system or transmitted in any form or by any means, electronic, mechanical, photocopying, recording or otherwise, without the prior written permission of the copyright holder for which application should be addressed in the first instance to the publishers. No liability shall be attached to the author, the copyright holder or the publishers for loss or damage of any nature suffered as a result of reliance on the reproduction of any of the contents of this publication or any errors or omissions in its contents.

A CIP catalogue record for this book is available from
The British Library

Cover and Design by Carnegie Book Production

Libri Publishing
Brunel House
Volunteer Way
Faringdon
Oxfordshire
SN7 7YR
Tel: +44 (0)845 873 3837
www.libripublishing.co.uk

Contents

About the Editors and Authors	vii
Chapter Summaries	xiii
Acknowledgments	xviii
Foreword	xix

Chapter 1 Blended Learning – A Strategic View   1
Professor Patrick McGhee

Chapter 2 Definitions and Applications of Models of Blended Learning   21
Dr Abigail Ayishetu Makoji-Stephen and Dr Brian Williamson

Chapter 3 A Learning Journey in Different Stages – Blended Learning in Action   33
Professor Russell Gurbutt

Chapter 4 Making a Clinical Diagnosis – A Blended Approach   47
Claire Goulden and Dr Mark Holland

Chapter 5 The Pursuit of Blended Learning Intervention Strategies through Professional Collaboration – Supporting TIRI and Campus Plus Strategy   65
Dr Mohammed Sadiq

Chapter 6 Staff Perceptions of the Transition to Blended and Online Teaching and Learning   85
Professor Paul Hollins, Dr Sarah Telfer & Daniel Edmondson

Chapter 7 Blended Learning – Authentic Assessment and Clinical Supervision   111
Dr Nick Wadsworth and Mel Greenhalgh

Chapter 8 Combining E-Learning and Face-to-Face Teaching in the Law School – The Digitally Enhanced Flipped Classroom for Teaching and Learning the Law   131
Dr Alicia Danielsson

Chapter 9 Lessons of How to Support Students Working on the Front-Line during the COVID-19 Pandemic – Blended Learning Support Strategies   163
Dr Joanne Smith

Chapter 10 Using Peer-Led Online Community Groups to Foster Connectedness during COVID-19   183
Dr Tara Chandler and Jo Luckhurst

Compilation of References   199

About the Editors and Authors

Dr Mohammed Sadiq

Mohammed Sadiq is an assistant teaching professor at the University of Bolton with extensive experience in blended and experiential learning technology, and a qualified teaching professional passionate about using his expertise to enhance the blended-learning body of knowledge. In addition, Mohammed has industrial knowledge to deliver and transfer essential accountancy/business skills to students of accountancy. Mohammed has served as a chief examiner and a subject-matter expert with a world-leading international qualifications body.

Professor Russell Gurbutt

Professor Gurbutt is a teaching professor at the University of Bolton. Russell is a creative and inspiring teacher drawing on decades of experience and continues to seek to inspire others. Formerly a Royal Navy Artificer (1977), having gained a 'Best all-round Apprentice' Award he was promoted to BRNC Dartmouth where he subsequently became the Senior Sub Lieutenant (General List Executive Branch). Awarded a ceremonial sword following graduation from BRNC Dartmouth, he saw service with the Hong Kong Squadron, the Armilla Patrol (Arabian Gulf), Far East (China Sea) and African deployments.

Dr Alicia Danielsson

Dr Alicia Danielsson is head of centre (contemporary coronial law) and assistant teaching professor in law, with particular interests and expertise in the areas of human rights law, EU law, international business and trade law, jurisprudence, legal research methods, international criminal justice and comparative law.

Dr Brian Williamson

After gaining his doctorate in mathematics in 1985, Brian Williamson was an independent full-time one-to-one mathematics tutor for 31 years. He joined the University of Bolton as a full-time lecturer in 2016. He holds a master's in special educational needs, is a fellow of the Royal Society of Arts (Innovative Education Network) and editorial board member of the *Educational Journal of Living Theories*.

Professor Patrick McGhee

Professor Patrick McGhee is assistant vice chancellor at the University of Bolton and chair of the Campus Plus Steering Group. Educated at the universities of Glasgow and Oxford, he was also a visiting fellow/scholar at the universities of Cornell, Yale and MIT in the USA in 2017. He is the author of *The Academic Quality Handbook* (Kogan Page) and *Thinking Psychologically* (Palgrave) and co-editor of *Accounting for Relationships* (Methuen). He has been an occasional columnist for the *Guardian*, the BBC and the *Times Higher* and is a UK National Teaching Fellow.

Dr Abigail Ayishetu Makoji-Stephen

Abigail Makoji-Stephen started her career as a supervisor of schools in her home country, Nigeria, before moving to the UK to pursue a postgraduate degree. She holds a bachelor of arts in English language and a master's in education (leadership and management) from Liverpool Hope University, UK. She recently graduated from the University of Bolton with a doctorate in education (EdD) with a focus on blended learning.

Dr Mark Holland

Mark is an associate TIRI professor and professional doctorate student at the University of Bolton. He qualified from St George's Hospital in 1988 and is a registered specialist in geriatric medicine and general internal medicine. Mark worked as a consultant in acute medicine until 2020. At Bolton he teaches advanced clinical practitioners. His research interest is in early decision making in acutely unwell medical patients. Outside of work his interests include family, cycling and trying in vain to keep his allotment free from weeds. Mark is the module lead for Diagnostics and Therapeutics and designed the *House, M.D.* whiteboard teaching.

Claire Goulden

Claire is a trainee advanced clinical practitioner at the University of Bolton and a registered physiotherapist. She qualified from the Manchester School of Physiotherapy in 2003 and during her junior rotations developed a specialist interest in respiratory medicine, in particular non-invasive ventilation. In 2009 she established the Sleep Service for Wigan Borough, which she continues to manage, and was clinical lead for the COVID-19 CPAP response on the Enhanced Respiratory Care Unit at Royal Albert Edward Infirmary. In her spare time, she enjoys outdoor activities with her family, playing tennis and attempting to learn Spanish. Claire was one of the top students in her diagnostics and therapeutics class.

Professor Paul Hollins

Professor Paul Hollins is responsible for supporting collaborative research activities across the School of Arts at the University of Bolton. Paul is an experienced academic and has published extensively across a diverse range of subjects in the arts, education, business and technology domains. He is currently engaged by the University in the EU Horizon 2020 project RAGE (Realising an Applied Gaming Ecosystem Europe), in chairing the Whitman 200 conference and in supporting the School of Arts' collaborative research projects.

Dr Sarah Telfer

Dr Sarah Telfer is an associate TIRI professor in education at the University of Bolton and operational lead for Initial Teacher Education programmes. She is an experienced educational leader and teacher educator with a background in ESOL and literacy teaching and learning, teacher training and staff development in a range of different educational contexts.

Dr Nick Wadsworth

Dr Nick Wadsworth is a sport and exercise psychologist, senior lecturer, and programme leader of the MSc Applied Sport and Exercise Psychology programme at the University of Bolton. He has worked within professional football for the past nine years and his research interests include practitioner development, athletic identity and coaching philosophy.

Mel Greenhalgh

Mel Greenhalgh is the programme leader and senior lecturer for the MSc/PGDip Cognitive Behavioural Psychotherapies courses at the University of Bolton. Mel is a practising cognitive behavioural psychotherapist, working in private practice for the last five years following an NHS career as a therapist in community and forensic settings for 12 years (and leaving the NHS in the position of clinical lead for CBT). Mel is accredited by the British Association of Behavioural and Cognitive Psychotherapists (BABCP) as an accredited psychotherapist. Mel began her academic career as a lecturer at the Open University in 2008, followed by an honorary role at the University of Chester in 2016, with Mel becoming programme leader and senior lecturer for the MSc/PGDip Cognitive Behavioural Psychotherapies courses at the University of Bolton in 2017.

Dr Joanne Smith

Dr Joanne Smith is an associate teaching professor at the University of Bolton. Joanne is divisional leader in health and society working with the teams in health and social care, community development and youth work, early years and childhood studies. Joanne graduated with a BA (Hons) in humanities and has since completed an MSc in sociology, PGCE qualifications and a PhD entitled 'The Work–Life Balance Experiences of Women Undertaking HE-level Work-based Learning' in June 2018. She is a senior fellow of the Higher Education Academy.

Dr Tara Chandler

Tara is a senior lecturer in psychology at the University of Bolton. She is a chartered psychologist (DARPT) and has held academic positions in teaching and research from 2008. Tara is particularly interested in social ecological models to explore student experiences in higher education. Due to adjustments in pedagogy based on COVID-19 regulations, Tara developed an interest in how to maintain the student experience using online measures.

Jo Luckhurst

Jo is a senior lecturer in psychology at the University of Bolton. She is a chartered occupational psychologist and has spent most of her career specialising in employment, working with those who have complex needs to help increase their employment prospects. Having moved into academia, Jo uses her experience from practice to support non-traditional students through the learning process. Having already recognised the importance of connectedness to campus for student outcomes, the COVID-19 pandemic was an opportunity to explore alternative methods for students to build and maintain connectedness to their university, peers and tutors.

Daniel Edmondson

Dan Edmondson is a lecturer, researcher and PhD candidate specialising in high-impact practices to support student retention in higher education. Dan also has research interests in the areas of Technology Enhanced Learning, Online Pedagogy and Student Engagement.

Chapter Summaries

Chapter 1: Blended Learning – A Strategic View
Professor Patrick McGhee

This chapter seeks to lay out the strategic considerations which have informed the development, implementation and review of our blended-learning strategy, which we have termed 'Campus Plus'. In that context we will consider in turn: What does 'strategy' mean in the context of a pedagogical approach in higher education? What evidence did we draw on to develop our blended-learning Campus Plus strategy? What were our core institutional strategic principles for blended learning? What practical actions did we take to implement the strategy? What might our experience of applying innovative teaching during lockdown to campus-based blended learning tell us about existing ideas and research about blended-learning strategies? The implications of our experience for a general understanding of strategic approaches to blended learning are explored.

Chapter 2: Definitions and Applications of Models of Blended Learning
Dr Abigail Ayishetu Makoji-Stephen and Dr Brian Williamson

In this chapter blended learning is defined and some models of how blended learning can be applied in education are discussed. The application of blended learning has been principally implemented by teaching practitioners at the University of Bolton as part of the Campus Plus strategy to (1) improve pedagogy, (2) improve engagement, (3) increase access and flexibility, and (4) increase educational gain. This chapter defines and critically evaluates blended-learning methodologies and provides a rationale for embedding blended learning into teaching practice at the University of Bolton.

Chapter 3: A Learning Journey in Different Stages – Blended Learning in Action
Professor Russell Gurbutt

This chapter showcases five contributions that have been developed during the pandemic and are being taken forward into the 2021–22 academic year. It commences with service-user integrated learning, championing a patient focus and then using Padlet for student engagement. Next, a decision-making interactive video is used to determine if students can make patient-focused decisions. Decision making under time pressure is developed through a midwifery escape room. Finally, a virtual wellbeing café illustrates self and peer care around handling stressful care situations. These examples showcase colleagues' creativity in developing learners' insights into professional practice (knowledge acquisition, development, application and reflection).

Chapter 4: Making a Clinical Diagnosis – A Blended Approach
Claire Goulden and Dr Mark Holland

Drawing inspiration from the TV series *House, M.D.*, COVID-19 was a catalyst to work with trainee Advanced Clinical Practitioners outside the classroom to develop clinical diagnostic skills. Adopting House's use of a whiteboard to think out loud, students are invited to watch episodes of the show prior to the first class. They are divided into groups of two-to-four students, and each week one group works through a short clinical vignette, following the conventional steps of history, examination, and requesting and interpreting investigations. At each stage the students seek further information from the tutor in an exchange of emails, until the diagnosis is reached. At the following week's class they present their analysis and diagnosis to their peers.

Chapter 5: The Pursuit of Blended Learning Intervention Strategies through Professional Collaboration – Supporting TIRI and Campus Plus Strategy
Dr Mohammed Sadiq

The Teaching Excellence Network (TEN) is a community of practice developed at the University of Bolton to complement TIRI (Teaching Intensive, Research Informed) and Campus Plus strategies. The platform supports the education and continuing professional development programmes and philosophies of the University. The aim of this community of practice is to create a platform from which teaching practitioners can collaborate, share ideas and discuss teaching interventions that would enhance the student and teacher experience. This study review indicates general satisfaction and belief in the initiative and its capacity to develop teachers and students. It is a simple programme which draws in professionals from both further and higher education to the principle of achieving improvement in teaching and learning, especially in the field of blended teaching and learning practices. It fits well into the philosophies of excellence which all institutions strive to attain.

Chapter 6: Staff Perceptions of the Transition to Blended and Online Teaching and Learning
Professor Paul Hollins, Dr Sarah Telfer and Daniel Edmondson

This chapter discusses the impact of the transition to blended and online teaching and learning on the teaching staff at the University of Bolton. It reports on the preliminary findings of a questionnaire which is part of an ongoing longitudinal study of staff perceptions of the support and guidance provided to them, both during the pandemic and in relation to the current implementation of the University's new strategy entitled 'Campus Plus'.

Chapter 7: Blended Learning – Authentic Assessment and Clinical Supervision
Dr Nick Wadsworth and Mel Greenhalgh

This chapter outlines two case studies from two postgraduate programmes delivered at the University of Bolton: Applied Sport and Exercise Psychology (MSc) and Cognitive Behavioural Psychotherapies (MSc/PGDip). Both programmes utilised core principles from the University's new Campus Plus framework to support students throughout the pandemic. On the Applied Sport and Exercise Psychology (MSc) the Campus Plus model and the GAME+ framework were both used to create authentic assessments, in line with the changing landscape of applied sport and exercise psychology, to improve the employability skills of students. On the Cognitive Behavioural Psychotherapies (MSc/PGDip) programmes, blended learning was used to refine the delivery of clinical supervision and lectures in a way that would enhance student self-determination and experience.

Chapter 8: Combining E-Learning and Face-to-Face Teaching in the Law School – The Digitally Enhanced Flipped Classroom for Teaching and Learning the Law
Dr Alicia Danielsson

Flipped classroom strategies are a convenient form of blended learning, whereby the content-heavy learning elements are provided via reading tasks which are to be completed by students before they attend their lectures, thereby freeing up valuable face-to-face class time for live problem-solving activities. In theory, this approach presents an ideal solution to assist teachers with the balancing of content and practical skills development and increased student engagement.

Chapter 9: Lessons of How to Support Students Working on the Front-Line during the COVID-19 Pandemic – Blended Learning Support Strategies
Dr Joanne Smith

The COVID-19 pandemic was described as unprecedented in our time, as we faced a situation where the UK population was 'locked down' to restrict people coming together to avoid infection. From an HE and University perspective, this meant an end to face-to-face, classroom-based teaching. From March 2020, teaching staff found themselves teaching online, which was a significant transition: for many staff this was not usual practice, as we had previously been classroom focused. Hence this method, previously only undertaken in exceptional circumstances, became a new norm. Teaching became embedded within the home, which was further altered as teachers and learners facilitated parallel activity, with their children at home. This required careful negotiation of time and space to allow for the facilitation of the different activities and commitments. I have been teaching for over 25 years and have experienced many changes but nothing so rapid. The pandemic might be seen as a watershed. Here I would like to share some of what happened and depict some of the adaptions which might be able to show us the potential for change.

Chapter 10: Using Peer-Led Online Community Groups to Foster Connectedness during COVID-19
Dr Tara Chandler and Jo Luckhurst

Having a strong sense of connectedness has been linked to increased health and wellbeing amongst the student population. A greater feeling of campus connectedness has been associated with increased rates of retention, which is influenced by higher levels of engagement in academic activities. Furthermore, a greater sense of campus connectedness is associated with an increased likelihood of accessing support services within the university and increased engagement with tutors and peer support. These positive associations with campus connectedness have been shown to lead to better academic outcomes and ultimately are predictors of successful graduate employment outcomes.

Acknowledgments

We thank the participants in our research studies and our co-authors for their chapters. Assistant Vice Chancellor Professor Patrick McGhee for his vision and leadership with TIRI and Campus Plus. The University of Bolton for funding and helping with some of this research. Dr Mohammed Sadiq, Professor Russell Gurbutt, Dr Alicia Danielsson, Dr Brian Williamson. Teaching colleagues at the University of Bolton group and to all the staff that support our students. The Students' Union for their continued support with TIRI and Campus Plus.

Foreword

This book explores the long-term innovations that have emerged across all faculties and subject areas of a higher education institution since the radical move to online teaching during the COVID-19 pandemic and the closure of university campuses between 2019 and 2021. *New Directions in Blended Learning* explores the use of blended-learning approaches, tools and methods within higher education by providing experiential insights into the teaching and learning practices of the University of Bolton, showcasing specifically selected experiences and reflections from academics from all faculties and subject areas of the institution. The chapters analyse key blended/hybrid teaching strategies, their outcomes, implications and recommendations for future developments in this area of teaching approaches and curriculum design in a variety of practical applied contexts which bring many of the associated conceptual models to life. While showcasing core themes like flipped learning, this book is primarily aimed at the practitioner but will be beneficial for higher education and college teachers, teacher trainers, administrators, practitioners, academics, researchers and students involved in pedagogy and the practical application of pedagogical tools.

The University of Bolton is a small-to-medium-sized university in Greater Manchester, UK, with a rather unique approach to the provision of higher education teaching and learning. As such, in contrast to the majority of universities across the country, the University of Bolton places its core emphasis on teaching excellence rather than scholarly research. According to this curriculum approach, the utmost priority is given to the effective support of students' learning. Prior to the COVID-19 pandemic, this focus involved over-average timetabled contact time, emphasis on academic tutorials and academic skills support, and a strong focus on social inclusion. This approach corresponded well with the key demographic of the University and the goal to widen participation, which is a central theme across all departments. As such, the University was also unique in its pre-pandemic mode of delivery, whereby the course provision of the University was solely face-to-face on campus.

The COVID-19 pandemic saw universities move their teaching entirely online in light of the imposed national lockdowns. For a university that had not previously engaged in online teaching provision, this case involved one of the purest adaptations in the sector. Considering the absence of pre-existing online delivery tools or necessary infrastructure, the University of Bolton developed its new approach to online teaching figuratively on a blank canvas. This has allowed the University to create a unique approach to blended learning and teaching models that sets this institution apart from others. Most notably, this university-wide step towards blended learning was not influenced by pre-existing facilities, yet benefitted from the specialisations of an institution that has dedicated more than two decades to the advancement of innovative teaching practices across all departments. Within a traditional on-campus face-to-face setting, it was always the University's goal to innovate teaching and learning within further and higher education by investing in the progression of innovative student-centred pedagogical approaches which placed students and the student learning journey at the heart of any curricular activities. In particular, the institution already had a previous track record of prioritising and following an individualised approach, including an emphasis on one-to-one tutorials for sense making, increased high-quality contact time, small group interactive and innovative class activities, and a focus on transferable employability skills within the entire curriculum, across the institution, to ensure graduate employment opportunities. As is the case with the philosophy of blended learning itself, the University of Bolton has sought to move away from traditional teacher-centred, lecture-based forms of teaching within on-campus settings. As such, they moved to solely online equivalents during the COVID-19 pandemic, which opened up new ways to embed these activities online.

Another unique characteristic of the development, specifically within the University, was the previous focus on physical teaching provision on campus. Considering the face-to-face, on-campus approach used by the University prior to the move to online teaching, the infrastructure and equipment provided may not have been as advanced as had been the case in other larger higher education institutions. This, however, places the University of Bolton in a unique position, such that the development throughout the pandemic and thereafter, when universities returned to on-campus teaching, is an excellent case study to showcase what is possible without the need for extensive investment in physical resources. As has been previously emphasised, the priority within the approach from this university is student learning and the student learning experience throughout their university journeys.

What is this book about?

Within this book, the University of Bolton showcases one of the purest moves from traditional on-campus teaching approaches towards new directions within the area of blended learning. The term 'blended learning' has been used within the literature for more than two decades. First and foremost, this suggests a combination of both face-to-face teaching alongside a variety of technological enhancements, most notably internet-based software applications as tools to enhance pedagogical design. Most literature in this area has focused strongly on the use of these approaches within educational disciplines. However, the radical shift that was prompted by the move to online teaching due to the COVID-19 pandemic meant that all disciplines and subject areas faced similar developmental educational needs while, at the same time, needing to adapt these to the specifics of the subject in question. Through interdepartmental and interdisciplinary collaboration, all faculties and departments within the University were able to implement novel ways to enhance the student learning journey in all subject areas.

Of course, there is not only one way, or one correct way, to design blended learning, as blended learning includes numerous concepts, techniques and methods. Moreover, the scope or spectrum of diversity amongst sector needs and subject matter requirements varies significantly between disciplines. It is natural that an approach in a subject such as engineering may differ significantly to learning and teaching requirements in subjects such as accountancy or law. Again, the

University of Bolton has been in a particularly advantageous position to showcase the range of different implementations of blended approaches across all faculties within the institution. As such, this book contains a collection of case studies which may provide inspiration and guidance for higher education institutions worldwide, to further enhance the implementation of blended-learning aspects, in many of their forms, within curricula.

Who is this book for?

Teaching and learning as a subject matter, and as a skill, are necessary and crucial for the progression of almost all aspects of human life. Naturally, this book would be a valuable resource for numerous audiences. Most notably, however, this book will be of relevance to universities or college faculty members who are seeking inspiration and exposure to novel ways to update, innovate and enhance pedagogical design and teaching practices. Moreover, academic staff or professionals specifically involved in the area of teacher training or technical staff employed for the enhancement of learning technology or learning designers will benefit from this book.

The chapters in this book represent a collage of case examples of a university's approach to pursuing excellent education through the Teaching Intensive, Research Informed approach to education, with cross-university contributions to the strategic agenda of developing excellent education that aligns to external benchmarks, which capture something of the richness of the student's learning journey and preparation or enhancement of graduate employment. Commencing with the context of a strategic institutional perspective, attention turns to some essential waypoints in this journey that can be represented as: the student at the heart of education design, considering effective blended learning, maintaining an employment focus, and supporting the student throughout their journey.

CHAPTER ONE

Blended Learning – A Strategic View

Professor Patrick McGhee

This chapter seeks to lay out the strategic considerations which have informed the development, implementation and review of our blended-learning strategy, which we have termed 'Campus Plus'. In that context we will consider in turn: What does 'strategy' mean in the context of a pedagogical approach in higher education? What evidence did we draw on to develop our blended-learning Campus Plus strategy? What were our core institutional strategic principles for blended learning? What practical actions did we take to implement the strategy? What might our experience of applying innovative teaching during lockdown to campus-based blended learning tell us about existing ideas and research about blended-learning strategies? The implications of our experience for a general understanding of strategic approaches to blended learning are explored.

What does 'strategy' mean in the context of a pedagogical approach in higher education?

Strategic planning is typically presented as involving the development of a long-range perspective with broad-brush goals, driven by a vision and supported by a guiding framework for priority actions. But strategies are also typically contested – and should be. Overall, strategic endeavour is an exercise in managing judgements under conditions of uncertainty, risk, ambiguity and contradiction. In practice, inputs are not only voluminous but come from different discourses, histories and methodologies. The overarching framework in this context becomes narrative rather than mathematical in form. Pivot tables give way to persuasion in a process which is essentially heuristic rather than algorithmic.

Despite this reality of uncertainty, to some extent the traditional strategic development model assumes a degree of stability, or at least predictable trajectories, in the operating environment. However, in spring 2020 the COVID-19 pandemic impacted on educational institutions globally at every level and, for a time at least, halted teaching systems in their tracks. How can a strategy be possible in such circumstances? Universities had to abandon or put on hold plans for portfolio, estate and staffing expansion. International recruitment strategies for universities in the UK, North America, Australia and elsewhere were particularly badly disrupted. Some basic ideas underpinning educational experience were not only disrupted but dismantled. Not only were the distinctive and in some cases definitional modes of educational transactions fractured, but the very idea of 'campus', which normally gives material effect to the abstract process of learning and engagement, became problematised. Both in the immediate sense in terms of the complicated logistics of access to delivery events and learning resources, but also in the wider sense of: what are campuses for?

As the world emerged out of lockdown and politicians sought to balance health and economic imperatives, universities, as largely autonomous institutions unlike state schools, were left to their own scheduling and management of the return to some kind of normality. What should the strategy be for the great 'Reopening' of campuses?

As COVID-related restrictions were lifted, universities were faced with the 'metastrategic' challenge of whether to (1) go back to their pre-COVID pedagogic and pastoral strategies, (2) embrace a 'pseudo-COVID' strategy by continuing to teach remotely as they did during lockdown, or (3) develop a genuinely post-COVID strategy, designing teaching and support in a way which incorporated what had been learned about learning that we did not know before – or had chosen not to notice.

While the complexities of the student and staff experience during the lockdown period have been examined extensively (e.g., Erlam et al., 2021; Cameron-Standerford et al., 2020) there has been less reflective consideration of the return to campus teaching. The question which remains, and the debate to which this volume seeks to contribute, is: how should we teach, given what we learned during COVID?

Many institutions drifted back to a pre-COVID strategy in piecemeal fashion, with some courses and departments returning to face-to-face teaching more rapidly, and more enthusiastically, than others. Students too varied in their responses, with younger students wanting the kind of university experience they had paid or borrowed for while more mature students, already facing challenges on travel, time and 360-degree caring responsibilities, felt attracted to extending the opportunity to study from home.

At the University of Bolton, we examined the options in the period of reopening after lockdown to see what choices we could make with our students to apply the experience of delivering digitally during lockdown to the post-pandemic environment. During 2020–21 we had initially sought to make our campus COVID-secure (see McGhee, 2020) and then, as the range of options for campus-based teaching expanded, developed our more expansive model of blended campus and online learning, which we describe as *Campus Plus*™ (McGhee, 2022). In that context, this chapter lays out the broader strategic considerations that inform that model and the way our staff and students continue to develop it. The case studies in this volume seek to demonstrate a key metastrategic principle for pedagogy: the best strategy is the one which lays out a framework for bottom-up innovation for staff and students.

What evidence did we draw on to develop our Campus Plus strategy?

Our strategy was to develop a model which confirmed our primary focus on face-to-face teaching but in the context of such learning being supported extensively by interactive digital activities. We aimed to promote local departmental solutions within an overall institutional framework which recognises variation in student expectations, skills, learning outcomes and professional-body expectations. This localised approach also made it easier for students to be more directly involved in the design, implementation and review of our model. We were not starting from scratch: the model reaffirmed our pedagogical philosophy of TIRI (Teaching Intensive, Research Informed) which prioritised evidence-based methods of treating students as individuals.

The initial impetus for the development of Campus Plus came from the University Vice-Chancellor, Professor George Holmes, who highlighted how the institution should be focusing on developing what had been learned during lockdown:

> Some of the innovative pedagogic practice which tutors and support staff were able to engage students in remotely over the last 18 months has been exemplary. We have had some excellent feedback from students. Our delivery on campus this year cannot therefore simply put the clock back to 2019; we must not lose the innovation which has been so well thought through by colleagues across the University.
>
> Vice Chancellor George Holmes, email to staff September 2021

Drawing on national research by JISC and their student digital experience insights survey, the QAA Building a Taxonomy for Digital Learning resources and our own regular internal polling of students during 2020 and 2021, a steering committee identified 12 strategic principles to guide our practical engagement with blended learning institutionally. These principles, and the accompanying action plan, were subject to institution-wide consultation (including live webinars which used an anonymous interactive polling platform) to gauge opinions and solicit suggestions for development and implementation.

A key plank of our Campus Plus model has been the move towards a delivery model for all our modules of 70% traditional on-campus face-to-face teaching alongside 30% remote digital – the latter principally through synchronous delivery.

The student voice was particularly important in shaping Campus Plus. In the chapter by Chandler and Luckhurst in this volume, we document how engaging directly and flexibly with the student voice enabled academic staff to intercept potential problems associated with accessibility, knowledge attrition and engagement. Additionally, the autonomy and empowerment associated with the student voice prompted students themselves to develop active learning, problem solving and enhanced motivation.

In national terms, the principal UK university network services and support organisation, JISC, carried out a large survey of students to explore their views of online teaching (JISC, 2020). This work had identified seven key issues which were important to students.

The first issue raised by students was what JISC characterised as "**get the basics right**". This included reliable, accessible Wi-Fi on campus and elsewhere; reliable hardware and software; clearly navigable learning content, timetabling and session scheduling; and proper audio and lighting for online sessions. One aspect of learning which lockdown made clear was that we probably routinely underestimate the general equalisation of access to resources that a campus, as a concentrated site of expertise and resources with considerable informal redundancy built in, routinely provides. Clearly, under-resourced students often lack access to technology and 'digital capital' which even a well-resourced campus will struggle to resolve. But in terms of access to basic technology and support, 'get the basics right' remains a sound principle.

Students also wanted their learning sessions to be more **interactive**. This probably reflects a desire to enjoy the learning experience but also an instrumental focus on succeeding. However, more and more large companies recognise that the route to consumer engagement and long-term relationships is increasingly about facilitating interaction before, during and after a purchase, in terms of interaction with both the company and other prospective or previous customers. Customers are encouraged to share ideas about improving products or how they have used the product at home. Customer reviewers research and debate the pros and cons of different purchase options and add-ons. At a time when so many educational institutions seek to succeed by treating students as customers, companies are learning the benefits of treating customers as students.

Another key element identified by students was that of **making recordings of teaching sessions available** to aid personal learning preferences, revision and catch up. This is not a surprise. Students routinely watch online videos live or on demand and 'on catchup'.

Free of the distraction of taking notes, students can in principle engage more directly with the themes and issues of the session with a focus on detailed aspects of the content deferred until later. The bounded nature of strategy here was clear. Our existing technology had not been designed to deal with the sheer scale and breadth of different sessions to be automatically recorded and so we invested in new scalable systems. There was also the issue that while the use of occasional, lecturer-led recordings was accepted as a useful complementary tactic to face-to-face campus lectures, a small section of the academic community was concerned that centralised, mass recordings and repositories could undermine the consensus on the centrality of academic teaching. We addressed this concern with a policy which retained the recordings for as long as they would be needed by students for a module, but not so long that they might be used to replace lecturing staff.

A further issue raised by the JISC survey was the support by students for lecturers to think about the **pace of delivery** and consider "shorter bursts with regular breaks". The experience of lockdown and novel online delivery put such issues on the agenda in a way they were not before.

In this context, there has been much anecdotal reference to the way in which online sessions can reduce student engagement or being fully present. Many of these debates appeared to be predicated on the questionable assumption that in the classroom all students are fully engaged and attentive and that any deviation from that will be noted. However, as the contribution by Sadiq to this volume makes clear, support via technologies such as AI-based systems can enhance student engagement.

Another interesting pointer to student needs which came out of the JISC research was the appetite amongst students to be offered opportunities to talk to and **ask questions of lecturers and peers**, and for there to be adequate individual and group support. Our adoption of Mentimeter, PebblePad, Flipgrid, Padlet and Zoom chat, and breakout-room functions, helped support all students participate in peer and tutor communications.

The final point highlighted in the JISC survey was another example of the need to get the basics right: "**improve communication**," providing "reminders of when sessions were going to start, when assignments were due" and "an accessible list of frequently asked questions (FAQs)". We addressed this (as many institutions did) with an FAQ which was updated on a daily, then weekly, basis.

What did our own students say they wanted? Our surveys of nearly 2,000 students across 2020 and 2021 highlighted clear patterns which informed our development of Campus Plus. The two best predictors of students' level of focus on employability was that their tutor online gave "a clear introduction at the beginning of the session on what will be covered and why" and checked that "all students are comfortable with the technology being used". The best predictors of low levels of contemplating dropping out and of high course satisfaction was positive agreement with the statement "Overall, I would say my tutors have increased the help they have given me in these areas during this year".

When asked in 2021 what features of learning during remote teaching during COVID should be retained post-pandemic, our students identified two key issues: (1) interactivity and (2) access to lecture recordings.

What are our core institutional strategic principles for blended learning?

On the basis of the JISC research, our own two internal surveys of staff and students, as well as consultation with staff across the institution in webinars facilitated by Mentimeter, we developed and refined 12 principles for our model of blended learning.

1. *Teaching-Led*
   The University is a teaching-led institution and as such places a particular emphasis on effective teaching, individualised learning and on student achievement that leads to positive outcomes – such as graduate employment. This latter element has never been more important, given the focus upon this by the regulator (Office for Students).

This strategic principle reaffirmed the value base of the institution while acknowledging the immediate regulatory priorities. This served to emphasise continuity as a means of addressing contemporary challenges.

2. ***TIRI and Student Centredness***

   TIRI should remain our primary philosophy – Teaching Intensive, Research Informed. Students – and their success and outcomes – are at the heart of all that we do. We will continue to seek to embrace a wholly inclusive approach in line with our Access and Participation Strategy and more generally. Students and the Students' Union will be key partners in our strategy.

This principle confirmed the central role of students not just as the focus of reforms and enhancements, but as partners in the change project. This principle was realised with students as full members of investment panels and the Students' Union joining the Steering Group.

3. ***Campus-Based***

   Given that students have an expectation of value for money and a fully rounded learning experience on campus, face-to-face teaching will be the principal delivery format for our programmes.

This principle provided a solid foundation for the expansion of digital delivery. In line with Vermeulen (2017) we were keen to specify what we would *not* be doing. Not only would we not be embracing a fully online delivery model, but we would also *not* be adopting an online-first model – the physical campus would be the heart of our delivery work.

4. ***Technology Core***

   Given the effectiveness and student appetite for interactive technologies that promote flexibility, individualisation, empowerment and fun, educational technology will be a core component of all of our delivery.

We were keen to separate the idea of a significantly more technologically informed pedagogy from the idea of remote digital delivery of courses. We were committed not only to exploiting technology to effect remote synchronous learning but also to connect students on campus with each other. We also were clear about exploiting the scope for technology to transform learning experiences – for example, by making it easier for less-confident students to have a voice in discussions, and to configure their contributions flexibly.

5. **A 'Campus Plus' Model**
   The University will adopt an approach to teaching and learning where approximately, but not prescriptively, 70% of scheduled teaching will be delivered face-to-face, in person, with the remaining 30% delivered using flexible, creative and innovation learning technologies.

This principle, in its specificity, highlighted the scale of the commitment and what we took to be the new default. As the contribution from Danielsson in this volume makes clear, it is not enough to manage campus and online educational inputs in parallel, they must be *blended* in what is effectively a "digitally enhanced flipped classroom".

6. **Local Solutions**
   The success or otherwise of our teaching and learning model for the coming year will depend upon local solutions by academics facilitating local variation, normally led by Schools and Deans, supported by central professional services alongside visible, consistent and imaginative leadership.

In line with research indicating the importance of devolution of decision making or subsidiarity, we knew that implementation needed to have local ownership because that was where the expertise and risk awareness lay.

7. **Centrality of Learning Support**
   The entire learning environment and support infrastructure – including specialist support staff, and for example library, IT and facilities professionals – is crucial to student success.

It is, or should be, self-evident, that a system which tries to harmonise on-campus and remote learning, and to make both of these more fully informed by technology, will require extensive support and redesign by specialists who manage the IT, physical and administrative environments.

8. **Success is Outcome**
    We will measure the success of our Campus Plus delivery in terms of the levels of student satisfaction, staff fulfilment and student outcomes particularly in relation to academic engagement, retention, success and employment.

While we recognise the interest and engagement of staff and students in giving momentum to the rollout of the model, we wanted to be clear that the model was a vehicle for delivery and not an end in itself. This strategic consideration ensured that outcomes would be clear and conspicuously aligned with our other institutional strategies. Imaginative uses of technology during remote delivery which can then be extended to a blended learning model are illustrated in this volume by the contributions on industry engagement (e.g., Sadiq). Similarly, Wadsworth and Greenhalgh highlight how two of our postgraduate programmes used the Campus Plus approach to integrate blended learning into clinical supervision and the creation of authentic assessments to improve employability skills.

9. **A 'Face-to-Face Base'**
    The learning experience for students benefits from a solid foundation established at the outset of the academic semester and year.

Some strategic organisational projects have sought to introduce significantly increased levels of digital remote delivery by focusing on getting the pace of technological change right. However, in this principle, we focused on the idea of making it clear that at the start of the academic year the gravitational centre of teaching and of the staff–student relationship generally would be the physical campus. This reflects the principle of interpersonal relations being a key basis for subsequent technologically mediated communication.

10. **Flexible Creation**
    Success in the development of flexible delivery often requires flexible development and support. In that context, academic and other staff may be best supported by intelligent time management, planned and supported across the academic year in collaboration with their line manager and academic colleagues.

This strategic principle reflected our desire to encourage staff to see Campus Plus not only as a new kind of flexibility for students, but also as an opportunity for more flexible working to support the creation of digital assets and related academic material. We enacted this principle though a range of competitive funding opportunities for staff to free up time in a block or distributed over a period to promote a transformation project. This aligns with research indicating the dangers of top-down asset creation for remote teaching (e.g., Aitchison et al., 2020).

11. *Resourced and Realistic*
    The University is committed to the development of creative, innovative, inclusive, collaborative and, where appropriate, disruptive teaching activities and engagements in order to foster informed and confident learners. This must be balanced with recognition of the academic learning outcomes of the given programme, the expectations of students, the logistical constraints of timetabling and the resources required to deliver the activity effectively and sustainably. This will include specialist facilities as well as IT support in general.

The importance of credibility in leading organisational change has long been recognised in leadership research (Hartney et al., 2022). The promotion of innovation and flexibility in new arrangements for delivery explicitly had to recognise resource constraints and academic standards.

12. *Attendance is Essential*
    Student attendance and engagement is essential to any form of learning. Students will be expected to attend on-campus events in person and online events with an appropriately high level of engagement.

This principle was primarily designed to balance the theme of remote access to learning providing additional flexibility alongside the commitment to teaching events and to other students. However, the work by Danielsson (this volume) highlights how synchronous video delivery – if managed well – can improve tutorial attendance and engagement.

What practical actions did we take to implement the strategy?

In order to make the strategy happen we took a number of decisions in summer and autumn 2021, following staff and student consultation. The most significant of these were: (1) setting up an equipment fund to provide all staff and students with the on-campus and off-campus equipment they needed which they could not otherwise access, (2) profiling all modules around a default of 30% of scheduled teaching remotely delivered, (3) setting up a series of Campus Plus training and development webinars led by professional services, academics and students, (4) revising our promotion criteria to explicitly reference excellence in managing blended learning under the Campus Plus model, (5) launching a Campus Plus Pedagogical Research Fund to identify evidence-based practices that supported excellent blended learning, (6) launching a competitive staff development fund to enable teams of academic or professional service staff to develop their skills and understanding around blending learning and related technologies, (7) installing software to record, store and provide access to all online lectures for a year, (8) formally adopting by Senate resolution the JISC Action Plan Framework for Remote Learning, and (9) developing an evaluation model of staff surveys, amended module evaluations and annual progress reports to Senate, as well review of progress on existing success indicators such as completion, student satisfaction and employment.

What might our experience of applying innovative teaching during lockdown to campus-based blended learning tell us about existing ideas and research about blended learning strategies?

We can more generally ask the question 'what makes blended learning strategies likely to succeed?' and in the present context what does our experience with the Campus Plus strategy tell us? Research suggests that institutional structure, resource support, technology infrastructure, management strategies and ethical considerations are important factors that predict universities' preparedness to promote blended learning initiatives in higher education (Bokolo et al., 2020). However, as with many institutional initiatives on blended learning strategies, these analyses are based on the idea that the transition to blended learning is one of moving from a model which is essentially campus-based to something that is essentially a combination of campus and digital. What we have faced with post-COVID reopening is the unanticipated and historically unique transition of moving *from* online only *to* a combination of campus and digital. The puzzle which most researchers have been trying to understand is how best to move from campus to digital, not from digital to campus plus digital.

This strategic inversion has meant that challenges around training and infrastructure have to some extent moved away from 'more' and towards 'different'. From 'how do we get lecturers more supported and engaged in digital delivery?' to 'how do we learn from those who have been immersed in digital delivery and develop that learning into embedded practices and policies?' In many ways, this is precisely what this volume is about.

As Rasheed and colleagues (2020) have pointed out, while training is one of the main challenges for staff, self-management and overcoming the difficulties in using learning technology are typically the key challenges faced by students. The challenge of synchronising staff, student and infrastructural support is articulated by Sannicandro and colleagues (2021): "it seems necessary to build a framework for the adoption and implementation of 'blended learning' strategies at the institutional level, starting from the construction of a concrete agenda setting shared between the actors of the innovation process". Similarly, Al-Ayed and Al-Tit (2021) have emphasised that a blended learning strategy depends not only on the technological aspects of the learning but also on the people doing the learning. Examples of this are illustrated in this volume by Smith on the development of student communities. As Smith points out, imaginative and holistic support systems were needed for nursing students who were not only learning but also working daily on the medical front-line and dealing with a public health crisis unknown in their life time.

Antunes, Armellini and Howe (2021) highlight the need to support blended learning implementation by *linking* different aspects of initiatives as well as focusing on initiatives per se. They found that the normalisation and effective embedding of digital technology and small group teaching were two of the most crucial factors in driving forward pedagogic transformation. Conversely, they found that inconsistent teaching practices and the lack of student engagement with learning activities were two of the main barriers. Our Campus Plus model enables very different components to be identifiably linked to each other (see for example Gurbutt, this volume).

Studies designed to systematically assess the strategic factors which have an *enduring* impact on the teaching and learning culture in the context of blended learning are difficult to carry out and consequently few and far between (see Ravenscroft & Luhanga, 2018; Han, Wang & Jiang 2019). Mihai and colleagues (2021), however, looked at a range of factors which could potentially support a blended approach across an extended period of time and found five key components. Their critical strategic factors for a mature blended-learning institutional implementation are reflected in our reopening strategy: an integrative approach, a gradual development model, a rigorous evaluation process, strong relations with the University and openness towards co-operation.

Hollins and Telfer (this volume) summarise their own evaluation research into how academic staff responded to the challenges of lockdown, the rapid transition to remote delivery and the development of pedagogical interventions which could be deployed in a blended environment such as that characterised by Campus Plus.

Similar observations have been made by Valantinaitė and Sedereviciūtė-Pačiauskienė (2020: 2) indicating that the challenges students face at the beginning of an engagement with blended learning are not necessarily the same as the challenges they feel they face as experience develops: "As students gain more experience in using an OLE for learning, it is not technical issues and computer literacy that become important, but students' and teachers' attitudes and the motivation to improve and learn". At the heart of this is inclusion. In principle, online learning can open up a wider range of options to enable fair and equitable access for all students. We sought the views of all students in our 2020 survey and explicitly asked learners if there were issues around our remote learning approach which would require additional individual support or adjustment to support plans.

One of the distinctive features of our experience of managing learning remotely and then subsequently during the transition to a more fully blended approach, was the way in which the enforced adoption of specific technologies allowed lecturers to promote in-depth, critical learning while maintaining student engagement and enjoyment. For example, Gurbutt (this volume) reports on the development and remote application of a decision-making interactive video used to assess students in making patient-focused decisions and of decision making under time pressure developed for midwifery. Again, in the health area, Goulden and Holland (this volume) report the use of digital remote whiteboards as a system for facilitating collaborative clinical diagnosis work for advanced care practitioners. In each of these cases, established pedagogic principles – problem orientation, collaboration, deconstruction and decision making – are supported by technologies but are taken in new directions in the context of a more flexible application within remote settings and extended time frames. This work aligns with earlier reviews and analysis which indicate the positive impact blended learning can have on nursing and related areas (e.g., Grønlien et al., 2021). These examples in Campus Plus also support work which suggests that while the increased use of technology in remote learning can lead to a demoralising and ineffective instrumentalism, it need not – but it does require insight and reflectiveness, supported by staff development (Almpanis & Joseph-Richard, 2022).

Reviewing data from 14 Australian universities, Aitchison and colleagues (2020) reported findings from three educational development groups: academic developers, academic language developers and online educational designers. They found that a central theme was the tension arising from a perceived shift in institutional priorities from 'people development' to 'product development'. A focus on learning resources was experienced as a disempowering one, as autonomy declined in relation to priorities and related skill sets. Our investment in staff-initiated proposals for training and development sought to offset this risk.

Kara (2021) has documented the practical challenges that academics and support staff faced during the COVID-19 pandemic: "unreliable internet connectivity and ICT infrastructure, equity in access to remote teaching and learning, staff and students' readiness, assessment of learning, resource constraints, delivery of field and practical courses and quality assurance in emergency remote teaching and learning".

She goes on to note the resultant gaps and inequalities "between learners, institutions and countries".

In summary – what lessons can be learned from the transition to lockdown-led remote digital delivery and then back to blended learning from our work on Campus Plus?

First, in a very fundamental sense it is too early to tell. It is doubtful that any institution has fully absorbed the technological, pedagogical, political, community and, for that matter, ethical dimensions of globally disrupted higher education. Yet some of the changes and challenges – and the international higher education sector's response – are so dramatic that we are able to stand back albeit provisionally and consider what appears to be emerging. For example, from our perspective, pedagogical principles are robustly valid whether informing campus, remote or blended learning. The need for rapid transition from campus to remote, and then cautiously from remote to blended has reminded us, if we needed reminding, that the technical and practical management of learning can masquerade as strategic until the point where the logistical assumptions of that management are swept away. In the future we now have a new test of what poses as a pedagogical principle or strategy: would it still be applicable in a pandemic? We also recognise now more than ever that, under conditions of uncertainty, ambiguity and novelty, devolution of innovation and implementation is the best strategy.

In the end, successful strategic approaches to blended learning are about *metastrategies* – strategies for strategies. What is the right process for the devolution of the adoption of online security for video conferencing is not going to be the same process for interactivity in online teaching sessions. There is no doubt that the pandemic not only illuminated differences in technological capital at the individual, institutional and community level, or that individual learners in too many cases were deprived of opportunities normally afforded by a resource-intensive and accessible university campuses. The cases of this volume, however, show that, equally, facilitating inventiveness under adversity can not only deliver effective alternatives immediately but can have powerful legacies which can benefit all students, and, if they want to embrace it, all institutions.

References

Abusalim, N., Rayyan, M., Jarrah, M., & Sharab, M. (2020). Institutional adoption of blended learning on a budget. *International Journal of Educational Management*, 34(7), 1203–1220. Available from: https://doi.org/10.1108/IJEM-08-2019-0326.

Aitchison, C., Harper, R., Mirriahi, N., & Guerin, C. (2020). Tensions for educational developers in the digital university: Developing the person, developing the product. *Higher Education Research and Development*, 39(2), 171–184. Available from: https://doi.org/10.1080/07294360.2019.1663155.

Al-Ayed, S. I., & Al-Tit, A. A. (2021). Factors affecting the adoption of blended learning strategy. *International Journal of Data and Network Science*, 5, 267–274. Available from: https://doi.org/10.5267/j.ijdns.2021.6.007.

Almpanis, T., & Joseph-Richard, P. (2022). Lecturing from home: Exploring academics' experiences of remote teaching during a pandemic. *International Journal of Educational Research Open*, 3, 100133. Available from: https://doi.org/10.1016/j.ijedro.2022.100133.

Antunes, V. T., Armellini, A., & Howe, R. (2021). Academic staff perspectives on an institution-wide shift to active blended learning. *Italian Journal of Educational Technology*. Available from: https://doi.org/10.17471/2499-4324/1248.

Bokolo, A., Kamaludin, A., Romli, A., Mat Raffei, A. F., A/L Eh Phon, D. N., Abdullah, A., Leong Ming, G., Shukor, N. A., Shukri Nordin, M., & Baba, S. (2020). A managerial perspective on institutions' administration readiness to diffuse blended learning in higher education: Concept and evidence. *Journal of Research on Technology in Education*, 52(1), 37–64. Available from: https://doi.org/10.1080/15391523.2019.1675203.

Cameron-Standerford, A., Menard, K., Edge, C., Bergh, B., Shayter, A., Smith, K., & VandenAvond, L. (2020). The Phenomenon of Moving to Online/Distance Delivery as a Result of COVID-19: Exploring Initial Perceptions of Higher Education Faculty at a Rural Midwestern University. *Front. Educ.*, 5:583881. doi: 10.3389/feduc.2020.583881.

Erlam, G. D., Garrett, N., Gasteiger, N., Lau, K., Hoare, K., Agarwal, S., & Haxell, A. (2021). What really matters: Experiences of emergency remote teaching in university teaching and learning during the COVID-19 pandemic. *Frontiers in Education (Lausanne)*, 6. Available from: https://doi.org/10.3389/feduc.2021.639842.

Grønlien, H. K., Christoffersen, T. E., Ringstad, Ø., Andreassen, M., & Lugo, R. G. (2021). A blended learning teaching strategy strengthens the nursing students' performance and self-reported learning outcome achievement in an anatomy, physiology and biochemistry course – A quasi-experimental study. *Nurse Education in Practice*, 52, 103046–103046. Available from: https://doi.org/10.1016/j.nepr.2021.103046.

Han, X., Wang, Y., & Jiang, L. (2019). Towards a framework for an institution-wide quantitative assessment of teachers' online participation in blended learning implementation. *The Internet and Higher Education*, 42, 1–12. Available from: https://doi.org/10.1016/j.iheduc.2019.03.003.

Hartney, E., Melis, E., Taylor, D., Dickson, G., Tholl, B., Grimes, K., Chan, M., Van Aerde, J., & Horsley, T. (2022). Leading through the first wave of COVID: A Canadian action research study. *Leadership in Health Services*, 35(1), 30–45. Available from: https://doi.org/10.1108/LHS-05-2021-0042.

JISC. Learning and teaching reimagined. August 2020. Available from: https://www.jisc.ac.uk/learning-and-teaching-reimagined.

Kara, A. (2021). Covid-19 pandemic and possible trends into the future of higher education: A review. *Journal of Education and Educational Development*, 8(1). Available from: https://doi.org/10.22555/joeed.v8i1.183.

McGhee, P. (2020) The University of Bolton on Opening its Campuses and Protecting Quality and Standards. June. Available from: https://www.qaa.ac.uk/news-events/blog/university-of-bolton-opening-campuses-and-protecting-quality-and-standards.

McGhee, P. (2022) 'Campus Plus' – An institutional model for success after Covid. April. Available from: https://www.qaa.ac.uk/en/news-events/blog/campus-plus-institutional-model-for-success.

Megahed, N., & Hassan, A. (2022). A blended learning strategy: Reimagining the post-Covid-19 architectural education. *Archnet-Ijar*, 16(1), 184–202. Available from: https://doi.org/10.1108/ARCH-04-2021-0081.

Mihai, A., Questier, F., & Zhu, C. (2021). The institutionalisation of online and blended learning initiatives in politics and international relations at European universities. *European Political Science*, 20(2), 359–377. Available from: https://doi.org/10.1057/s41304-020-00307-5.

Muhuro, P., & Kang'ethe, S. M. (2021). Prospects and pitfalls associated with implementing blended learning in rural-based higher education institutions in southern Africa. *Perspectives in Education*, 39(1), 427–441. Available from: https://doi.org/10.18820/2519593X/pie.v39.i1.26.

QAA in June 2020. Building a Taxonomy for Digital Learning. https://www.qaa.ac.uk/docs/qaa/guidance/building-a-taxonomy-for-digital-learning.pdf.

Rasheed, R. A., Kamsin, A., & Abdullah, N. A. (2020). Challenges in the online component of blended learning: A systematic review. *Computers and Education*, 144, 103701. Available from: https://doi.org/10.1016/j.compedu.2019.103701.

Ravenscroft, B., Luhanga, U. (2018). Enhancing student engagement through an institutional blended learning initiative: A case study. *Teaching and Learning Inquiry*, 6(2), 97–114. Available from: https://doi.org/10.20343/teachlearninqu.6.2.8.

Sannicandro, K., De Santis, A., Bellini, C., & Minerva, T. (2021). Blended learning design for teaching innovation: University teachers' perceptions. *REM: Research on Education and Media*, 13(2), 36–45. Available from: https://doi.org/10.2478/rem-2021-0011.

Valantinaitė, I., & Sederevičiūtė-Pačiauskienė, Ž. (2020). The change in students' attitude towards favourable and unfavourable factors of online learning environments. *Sustainability (Basel, Switzerland)*, 12(19), 7960. Available from: https://doi.org/10.3390/su12197960.

Vermeulen, F. (2017) Many Strategies Fail Because They're Not Actually Strategies. *Harvard Business Review*. November. Available from: https://hbr.org/2017/11/many-strategies-fail-because-theyre-not-actually-strategies.

Acknowledgments

The University of Bolton Campus Plus Steering Group comprised: Janet Galligan, the Students' Union, Dr Julian Coleman, Dr Greg Walker, Dr Gill Waugh, Dr Jane Howarth, Claire Window, Simon Wiggins, Sharon Germaine-Cox, Chris McClelland, Professor Patrick McGhee (Chair).

CHAPTER TWO

Definitions and Applications of Models of Blended Learning

Dr Abigail Ayishetu Makoji-Stephen
and Dr Brian Williamson

The application of blended learning has been principally implemented by teaching practitioners at the University of Bolton as part of the Campus Plus strategy to (1) improve pedagogy, (2) improve engagement, (3) increase access and flexibility, and (4) increase educational gain. This chapter defines and critically evaluates blended learning methodologies and provides a rationale for embedding blended learning into teaching practice.

There has been much pedagogical discussion about the term 'blended learning' in recent years, yet there seems to be no agreed concise definition of the phenomenon. Nevertheless, the literature reports that 'blended learning' as an instructional approach benefits students and institutions (Poon, 2013) and can facilitate improved learning outcomes, enhance flexibility in teaching and learning, facilitate a sense of community and connectivity, support the effective use of resources, and improve student satisfaction. Blended learning has 'proved' beneficial in several ways. Osguthorpe and Graham (2003) identified six reasons for using blended learning: (1) pedagogical richness, (2) access to knowledge, (3) social interaction, (4) personal agency, (5) cost-effectiveness, and (6) ease of revision. A further examination of these six reasons by Graham, Allen and Ure (2003) suggests that the dominant motives for the implementation of blended learning are (1) pedagogical richness, (2) access to knowledge, and (3) cost-effectiveness.

In contrast, Beck's (2010: 282) findings pointed to the fact that students were "especially prone to falling behind on their assignments since the relative amount of outside-the-classroom work is greater". The multiplier effect of this increase in workload is that inadequately prepared students could feel disenchanted with the course. Corroborating, Parsons (2016) notes that students using mobile and blended learning innovations can experience an increase in their stress level, owing to the introduction of mobile apps and could get disoriented in the process.

However, despite all of these perceived benefits and drawbacks, there is still a concern regarding this instructional approach as it is yet to be defined or commonly understood by teachers, administrators and managers in schools and universities. In this chapter, some conflicting definitions and a set of models for the phenomenon we call 'blended learning' are considered because we feel that with its growing popularity as an instructional approach, it is important to attempt to create and explore definitions and pedagogical models to understand how it could contribute optimally to effective teaching and learning.

Conflicting definitions

As explained by Olivier (2011) the concept of blended learning is derived from two words, blended and learning. To blend means to combine things and learning refers to the process of assimilation of new knowledge. According to Milakovich and Wise (2019) blended learning allows students to engage in learning outside the confines of the classroom; with synchronous tools, such as web conferencing, Skype and group chats, and asynchronous tools that include discussion boards, blogs and social networking sites. Kop and Hill (2008), Kliger and Pfeiffer (2011) and Al-Ani (2013) describe blended learning as a hybrid between face-to-face learning and the integration of technology, as a student-centred approach that is framed in constructivism and, in particular, social constructivism learning theories. Bersin (2004: 323) writes that blended learning "is generally looked at as a combination of different training media including technologies, activities and types of events, to create an optimum training program for a specific audience". Commenting further, Bersin (2004: 323) maintained that blended learning "is an instructor-led training supplemented with other electronic formats or vice-versa". The view of blended learning put forward by Bersin appears to be broader than that advanced by authors such as Neumeier (2005: 164), who defines blended learning "as a combination of face-to-face and computer assisted learning in a single teaching and learning environment or different learning environments". This lends credence to the position expressed by Sharpe and colleagues (2006: 18) that, "scholars have difficulty in reaching a consensus around the definition of blended learning".

Making blended learning your own

Some institutions have developed their own language, definitions or typologies to describe their blended practices. Sharpe and colleagues (2006) consider that this lack of clarity with regards to what 'blended learning' actually is may be a strength. It could even be part of the reason why the term is being accepted, as a lack of definition allows institutions to adapt and use the term as they deem fit, and to develop ownership of it. This position appears to agree with the views of Heinze (2008: 8) who, apart from noting that there is no single commonly accepted definition of blended learning, maintained that the lack of a commonly accepted definition affords practitioners the leverage to "negotiate their own meaning" according to the needs of their contexts of practice.

Blended learning and technology

All said, blended learning emerged in the educational context as a result of a combination of factors ranging from the accessibility of computer technology in and outside the classroom and the expansion of the pedagogical potential of ICT for teaching and learning to the disillusionment generated in online learning with the stand-alone adoption of online media (MacDonald, 2008; Hong and Samimy, 2010). From the foregoing definitions, technology appears to be a common component in the use of the blended-learning instructional model. However, Sloman (2007) argues that there is more to blended learning than just the use of technology and it must be as much about varying learning methodology. In addition, blended-learning instructional approaches must be aligned with what motivates learners, as well as the tools necessary to support student learning.

Blending learning and learning interactions

Bergmann and Sams (2012) noted that the new blended models are leveraging the technology to increase student–teacher engagement by providing instruction online. They assert that these models provide a robust platform for teachers to have more time and interact further with the students as this involves the traditional face-to-face learning with online learning.

There is evidence in the literature that research relating to blended learning has been conducted at all levels, looking at the use of both web-based and classroom-based techniques. One such study was conducted by Kitchenham (2005). His study sought to examine teachers' implementation of a blended-learning approach to instruction in three elementary schools, which included the use of technology within classrooms as well as an examination of the degree to which teachers experience perspective transformations due to their engagement with educational technology. Generally, the study suggested that specific components of blended learning were successful when implemented within teachers' classrooms. Similarly, Mirriahi and colleagues (2015) in their study explored a course which was developed to give support to teaching staff and their utilisation of a blended learning model used to interact, mentor and share knowledge with one another. It was also intended to bring to life online and blended learning experience that would effectively offer their students support, using technology and blended learning. The online course, which was titled 'Learning to Teach Online', was designed to offer professional development to teaching staff as well as to support the learning of pedagogic principles related to online and blended learning practices. Key findings from the study suggest that blended learning provides (1) participants an opportunity to gain understanding of theoretical rationale and practical applications, (2) hands-on experiences in lab and simulation environments, and (3) interaction amongst colleagues to gain knowledge of instructional practices.

Models and application of blended learning

Benefits of blended learning relate to the additional time, the increase in student performance as well as the opportunity afforded to students and teachers as a platform for engagement. Others argue that there is a lack of empirical evidence into blended learning. Yeigh and colleagues (2017) comment that blended learning methods are still quite vague and remain a challenging task for most faculties. Another area where blended learning models have been criticised is in the area of workload (Yilmaz, Durak & Yildirim, 2022). Even though there is evidence that blended learning provided students with the ability to review, work collaboratively and extend their learning beyond the frontiers of the classroom, there is the belief that its implementation constitutes an increase in the workload for already challenged students.

The need to identify and clearly define the models of blended learning has continued to evolve over the years. Earlier attempts classified blended learning models into seven categories (Tucker, 2012). However, because of the existence of other definitions of blended learning which appeared to have overlapped, the more recent attempts at defining blended learning have classified the models into four categories, namely rotation, flex, self-blend and enriched-virtual (Staker and Horn, 2012; Kafer, 2013). Even though an attempt was made by Bailey and colleagues (2013) at further simplifying these models, most research in blended learning continues to refer to the four models of blended learning (Watson et al., 2013). The revised blended learning taxonomy according to Staker and Horn (2012: 8–15) includes the following models.

1. **Rotation model**: under this model, in a specific programme within a given course or subject, students are made to rotate on a fixed schedule or at the discretion of the teacher between learning modalities, with at least one of these rotations being

online learning. Under this model, there are different types of rotation, discussed below.

a) **Station rotation**: this is a rotation model implementation in which students are expected to rotate on a fixed schedule or at the discretion of the teacher among classroom-based learning modalities, with at least one of these stations being for online learning.

b) **Lab rotation**: in this rotation model implementation, students rotate on a fixed schedule or at the discretion of the teachers among locations on the brick-and-mortar campus, with one of the spaces being a lab reserved predominantly for online learning.

c) **Flipped classroom (FC)**: this is a rotation model implementation where within a given course or subject, students are made to rotate on a fixed schedule between face-to-face teacher-guided practice on campus during the standard school day and online delivery of content and instruction of the same subject from a remote location (often home) after school.

d) **Individual rotation**: as a rotation model implementation, students here are made to rotate on an individually customised fixed schedule among learning modalities, at least one of which is online learning within a given course or subject. The difference between the individual rotation and the other rotation models is that students do not necessarily rotate to each available station or modality.

2. **Flex model**: in the flex model, content and instruction delivery is primarily by the internet, with students moving on an individually customised, flexible schedule among learning with the teacher on-site. The teacher here provides face-to-face support on a flexible basis through activities such as small-group instruction, group projects and individual tutoring. Here, there are some implementations that have substantial face-to-face support, while others have minimal support.

3. **Self-blend model**: this describes a situation in which students, on their own volition, choose to take one or more courses entirely online to supplement their traditional courses and the teacher serves as the online teacher. Students here are at liberty to take the online courses either on the brick-and-mortar campus or off-site. There is a marked difference between the full-time online learning and the enriched-virtual model in the sense that it is not a whole school experience. Here, students self-blend some individual online courses and take other courses at a brick-and-mortar campus with face-to-face teachers.

4. **Enriched-virtual model**: this is a whole-school experience in which students divide their time between attending a brick-and-mortar campus and learning remotely using online delivery of content and instruction within each course. It is important to note that many enriched-virtual programmes began as full-time online schools and then developed blended programmes to provide students with brick-and-mortar school experiences. There is a difference between the enriched-virtual and the FC because, in enriched-virtual programmes, students seldom attend the brick-and-mortar campus every weekday. It also differs from the self-blend model because it is a whole-school experience, not a course-by-course model.

Blended learning and the 'personal touch'

There are suggestions in the literature that students are more amenable and enthusiastic about accessing online resources prepared by the lecturer personally known to them when using an FC rotation model, with the 'personal touch' acting as the dominant factor. Williamson (2018) explores three stages of student engagement in a flipped classroom environment, and since the FC is a relatively new model of learning, there appears to not be much detailed information on how this is done – suggesting a need for 'flipped professional development' which Williamson (2018) identifies in his research.

Blended learning and inclusiveness

Issues regarding student access to the materials critical to a successful implementation of blended learning instruction have also been raised. Ololube (2015) notes that there are challenges in the supply of technology-aided materials in the education system in developing countries which stem from an inadequacy of materials either in the finished or raw form and their associated high cost. In an earlier research study, Ololube, Ubogu and Egbezor (2007) point out that almost all sub-Saharan countries are poor and indebted, thereby exacerbating an inability to make use of ICT products especially those related to educational technology. Stone (2008) adds that, given the financial and family status of students, their access to the internet may be non-existent at home and only available in school. Singh, Steele and Singh (2021) also add that the inability of students to access internet-based materials owing to their financial status would put students at a disadvantage relative to their peers. Cevikbas and Kaiser (2020) observed that part of the difficulty for FC implementation is to have the technical requirements for teaching and learning. The technical problems they assert lie with accessing the internet and mobile devices in the sense that these devices cannot be underestimated and may destroy the structure of FCs.

Conclusion

Blended learning has been principally implemented for (1) improved pedagogy, (2) increased access and flexibility, and (3) increased cost-effectiveness. Even though effective teaching practice is hinged on innovative and effective teaching approaches and strategies, it appears that the successful implementation of the blended learning model in the classroom faces many questions and challenges. It is therefore relevant to put in place strategies that will help meet these implementation challenges. When these challenges are addressed, it could lead to meaningful strategic teaching and learning processes for staff and students generally.

References

Al-Ani, W. T. (2013). Blended learning approach using moodle and student's achievement at Sultan Qaboos University in Oman. *Journal of Education and Learning*, 2(3), 96.

Bailey, J., Martin, N., Schneider, C., Vander Ark, T., Duty, L., Ellis, S., & Terman, A. (2013). Blended learning implementation guide 2.0. *Digital Shift*.

Beck, R. J. (2010). Teaching international law as a partially online course: The hybrid/blended approach to pedagogy. *International Studies Perspectives*, 11(3), 273–290.

Bergmann, J., & Sams, A. (2012). Before you flip, consider this. *Phi Delta Kappan*, 94(2), 25–25.

Bersin, J. (2004). *The blended learning book: Best practices, proven methodologies, and lessons learned*. John Wiley and Sons.

Cevikbas, M., & Kaiser, G. (2020). Flipped classroom as a reform-oriented approach to teaching mathematics. *Zdm*, 1–15.

Christensen, C. M., Horn, M. B., & Staker, H. (2013). Is K-12 Blended Learning Disruptive? An Introduction to the Theory of Hybrids. *Clayton Christensen Institute for Disruptive Innovation*.

Graham, C. R., Allen, S., & Ure, D. (2003). Blended learning environments: A review of the research literature. *Unpublished manuscript, Provo, UT*.

Heinze, A. (2008). *Blended learning: An interpretive action research study*. University of Salford (United Kingdom).

Hong, K. H., & Samimy, K. K. (2010). The influence of L2 teachers' use of CALL modes on language learners' reactions to blended learning. *Calico Journal*, 27(2), 328.

Kafer, K. (2013). *The rise of K-12 blended learning in Colorado*. IP-5-2013). Denver, CO: Independence Institute.

Kitchenham, A. (2005). Adult-Learning Principles, Technology and Elementary Teachers and their Students: the perfect blend? *Education, Communication and Information*, 5(3), 285–302.

Kliger, D., & Pfeiffer, E. (2011). Engaging students in blended courses through increased technology. *Journal of Physical Therapy Education*, 25(1), 11–14.

Kop, R., & Hill, A. (2008). Connectivism: Learning theory of the future or vestige of the past? *International Review of Research in Open and Distance Learning*, 9(3).

MacDonald, J. (2008). *Blended learning and online tutoring: Planning learner support and activity design*. Gower Publishing, Ltd.

Milakovich, M. E., & Wise, J. M. (2019). Overcoming the digital divide: Achieving access, quality, and equality. In *Digital Learning*. Edward Elgar Publishing.

Mirriahi, N., Alonzo, D., McIntyre, S., Kligyte, G., & Fox, B. (2015). Blended learning innovations: Leadership and change in one Australian institution. *International Journal of Education and Development using ICT*, 11(1).

Neumeier, P. (2005). A closer look at blended learning—parameters for designing a blended learning environment for language teaching and learning. *ReCALL*, 17(2), 163–178.

Olivier, J. (2011). *Accommodating and promoting multilingualism through blended learning* (Doctoral dissertation, North-West University).

Olokooba, I. N. (2015). Availability and Use of Computer-Based Instructional Materials (CIM) by Upper Basic Social Studies Teachers in Ilorin, Nigeria. *Nigeria Journal of Educational Foundations*, 14(1), 16–28.

Ololube, N. P., Ubogu, A. E., & Egbezor, D. E. (2007). ICT and distance education programs in a sub-Saharan African country: a theoretical perspective. *Journal of Information Technology Impact*, 7(3), 181–194.

Ololube, N. P. (ed.) (2015). *Handbook of Research on Enhancing Teacher Education with Advanced Instructional Technologies*. IGI Global.

Osguthorpe, R. T., & Graham, C. R. (2003). Blended learning environments: Definitions and directions. *Quarterly review of distance education*, 4(3), 227–233.

Parsons, D. (ed.) (2016). *Mobile and Blended Learning Innovations for Improved Learning Outcomes*. IGI Global.

Poon, J. (2013). Blended learning: An institutional approach for enhancing students' learning experiences. *Journal of Online Learning and Teaching*, 9(2), 271–288.

Sharpe, R., Benfield, G., Roberts, G., & Francis, R. (2006). The undergraduate experience of blended e-learning: a review of UK literature and practice. *The higher education academy*, 1–103.

Singh, J., Steele, K., & Singh, L. (2021). Combining the Best of Online and Face-to-Face Learning: Hybrid and Blended Learning Approach for COVID-19, Post Vaccine, & Post-Pandemic World. *Journal of Educational Technology Systems*, 50(2), 140–171.

Sloman, M. (2007). Making sense of blended learning. *Industrial and commercial training*, 39(6), 315–318.

Staker, H., & Horn, M. B. (2012). Classifying K-12 blended learning. *Innosight Institute*.

Stone, A. (2008). The holistic model for blended learning: A new model for K-12 district-level cyber schools. *International Journal of Information and Communication Technology Education (IJICTE)*, 4(1), 56–71.

Tucker, C. R. (2012). *Blended Learning in Grades 4–12: Leveraging the Power of Technology to create Student-centered Classrooms*. Corwin Press.

Watson, J., Murin, A., Vashaw, L., Gemin, B., & Rapp, C. (2013). Keeping Pace with K-12 Online and Blended Learning: An Annual Review of Policy and Practice. 10 Year Anniversary Issue. *Evergreen Education Group*.

Williamson, B. (2018). Three stages of student engagement in a flipped classroom environment. *Journal of Learning and Student Experience*, 1: 2.

Yeigh, T., Sell, K., Lynch, D., Willis, R., Smith, R., Provost, S., & Turner, D. (2017). *Towards a Strategic Blend in Education: A review of the blended learning literature*. Lulu. com.

Yilmaz, Y., Durak, H. I., & Yildirim, S. (2022). Enablers and Barriers of Blended Learning in Faculty Development. *Cureus*, 14(3).

CHAPTER THREE

A Learning Journey in Different Stages – Blended Learning in Action

Professor Russell Gurbutt

This chapter showcases five contributions that have been developed during the pandemic and are being taken forward into the 2021–22 academic year. It commences with service-user integrated learning, championing a patient focus and then using Padlet for student engagement. Next, a decision-making interactive video is used to determine if students can make patient-focused decisions. Decision making under time pressure is developed through a midwifery escape room. Finally, a virtual wellbeing café illustrates self and peer care around handling stressful care situations. These examples showcase colleagues' creativity in developing learners' insights into professional practice (knowledge acquisition, development, application and reflection).

Introduction

The student journey in the health and social care sector leads towards a public-facing role that has at its heart an essential focus on the individual. People who embark on professional pre-registration education often, but not always, have this destination in mind.

Through various means, education has the challenge of countering the potent social-media influences that veer towards individualism and self-interest over service and the public interest. This chapter, therefore, unpacks five steps that can inform educators about ways in which they might think about small but meaningful steps towards professional education that keep in sight the individual at the heart of health and social care. To do otherwise risks rendering the client/patient as an object and relegates the use of professional knowledge to task-driven approaches towards care and support. These steps are presented in a logical sequence that commences with an attempt to bring the patient experience into centre stage, and then involves facing up to information seeking around dealing with challenging situations encountered in practice. Given that information seeking is a part of decision making, the next step is a decision-making interaction that helps students to make decisions and understand what else might be considered. If professional decision making is the norm in practice, it is more exacting during urgent situations, perhaps where life or death is at stake. Making decisions under pressure is thus a useful step to test out students in a safe environment. Finally, it is necessary to not underestimate the emotional toll that front-line health and social care exacts on individuals. The 2020 pandemic brought this to the fore but it was not a new phenomenon. Being expected to undertake sometimes-distressing professional work without finding a space to talk and 'off load' those emotions will not prevent them from 'catching up' with the individual at some time. The final step, therefore, is about wellbeing, which is currently enjoying a centre ground in the light of recent events but is always vulnerable to being displaced by the next major issuer of the day.

Blended learning that brings the service user into focus

The service user (AKA 'patient' or 'client') is the focus of care and support but often the sheer complexity of an organisation can render the individual an object that the professional services do things for as they 'process' them through a 'system' of care. This has been noticed in the past and measures have been taken to bring this back into focus. Publications such as 'No decision about me, without me' (DH, 2012) effectively signal that the service can subsume the service user.

Major service failings set out in the Francis Report (Francis, 2013) and Ockenden Review (DHSC, 2022) further signal consequences of displacing service users from the focus of care.

In order to make learning as flexible as possible and efficient too, a blended approach to learning journey design was taken as part of a broader initiative at the University of Bolton of flipping a pre-registration nursing curriculum prior to the 2020–22 pandemic. Whilst blended learning means different things to different people, it essentially is a curriculum designer's choice to determine a mix between where learning takes place and in what ways that is deemed to be the most effective for students. In this case the blend was to introduce students to a real-world patient story via an asynchronous online learning package. The tool used to deliver this content was Articulate, a content creation package that allows integration and sequencing of text, images, video and documents.

The service-user story was sequenced through a series of 'slides' that gradually unfolded a narrative about the suicide of a relative. Through this, students were prompted to read and consider the information provided, think about its implications and how it might feel for the relative presenting the story. Next, links were provided to online embedded forums and quizzes to check the students' understanding. Through this, the first part of the learning journey was completed. Online independent learning allowed students to work through it at a time, place and pace that suited them, within a designated completion period. Following that, a live campus classroom-based session took place where the students could meet face to face the service user's relative who featured in the learning package. Whilst this could be undertaken on Zoom, and probably would facilitate the logistics of managing timetabling and class-size management, there is something important about being able to engage in dialogue with a service user. Especially in a social space that replicates real-world care where interpreting the environment, the other people within it and the nuances of reading non-verbal cues is easier than on a platform such as Zoom.

The sessions have been evaluated following each student cohort for content, learning experience and technical ease of use. This has resulted in a meaningful learning experience that brought a real-world story into the students' domain, and corroborated with other times when students paused to think deeper about their dialogues with service users. Moreover, it balances the vast amount of practice-based information being acquired with a focus on what really matters – the person at the heart of health and social care.

Applications for engagement in information acquisition

A decision-making process includes information acquisition, information processing and identifying issues that need addressing. In the cycle of 'assess, plan, implement and evaluate', the process of assessment is often tacit but can be linked to aids that prompt a person to remember to check out specific types of information. However, such aids represent one way of developing an understanding about the service user, a lens through which one looks at the individual. Depending on the information sought and the information not attended to, different understandings of the service user, and thus of their needs, can develop. That naturally can lead to diverging views on what care and support they need or consider acceptable.

Two relatively simple approaches can be used here, both employing applications used to post and sort information. These are Slido (2022) and Padlet (2022). Slido is a live polling platform that enables interaction with an audience. It allows polls to be undertaken and live visual feedback given such as in bar charts or percentages of responses to poll questions. Additionally, there are quiz tools that enable 'fun' to be included in sessions. A word-cloud feature also enables the capture and visualisation of common text responses to questions.

In relation to developing students' information seeking and processing, Slido offered a way in for students to engage with sensitive topics in an online classroom. Asynchronous learning such as the service-user story discussed earlier presented an interactive sequence in a content-creation package that fed forward into a synchronous session during which an application such as Slido could be used.

During the synchronous session, students were guided to explore sensitive care topics. If this was undertaken in a face-to-face classroom, a few individuals might verbally contribute, but the online application use facilitated a whole class to be able to post responses to questions that were chosen to check their understanding, and that explored views on ethical concepts and associated legal aspects of care (such as what the registered practitioner's boundaries of decision making were in relation to the law and regulation). The word-cloud option allowed students to post a range of related descriptions of issues that they considered to be associated with a given sensitive topic. The visual summary provided a starting point for a tutor-led discussion about ideas that emerged from the group based on the key terms in the exercise. This, whilst it began with the students' perspectives, allowed other things to be introduced to alert them to an array of information that is both interlinked and relevant in decision making.

Class evaluations suggested that there was more engagement than was previously experienced in physical-classroom-based activities, and post-session learning checks indicated that deeper learning was beginning to occur, along with students reporting high levels of satisfaction and tutors reporting that there was more depth of handling of sensitive topics demonstrated in students' written work. Whilst this was just one small teaching intervention, it is nonetheless a useful tool that facilitates discussion and simultaneously helps students to see the registered professionals and lecturers as role models, in terms of professional decision making, who can help them to appreciate the need to develop effective interpersonal skills, such as interview questioning, so that a range of information can be gained in order to interpret the service user's needs.

A second application, Padlet, was also used specifically to facilitate group work so that students could be given tasks to complete and present their responses in a shared space. Padlet allows text, files and images to be posted into a shared space and for real-time interaction with live updates by participants.

In the example of developing knowledge about different service users and their needs, some case examples were given and students were instructed to work in the virtual shared space in groups. Each group produced an account of the information relevant to interpreting the needs of each individual in the given case and produced for other groups a summary of what that information signalled in terms of interpreting needs and challenges around decision making. This exercise created an evidence-informed resource (in which students demonstrated some skills of being consumers of peer-reviewed materials) that was reviewed by the lecturer to identify any errors or inaccuracies. This resource was saved as a PDF for students to access later. The scope of a student's learning also encompassed several case examples beyond the one that they had worked on. Lecturers reported that they noticed an inclusive element. Some students who struggled or had social anxiety issues and were reluctant to engage with others found the variety of interaction helped their learning.

In summary, application use in synchronous learning sessions can be an effective means of promoting greater student engagement through enhanced interaction with the lecturer and collaboration with each other. Its advantages are that it allows a lecturer to know the extent of engagement (through online polls, for example) and facilitates students posting responses anonymously, thus reducing a sense of vulnerability when offering a view or response without perceiving it will be somehow wrong and therefore attract adverse attention. Overall, however, it draws students into greater dialogue with peers and lecturers, which in the process helps them to see lecturers as professionals and role models when it comes to learning about how to make safe and effective service-user-focused decisions.

That is especially important as students are not just learning subject-specific information or undertaking tasks to pass a module. Rather, they are moving towards a public-facing accountable role where their skills of knowledge acquisition and interpretation sit at the heart of clinical decision making. In this way the graduate destination is brought into focus that in itself should underline the relevance and importance of specific experiences in the learning journey.

In these case examples students have been learning about knowledge acquisition and processing to understand the service user as an individual so as to be able to identify their needs. A further step in the learning journey about decision making is to see whether a student could follow a real-time decision process and identify accurately whether there was a serious life-threatening event developing that required a timely response.

Operating department (OPD) urgent decision making

The challenge of real-world practice is that the routine non-urgent everyday decision making is interspersed with more rapid health changes that an individual might experience. In these cases, a clinician has to be able to make sense of the situation (through information acquisition and processing) and identify the key care issues. Different issues will have different levels of risk associated with them and one such example is seen in the case of a person who develops an anaphylactic reaction. Anaphylaxis is a response to an allergen (such as peanuts) that can cause rapid severe physical and life-threatening effect (NHS UK, 2022).

An approach to assessing whether students could apply their knowledge in such situations was developed through the creation of a decision tree scenario. It was based on a real-world case example in which a patient's health begins to deteriorate. This was set in an operating department context where serious incidents do occur, such as the 142 'Never Events' reported in NHS operating departments between April and July 2022 (NHS England, 2022). Whilst many relate to surgical procedures, they serve to remind students that this is a high-risk area requiring vigilance in decision making.

In real-world practice there are signs about a patient's health that indicate that a change is occurring. The speed of that change introduces an urgency in accurate decision making around which action to take and when. A branched decision-making scenario can be made using a versatile tool such as Microsoft PowerPoint, or more expensive content-creation products such as Articulate. The underlying principle in design remains the same though. A story is built up in a sequential order, with stages of information seeking and acquisition, information processing and information labelling. A series of questions posed at each stage of the unfolding sequence prompts the students to think about whether they need more information or to ask what they think the information means (that they have made sense of). Additional questions are introduced presenting the student with action options. For example, they could run some test, record some observations or administer a drug. There are different question options for nodes where the story can unfold in a different direction. This could be a loop that returns to the main story after having explored a specific aspect of the patient's health. Alternatively, it could be a branch that leads to the patient's deterioration, the student having missed certain vital cues and questions that should have prompted them to act.

As a decision learning tool, the student has to apply their information-seeking skills and pursue options to acquire what they think is sufficient information to interpret and identify the patient's needs. The questions posed to the student prompt them to think whether the information acquired is actually a cue to recall other retained knowledge about what the issue is. This draws on previously learnt information including anatomy and physiology as well as a range of health conditions.

Depending on the answer selected from the choices offered, students were given video feedback clips that explained what was happening (affirming a correct choice) or questioned their choice and asked them to think again. In this way, it replicated the experience of professional peer review that occurs in real-world practice. Such review serves to compound a student's learning to cause them to think and, where relevant, consider the information that they seek, or review how they have made sense of the patient's health issues.

The urgency of decision making is introduced when the student realises the consequences of either an action or an inaction. This is developed as they follow specific branches of the decision scenario. The challenge for the student was to recognise what to do and then how urgently an action should occur. Once again, deciding the action to take drew upon a different knowledge base about intervention options and associated risk weightings of the likelihood of the range of anticipated outcomes. In this way, the scenario required students to apply skills (information seeking and processing) and draw on knowledge (anatomy, physiology, health and illness) and on intervention knowledge (what to do) in order to correctly identify the health change and correctly respond in a developing high-risk scenario.

In summary, the branched interactive decision scenario offers many advantages to the student. As an asynchronous learning tool, it allows for several attempts to be made and to gain video feedback corresponding to different choice options. It also helps the student to recognise the integrated curriculum where different types of knowledge and experience are drawn upon within a decision task. This in turn should help a student to identify their own learning needs and thus be a prompt to address those gaps. Furthermore, the decision scenario feeds forward into synchronous learning sessions where the students can discuss their own stories of practice where similar events and urgent decisions have occurred. In this way the learning serves to embed real-world practice into the curriculum as well as to allow students to make clear connections between what they observe in practice and thinking through what they need to do when confronted with urgent decision making themselves.

If the urgent decision-making exercise demonstrates how students could *apply* a range of knowledge types that they have acquired throughout theoretical and practical experience, then the next logical step is to place that process under pressure. This indeed would replicate some of the experiences that they would encounter in practice.

Decision making under pressure: a midwifery escape room

This approach to decision making is nothing particularly new. Being prepared to deal with emergency situations is necessary whether it be in the military, aviation or healthcare. As a military veteran, I'm aware that simulation training already exists around naval damage control. The scenario is that a ship is taking in water after combat damage and a team have to problem solve to stop the flooding, and secure the damaged area. The simulation is a physical section of a ship that actually floods and lists (under strict control); if the team of learners do not work together, communicate effectively and apply practical skills in damage control, the situation becomes irretrievable. In real life, this has obvious consequences and there is only one opportunity to get it right. So it is in clinical practice, too, when the life of a patient or unborn baby is at stake. (If you are interested in viewing the actual real-life military simulation of damage control, take a look at the Phoenix repair damage control unit – MOD UK, 2022.)

CHAPTER THREE

Escape rooms have become a popular entertainment in recent times, and have been popularised through some TV programmes (Wikipedia, 2022). The idea is uncomplicated, in that a series of puzzles need to be solved to find a solution to be able to open a door and escape from the 'room'. Puzzle solving is a popular pastime and the skill of being able to do that has in the past led to contributions to major historical events. One example comes from the intelligence services, where code-breaking teams were developed, drawing on people with mathematical backgrounds and their ability to rapidly solve crosswords (see Imperial War Museum, 2022). In itself, problem solving is a skill that all students need to develop because the complexity of real life means that simplistic linear responses do not account for complexity and variation in a given scenario. Indeed, a rule-driven approach to clinical decision making falls into this error. What is actually needed are clinicians who can think their way through complex 'puzzles', often in teams where collaboration and good interpersonal relations are important. Lecturers, therefore, continue to seek innovative ways of designing a learning journey that is effective for students to be able to solve complex problems under pressure. That is where an escape-room approach has proved to be useful in identifying an approach that can be applied to a dimension of learning in a different field, namely clinical midwifery.

The scenario was designed as an online 'delivery escape room' containing a set of puzzles to be solved. It was time limited to one hour, during which a group of students had to find clues and answer the questions. Each puzzle generated a numerical answer and the sum of all the answers created the code needed at the door in order to successfully escape. The group had to explore the room and check out hot spots when they found them. Some of these were information deliberately placed that had no relevance to working out the answer to specific puzzles and thus acted as 'dead ends' in problem solving. Other areas had voiceovers to give verbal rather than textual information. An example of a hot spot is a question about the weeks of a pregnancy that anomaly scans usually took place in, requiring the figures for the start and end weeks.

During the scenario, students worked together online, discussed the questions and decided which information was irrelevant to the task. They were not allowed to check out information online by 'spoking out' to confirm evidence-based accurate responses because the task was a method of evaluating the extent to which students had retained a range of information that had previously been taught in class. It is important to note that in clinical practice there is a body of knowledge that is gradually evolving but nonetheless needs to be learnt. Examples are the anatomy and physiology of the reproductive system or foetal circulation. Later on, when undertaking higher levels of study, students will learn more about the nature of knowledge, how it is created and how its value can be evaluated, but at this pre-registration level the foundations need to be established so that they can be applied in decision making. The escape room thus proved to be a fun way of assessing the extent to which students had retained a specific body of knowledge and positive feedback was given in a local evaluation of the intervention.

In summary, an edutainment approach can offer a useful way to check whether students have retained knowledge and can work together to solve a range of problems under time pressure in order to 'escape'. The next stage in the learning journey is to find a place for free exploration of thoughts and feelings.

Caring for the carers – a wellbeing café

So far, a series of learning interventions have been described that commenced with placing the service user at the heart of decision making, followed by developing information seeking, acquisition and processing and providing various means of feedback to support students being able to identify issues that will be addressed as decisions. The actual people that students encounter in practice raise ethical and challenging dilemmas that are not amenable to simplistic decision making. The emotional burden that comes with such situations points towards a natural need to discuss this with peers. In registered practice, this is (or at least should be) both a formal and an informal action. It is formalised in clinical supervision (a process where a clinical extent is deconstructed and learning derived from discussing it) and it also occurs in multiple informal interactions. These take place in rest rooms, offices, quiet places away from others. Places and spaces where the emotional load of care can be expressed in a supportive and non-judgemental environment, where decompression can happen and thoughts and feelings can be dealt with. In a similar way, students need to be able to do this as part of their university-based education.

Where there is a campus-based experience there are social spaces where this might occur in a low-key natural way such as cafés, dining rooms, gardens, bars. However, it is not infrequent that students who are sitting together in social spaces are often all absorbed in looking at a mobile device, scrolling through images, different news and blog feeds. In this way they might be together but not actually present and developing close social connections with the people that they are actually with. The online environment can actually break into this and bring people together in a space where they have chosen to be, regardless of geography.

The wellbeing café was an online area that students visited at designated times for a specific purpose to share traumatic experiences. During the COVID-19 period this included needing to discuss the high-intensity care for patients who were nursed at times on their front (prone position) to aid respiration. Other students had been on wards where several patients had died on the same day.

It was student led, and the facilitating lecturer established the ground rules for the café and shared an activity as an example of what they had done to support their wellbeing. Other students shared their experiences and ideas for wellbeing. For example, one used the café to share about an online choir and subsequently four other students joined it. The value of the café was that it got students sharing and there was not a one-size-fits-all response to supporting wellbeing, nor prescriptive giving steps that magically led individuals to attaining wellbeing. Rather, it opened up participants to consider approaches that might be helpful and at the very least others listened to experiences expressed. It is now embedded as part of the curriculum into modules, with lecturers being provided with a guidance template.

Conclusion

This chapter sought to describe a range of learning interventions that were developed during the switch to online learning during the COVID-19 pandemic. Professional education is not a curriculum of things. It has a focus and purpose to prepare individuals for a registered and accountable role. As such, the learning journey needs to find ways of developing the requisite initial knowledge base that will continue to be built once registered and thereafter throughout a professional career. The graduate should know what and 'know how', and be able to demonstrate this to others and 'tell how' (i.e. explain their professional actions). The sequence of teaching interventions described offers pauses for thought for the reader to decide what ideas, if any, could be adopted and adapted for their own learning design. The impact of education is measured in many ways, but a key outcome measure for professional registrants is that they are competent to practise. At the heart of practice lies the service user, and around them the professional makes decisions with and sometimes for them, depending on the circumstances. Steps that engage students online, to communicate together, collaborate together, problem solve together and decompress together, underpin exactly what is needed in practice. Thus being creative in education design is always worth pursing to bring about the enduring outcomes that are required for professional practice.

Acknowledgments

Acknowledgments are given to academic staff at the University of Bolton who shared these interventions: Helen Lord and Sean Freeman for service-user integrated learning; Liz Wheatley for Padlet and Slido for engagement; Jo Wroe for an OPD decision-making tool; Gemma Moss for the midwifery escape room and Aleeza Khan for the Student Wellbeing café.

References

DH (2012). Liberating the NHS: No decision about me, without me. Government response [Online]. Available from: http://data.parliament.uk/DepositedPapers/Files/DEP2012-1873/LiberatingtheNHS-Nodecisionaboutmewithoutme.pdf [Accessed: 22 September 2022].

DHSC (2022). Ockenden review: summary of findings, conclusions and essential actions [Online]. Available from: https://www.gov.uk/government/publications/final-report-of-the-ockenden-review/ockenden-review-summary-of-findings-conclusions-and-essential-actions [Accessed: 22 September 2022].

Francis, R. (2013). Report of the Mid Staffordshire NHS Foundation Trust Public Inquiry [Online]. Available from: https://www.gov.uk/government/publications/report-of-the-mid-staffordshire-nhs-foundation-trust-public-inquiry [Accessed: 22 September 2022].

Imperial War Museum (2022). Turing Enigma for an example [Online]. Available from: https://www.iwm.org.uk/history/how-alan-turing-cracked-the-enigma-code [Accessed: 22 September 2022].

MOD UK (2022). Phoenix damage repair instructional unit [Online]. Available from: https://www.royalnavy.mod.uk/our-organisation/bases-and-stations/training-establishments/hms-excellent/phoenix-damage-repair-instructional-unit [Accessed: 22 September 2022].

NHS England (2022). Provisional publication of Never Events reported as occurring between 1 April and 31 July 2022. Published 8 September 2022 [Online]. Available from: https://www.england.nhs.uk/wp-content/uploads/2022 September Provisional-publication-NE-1-April-31-July-2022.pdf [Accessed: 22 September 2022].

NHS UK (2022). Anaphylaxis [Online]. Available from: https://www.nhs.uk/conditions/anaphylaxis/ [Accessed: 22 September 2022].

Padlet (2022). It's a beautiful day. Make something beautiful [Online]. Available from: www.padlet.com [Accessed: 22 September 2022].

Slido (2022). Your go-to interaction app for hybrid meetings [Online]. Available from: https://www.slido.com/ [Accessed: 22 September 2022].

Wikipedia (2022). Fort Boyard game show [Online]. Available from: https://en.wikipedia.org/wiki/Fort_Boyard_(game_show) [Accessed: 22 September 2022].

CHAPTER FOUR

Making a Clinical Diagnosis – A Blended Approach

Claire Goulden and Dr Mark Holland

Drawing inspiration from the TV series *House, M.D.*, COVID-19 was a catalyst to work with trainee advanced clinical practitioners outside the classroom to develop clinical diagnostic skills. Adopting House's use of a whiteboard to think out loud, students are invited to watch episodes of the show prior to the first class. They are divided into groups of two-to-four students, and each week one group works through a short clinical vignette, following the conventional steps of history, examination, and requesting and interpreting investigations. At each stage the students seek further information from the tutor in an exchange of emails, until the diagnosis is reached. At the following week's class they present their analysis and diagnosis to their peers.

Introduction

Workforce planning is a leading priority for the National Health Service (NHS), with staff shortages across all the traditional healthcare professions. In tandem is a modernisation programme where roles traditionally reserved for doctors are now undertaken by advanced clinical practitioners (ACP) (NHS, 2017) and physician associates. ACPs are registered healthcare professionals from a variety of backgrounds, including nurses, pharmacists, paramedics, physiotherapists, occupational therapists and podiatrists. After completing a two-year, part-time master's degree that includes independent prescribing, ACPs work as autonomous clinicians.

In March 2020, COVID-19 led to an abrupt cessation of our programme, as students returned to clinical practice to fight the pandemic. As the first wave of the pandemic eased, studies resumed online via the video conferencing platform Zoom. This chapter describes an interactive teaching activity whose primary aim is to develop clinical diagnostic and decision-making skills, in a way that is engaging, entertaining and of course educational.

The advanced clinical practitioner programme

Students can register for either the Advanced Clinical Practice MSc, Clinical Practice MSc or standalone continuing professional development (CPD) modules. In year one, semester one, two core clinical modules run concurrently: Clinical Examination Skills and Biological Basis of Disease. These modules equip students with the skills to examine patients and an understanding of the breadth and pathophysiology of diseases. In semester two the final core clinical module, Diagnostics and Therapeutics, consolidates the learning from the first two modules, with the emphasis on synthesising clinical information to make a diagnosis, as well as understanding how to interpret common clinical investigations.

The expectation of many students enrolled on the Diagnostics and Therapeutics module is that diagnostic acumen will simply emerge from their recently acquired clinical examination skills and knowledge of disease. However, making a diagnosis is more complex. Students are introduced to uncertainty, including statistical and probability models, for example sensitivity, specificity and Bayesian theory. To tie all these strands together, case-based learning is arguably the best vehicle.

Case-based learning

Teaching diagnostic thinking and skills to healthcare professionals other than doctors is relatively new. Although lectures and clinical textbooks might describe diseases in detail, there is a bridge to cross before applying this information in routine practice; simply being armed with knowledge does not make even the best student a competent practitioner. Case-based learning provides a safe transition from the classroom to the clinic, affording students the opportunity to explore the application of their newly found knowledge (Thistlethwaite et al., 2012). Whether it be theoretical patients in case-based learning or real-life patients in a clinical setting, generations of medical students have been taught to see their patients as 'coat hangers', to contextualise their skills and knowledge. To become a diagnostician, one must integrate theory and practice.

We live in an age of technology with sophisticated investigations readily available in every acute hospital. Sadly, these tests are frequently requested in error. In this module I emphasise to my students, ad nauseum in their opinion I suspect, that the greatest diagnostic tool is the clinical history, followed by a physical examination, with investigations requested to test or refute the initial *working diagnosis*. The 'father of modern medicine', Dr William Osler (1849–1919) is famous for a multitude of contributions to modern medicine, none more so than his insistence that medical students learn from talking to and examining patients (Bliss, 1999). The importance of the clinical history cannot be overemphasised. Whether Osler would approve of blended learning on a video conferencing platform is impossible to say, but I hope he would acknowledge my attempt to adhere to the spirit of his teaching during a time of adversity.

House, M.D.

House, M.D. was a television series which ran for eight seasons between 2004 and 2012 on the Fox network (House, n.d.). While a plethora of medical dramas exist, a genre probably second only to crime fiction in popularity, *House, M.D.* was unique. Each week a complex patient presented to Dr Gregory House and his team, and in the ensuing 45 minutes they would invariably struggle, albeit ultimately successfully, to diagnose what was wrong. Of course, there were the usual ingredients of interpersonal relationships, and moreover Dr House fighting his own inner demons, but above all was the central clinical case. House and his team would think out loud in a team meeting, expressing their thoughts using a whiteboard, for which only House himself had control of the marker pen. As each episode progressed, further medical history about the patient was sought and investigations were performed to confirm or refute potential diagnoses. Speculative hunches would lead to empirical treatment regimes, often ending spectacularly badly.

House was, by his own admission, a supreme diagnostician. However, he lacked other key attributes required by a doctor, including communication skills and compassion. The character House is based on Sherlock Holmes (House Trivia, n.d.), a man who is similarly flawed, although probably not the sociopath he is often thought to be (Ryan, 2018). It was made clear to my students that they were not being asked to adopt House's human frailties; instead they were being asked to observe and learn from a brilliant clinical mind.

The association between House and Sherlock Holmes is interesting. Holmes' creator, Sir Arthur Conan Doyle (1859–1930), studied medicine at the University of Edinburgh and based the character on his teacher and inspiration, Dr Joseph Bell (1837–1911) (Cirillo, 2014). Bell was renowned for his powers of clinical observation and diagnostic acumen, as well as helping the police with their investigations. In fact, Bell was a clinical genius. I still get goose bumps listening to Abraham Verghese's 2011 TED talk, 'A doctor's touch', where he beautifully describes Bell's brilliance (Verghese, 2011). Verghese's talk is played to all my students; I tease them that Dr Joseph Bell is the standard I expect of them when they graduate. The connection between House, Bell and Verghese is vital. For most viewers, House is a work of pure fiction but dig a little deeper and one can start to see more than an element of truth in the way he thinks and works; through Bell, Verghese affords Dr Gregory House credibility. For me, as the teacher for a class of budding clinicians, this credibility is vital, as it makes the undeniable clinical excellence of House a palpable reality, as opposed to a hopeless, futile conquest. Putting House's rudeness and social ineptitude to one side, he does provide a role model for any student who wants to be the very best diagnostician they possibly can be.

An in-joke among doctors is the assertion that watching medical drama contributes to their CPD, a notion that is not entirely frivolous. *House, M.D.* has been academically appraised and the conclusion seems to be that structured, facilitated learning based around our antihero provides a positive educational experience. The first series was assessed for content that would be useful to help teach clinical pharmacology (Baños et al., 2019). The authors found that most episodes had drug-related information; in their opinion five episodes were very useful for clinical pharmacology teaching, although they felt the overall pedagogical value of using medical drama required further evaluation.

Arawi (2010) scrutinises *House, M.D.* in much greater depth from the perspective of biomedical ethics, arguing that medical drama enhances emotional engagement, cognitive development and moral imagination. She defends her choice of *House, M.D.* over more benign dramatisations of doctors. Acknowledging that he is not an obvious ethical role model, his odd behaviour can actually highlight what *good* looks like; ultimately, she thinks he does *care* – an assertion I support. She also compares House with his colleague and best friend, Dr Wilson, a reincarnation of Sherlock Holmes' Dr Watson. Wilson is an archetypal caring, lovely doctor. He is a matinee idol who would only harm a patient by making them swoon. However, his gift of kindness is so often his Achilles' heel. On the surface, defending House is not easy. That said, placing bad-ass House next to angelic Wilson at the very least allows my students to decide for themselves what is good, what isn't good and, more likely in their world, what is acceptable. I am particularly drawn to one of Arawi's (2010) key points: "Case-studies objectify patients and render them soulless while medical drama narratives objectify them to bring them to life". This quote precisely and succinctly endorses House's presence in my classroom. That said, medical drama is but one tool at our disposal to learn from clinical cases. In a separate module, the students need to complete a portfolio of 50 real-life cases to complete their master's degree. The clinical vignettes I provide (Figure 1) for their whiteboards also contribute, although my students definitely make their fictitious patients come to life – *soulless* they are not. Wicclair (2008) is far less forgiving of House's behaviour but accepts that as the antithesis of good ethical practice, his presence in class is justified in showing students how things shouldn't be done.

I am not a fan of polarising medical practice as simply good or bad. Clearly there are definitive examples of both, but so often, like diagnostic decisions themselves, things are very grey. I often go to meetings and conferences where a medical educationalist plays a short clip from the 1954 feature film *Doctor in the House* (*Doctor in the House*, 1954). The bombastic Sir Lancelot Spratt arrives at the hospital in his Rolls Royce and conducts a ward round, where he proceeds to frighten the staff and more importantly the poor patient. Now clearly this is a comedy film, relying on characterising and stereotyping as staples for comic effect. Not unreasonably, Sir Lancelot is held up as a bully and a poor communicator. Despite clearly despising him, contemporary educationalists are all too happy to make their audience laugh, undoubtedly enhancing their feedback, but they are less keen to look at the *positives*. A film clip is a soundbite, nothing more. I show this clip to my classes too, but ask the students to balance things they don't like and things they do like, such as a ward round that everyone attends. I also remind my students that in the other unseen 90 minutes of the film, Sir Lancelot shows his softer side when defending the high jinks of a student who the dean of the medical school wants to expel. Sir Lancelot discretely blackmailing the dean comes over as entirely reasonable. Both House and Sir Lancelot do show they can care, in fact they do care; their problem is that they display this through *tough love*. They also show that life is ambiguous and only when we fully get to know this pair of rogues can we truly judge them – certainly, we must shy away from headlines and take on a full narrative, in the same way as when we make a diagnosis. We can learn a lot from mavericks.

So far, my support for using House in an educational setting has been very much based on opinion – hopefully, the irony of this is not lost on you, the reader. However, empirical evidence to vindicate medical drama as a positive educational tool is easily found. Jerrentrup and colleagues (2018) report their experience of using *House, M.D.* with medical students. In a Likert-scale questionnaire study comparing House and traditional seminar teaching, students reported improved learning (69.9%), better concentration (89.7%), higher motivation to participate (88.7%) and more fun (86.7%) ($p<0.001$). While recognising his diagnostic and therapeutic brilliance, the students were reassuringly less enamoured by his interactions with colleagues and patients. The authors concluded that this teaching was a vehicle for students to discuss ethical and controversial issues and learn about rare conditions.

In evaluating the success of an education event, one of my preferred tools is Kirkpatrick's Model. Jerrentrup and colleagues (2018) provide convincing evidence for achieving Level 1, participant reaction, which was positive. Level 2, participants learning, is partially achieved in my view, as the assessment of perceived learning was self-reported. But is there evidence to bridge clinical practice? Perhaps, the apex of the model is results, or Level 4. In a case report by Dahms and colleagues (2014) published in the *Lancet*, the authors report a patient with heart failure secondary to cobalt poisoning. The cobalt had entered the patient's body following hip-replacement surgery. When faced with heart failure, fever, lymphadenopathy, deafness, blindness and hypothyroidism, the authors, who had already introduced House to teach their medical students, turned to the great man again, remembering a similar case from Season 7, Episode 11. The summit of Level 4 was duly reached, and more importantly a life saved.

Beyond House, the role of medical drama in education appears to be well established now. Overall, the evidence is predominantly from undergraduate medical education. A guide has been published in *Medical Teacher* for those wishing to roll out this pedagogical approach (Hirt et al., 2013). In contrast to House and his predilection for rare cases, much of the learning is associated with *softer* skills. In an opinion piece, Kwong (2013) states the positive role of medical drama in teaching psychotherapy, communication and professionalism, and goes on to argue how these shows allow students to develop emotional connections. He also provides an example of teaching obstetrics to medical students by embedding standard didactic teaching in an episode of *ER*, where the case goes horribly wrong.

There are drawbacks in educating people through medical dramas. This is especially true for the general public. Serrone and colleagues (2018) argue that in the show *Grey's Anatomy* (*Grey's Anatomy*, n.d.), the portrayal of recovery from major trauma is too positive, leading to unrealistic expectations among patients and their families. The same message came from Spurgeon (2002), who highlighted that the survival rate from cardiopulmonary arrest in medical dramas was two-to-six times higher than in real life. It seems a shame to let the truth spoil a good storey, or as Williams, Evans and Alshareef (2015) put it, the "Hollywood effect". These authors voice further concerns, for example squeezing a completed event into one hour, exaggerating accepted norms, failing to appreciate the nuances of real-life medicine and promoting unintended learning outcomes. That said, when delivered appropriately and safely, medical drama does add to the richness of my students' education.

Bringing *House, M.D.* to class

House, M.D. is introduced to the class in the first week of the module (Figure 2); most of them have at least heard of the show. Between week one and week two, students are asked to watch available licensed episodes of the show, particularly Episode 3 from Season 1, 'Occam's Razor' (see below). In week one, they are told that House and his team will provide a model for a weekly class activity where students work in small teams to solve a complex clinical problem. The teams are randomly allocated to three or four students using the breakout rooms function in Zoom. Each team is allocated a week to study a case and present to the class. During each 15-week module, there are approximately ten presentations, each recorded on Zoom, with a link uploaded to the learning management system Moodle.

The first case is available to the whole class at the end of class in week two. The case is a short clinical vignette (Figure 1). Only the team allocated to week two will work on the case with me. The team are invited to dissect the case vignette using House's whiteboard approach. The team meet virtually on Zoom or their preferred social networking platform. The next step is for them to summarise their initial thoughts from their whiteboard and seek further information via a group email with me, which usually occurs between 24 and 48 hours after class. This step is vitally important in developing the students as diagnosticians. Inexperienced clinicians will jump straight from the vignette to requesting investigations. However, the next step must be to acquire more clinical history, asking questions pertinent to the case at hand. As stated already, ad nauseum, the clinical history is recognised as the key step to make a diagnosis.

The exchange of emails continues following the conventional approach of history, physical examination findings and investigations. Again, requesting investigations often proves problematic. Students are inclined to ask for investigations in a scatter-gun approach. It is made clear to them that they must justify every request. This is particularly important when they request potentially harmful investigations, for example high doses of ionising radiation associated with CT scans. To add a sense of real-world practice, I might play with the students, for example agreeing to a CT scan but saying it cannot take place for 24 hours as the scanner is being repaired or more urgent cases are waiting, thereby prompting students to consider a plan B.

Emails are exchanged between the students and myself for about two to three days. Towards the final exchange of emails, students are prompted to pull together all of the information they collected and make a final diagnosis or at least a short-list of plausible differential diagnoses. Managing this step is vital. I am aware that students may struggle to get the final diagnosis over the line, which can be a source of angst, especially when they are due to present their case to their peers at the next class. Therefore, as the exchange of emails progresses, I will drop hints if the students are heading off course. Invariably, albeit with an occasional small nudge, students complete the task and prepare a PowerPoint presentation. In presenting the case, students are asked to outline their thought processes as they unravel the diagnosis and give a brief overview of each of their differential diagnoses to educate the class. The class are encouraged to ask questions at the end of the presentation. Finally, the presentation slides and a link to the Zoom recording are uploaded to Moodle.

The first case is presented to the class at the start of week three and at the end of week three the second case is revealed. Most students are not actively participating with a case but are still provided with the vignette to allow them to practise their whiteboard skills before we next meet. If there are two cohorts of students undertaking the module, they are each provided with the same vignette but with a different outcome – an entirely possible feat with some thought and planning on my part.

Exploring hypothetical cases has several advantages. One is the ability to 'see' cases less commonly encountered in day-to-day practice (Figure 1). Secondly, students learn how to *request appropriate investigations* and how to *request investigations appropriately* – meaning providing sufficient clinical information to justify the request and sufficient clinical information to allow the result to be interpreted in context, for example a radiologist reporting the result of a CT brain scan in a patient with a headache.

Occam's razor

Simply put, Occam's razor argues that when two explanations are provided for a given problem, the simpler of the two should be chosen (Mani, Slevin & Hudson, 2011). As an aside, this philosophical principle affords the students an interesting titbit of historical knowledge, discovering that this important tool in their twenty-first-century diagnostic armoury is attributed to the English Franciscan friar William of Ockham (1285–1348). In medicine, Occam's razor is used to combine clinical information to provide a single unifying diagnosis, which is intuitively the simplest solution. For example, if a patient presents with fever, a cough productive of sputum and chest pain, one will make a diagnosis of a chest infection or pneumonia, but one will not initially consider all the causes of fever and all the causes of chest pain. This example is simple and used to illustrate a point. However, in practice diagnostic uncertainty is common with seemingly disparate information at the clinicians' disposal; Occam's razor is employed to cut through the prevailing complexity and provide a simple, single answer. Hickam's dictum is the opposite of Occam's razor (Mani, Slevin & Hudson, 2011): Dr John Barber Hickam MD (1914–1970) is quoted as saying a patient "can have as many diseases as he damn well pleases". Only a very foolish physician would live their clinical life solely by the rules of William of Ockham or Dr John Hickam; in practice both are relevant. However, as personified by House in Season 1, Episode 3, there is immense professional satisfaction in tying everything together.

A Student perspective

House is a rebellious, opioid-addicted doctor with a complete lack of people skills, and thus may seem a strange choice with which to illustrate the world of diagnostics and therapeutics; strangely however, he proved to be an effective catalyst for thought-provoking discussion.

House's often-chaotic approach offered the opportunity to introduce and explore some of the principles utilised in medicine, such as Occam's razor, and to think how they can potentially be applied to our own patients and their management. The 'Occam's Razor' episode of *House, M.D.* set for pre-session learning provides several key learning points, primarily emphasising the fundamental importance of good history taking when trying to formulate a diagnosis and to guide clinical decision making. It shows how simple things, such as enquiring about over-the-counter medications, can have a profound impact on your diagnosis and future care. This resonated with my own experiences, for example where patients often don't consider inhalers or antihistamines as medication, so won't necessarily volunteer this information unless it's actively sought out. A further discussion point was around whether we always need to treat, or if there are times when the best option is to do nothing at all; the condition may self-resolve or perhaps the proposed therapeutic intervention carries more risk than benefit, all of which should be carefully considered in our daily practice.

The use of House's whiteboard approach for the case studies was an engaging, practical way to challenge our diagnostic skills. From a basic two-line synopsis, it was then up to us to solve the puzzle. This was not just about asking questions, but asking the *right questions*; and simply put, if you didn't ask, you weren't told. Only once you had obtained your relevant history could you proceed to requesting investigations, clinically justifying why you wanted each one. It prompted you to think about the appropriateness and value of each diagnostic test; anyone can run a battery of investigations in the hope of returning a positive result, but to know what specific tests to ask for is a nuanced skill. Consideration of implications such as cost, the time required to get results and most importantly the impact on the patient, are all factors that pertain to our real-life patients and need to be integral to the clinical decisions we will go on to make as advanced clinical practitioners.

When piecing together the symptoms and investigation results, the use of the whiteboard method helped to focus and simplify all the information. Using tools such as the 'VITAMIN CDIP',[1] a differential diagnostic pneumonic previously taught in the Biological Basis of Disease module, and the occasional bit of help from Dr Google, it helped facilitate the diagnostic reasoning process by making you take logical steps to rule-in or rule-out any potential diagnoses, until you

---

[1] VITAMIN CDIP: Vascular, Infective, Trauma (Including chemical and radiation), Allergy/Immunological, Metabolic/Endocrine, Iatrogenic, Neoplastic, Congenital, Degenerative, Idiopathic, Psychogenic

finally arrived at an answer you had long given up all hope of ever reaching.

In summary, although I certainly won't be adopting his bedside manner, the use of House's whiteboard has provided a structured approach to diagnostics and has proved to be a novel yet valuable learning tool.

Where next?

Having invited House into our classroom I am keen to engage my students with other forms of media, both fictional and non-fictional, going beyond traditional textbooks. Paperbacks are starting to appear in the non-compulsory section of my recommended reading list for students. Generations of doctors have grown up reading the legendary novel *The House of God* (Shem, 1978). In his first year as a doctor, Dr Roy, MD fears for his own survival as much as he does for that of his patients, a feeling that resonated with many of my peers back in the day. It is uncommon to find a doctor who cannot quote at least one line from the book. While most of us would agree that the book is 'two standard deviations from the mean' in its true reflection of the reality of life in a hospital, there is undoubted authenticity in its depiction of the dark humour and cynicism of medical culture. What makes this book so appealing, however, is the description of social context. I am acutely aware that my teaching needs to be three-dimensional, loaded with clinical examples and stories, to bring what is otherwise dry theory to life. But however hard I try, the students need more help than I can ever provide to enhance their understanding of the complex concepts presented to them. House's presence in our classroom offers a layer of contextual support which I can only dream of providing for my students. I contest that the popularity and success of using drama as a teaching aid rests on the juxtaposition of the mystique of medicine with visceral social contexts, with the latter being something we can all understand. When trying to demystify medicine, having off-the-shelf social contexts to support learning is a gift.

I am also introducing a relatively new genre of reading to my class, that of the clinical expert writing about their experiences and medicine, sometimes alongside an autobiographical account of their life in general. These authors share a literary gift in their ability to present relatively complex medical concepts in simple language that lay people easily understand, without ever appearing to patronise their reader. Personally, I find these books real page turners: once started, you can't put them down. Retired neurosurgeon Mr Henry Marsh was a trailblazer of this form of writing (Marsh, 2014). Who wouldn't want to read about his exploits? He teaches the reader about all the common neurosurgical conditions and makes it clear that to survive in his specialty, humbleness and humility are musts, which may be at odds with the public's expectations. Dr Kathryn Mannix (Mannix, 2017) shares a casebook of her life in palliative care. I need to correct myself here and point out that this is a book I frequently did put down, as I was reduced to tears reading it on a train journey from Manchester to Newcastle. More recently, Dr Lucy Pollock (Pollock, 2021) has written about growing old in a book aimed at the public and from the perspective of a geriatrician. I teach a module on the health of older people and her book is now compulsory for my class. (I will whisper it, but they only need her – I'm probably redundant now!)

In summary

Adversity is a catalyst for innovation, and without doubt COVID-19 was a major cause of adversity. However, as the calypsonian David Rudder once sang (Rudder, 1993): "Out of a muddy pond, ten thousand flowers bloom". Forced to interact with my students on Zoom, *House, M.D.* came to the rescue. I doubt that this cantankerous genius of a man would welcome our plaudits, not openly anyway, but he must take the credit for inspiring a simple blended learning approach that is now well established in the teaching of the Diagnostics and Therapeutics module at the University of Bolton. I have also opened my eyes to untapped resources that I had previously overlooked, combining medicine with the arts. As an Associate TIRI Professor (Teaching Intense Research Informed) I am fortunate to observe the teaching of colleagues across many disciplines. My experience with House has inspired me to go and bring to my class everything good I see in the teaching of my peers.

When I mentioned to my kids that I was using House to teach my students, one of them replied "House is in da house". I guess he is.

Figure 1. Examples of fictional clinical vignettes and cases

Clinical vignette	Final diagnosis
You are asked to see Caitlin, an 18-year-old woman who presents to the ED with black motions. She is triaged as a GI bleed with melaena. A complicating factor is Caitlin's mum, who is angry that she has had this condition in the past and on one occasion was told that "she is putting this on and just making it all up". Initially, what more do you want to know?	Group 1 – Meckel's diverticulum Group 2 – splenic thrombosis
Bernard is a 54-year-old solicitor. He is a very intelligent man but maybe he could look after himself better. He was diagnosed with type 2 diabetes mellitus four years ago. He is not one to complain but has come to see you in primary care as he feels exhausted and his ankles are starting to swell.	Group 1 – renal amyloid Group 2 – diabetic nephrotic syndrome
Rosie is a 23-year-old lady who comes to see you in primary care for blurred vision in her left eye.	Group 1 – multiple sclerosis Group 2 – neuromyelitis optica
You are an ACP working in ambulatory emergency care. George is a 36-year-old man who has been referred in with total swelling of his left leg.	Group 1 – May-Thurner syndrome Group 2 – testicular cancer
You are an ACP working in A&E. You are asked to see Leah, who has just returned from a six-month trip to India and the far east. She has a temperature of 38.8°C and feels awful.	Group 1 – dengue fever Group 2 – chikungunya
Ron is a 56-year-old man with hypertension, who presents with confusion. He has no focal weakness and has been declined by the stroke team. He is to be seen by you, the medical ACP.	Group 1 – posterior reversible encephalopathy syndrome Group 2 – progressive multi focal leukoencephalopathy

Figure 2. Timeline of bringing *House, M.D.* to class

Week	Activity
Week 1	· Introduction to *House, M.D.*
	· Students are asked to watch two or more available licensed episodes of the show, in particular Season 1, Episode 3 – 'Occam's Razor'
	· Introduction to the 'whiteboard' in collating and analysing clinical information
	· Random allocation of two-to-four students per group
	· Allocation of week when students will present
	· Overview of diagnostic principles and tools, including sensitivity and specificity, positive and negative predictive value, area under the receiver operating curve (ROC), Occam's razor, Hickam's dictum, Bayes' theorem, gestalt and heuristics
Week 2	· Clinical vignette provided to the whole class
	· If there are two cohorts of students, both classes will have the same clinical vignette but with a different final diagnosis
	· First group of students work with the vignette outside class using a whiteboard approach
	· When ready, students collectively email their tutor to seek more clinical history – usually 24 to 48 hours after class
	· Tutor responds and a series of emails are exchanged, including clinical history, examination and investigations – usually over two to three days
	· A differential and preferred diagnosis are presented to the tutor – the students will have been supported to reach the correct diagnosis during the exchange of emails
	· Students prepare a PowerPoint presentation

Week	Activity
Week 3	· First case presented at the start of class and recorded on Zoom, followed by questions from peers, with further discussion facilitated by the tutor
	· PowerPoint presentations and Zoom recordings for participating cohorts uploaded to joint Moodle page
	· Second case provided at the end of class for a new group of students as per week 2
Week 4 onwards	· Repeated until all students have completed a whiteboard
	· Usually completed in week 12, depending on class size

References

Arawi, T. (2010). Using medical drama to teach biomedical ethics to medical students. *Medical Teacher*, 32(5), e205-e210. Available from: https://doi.org/10.3109/01421591003697457.

Baños, J., Lucena, M. I., Farré, M., & the Group for the Study of the Teaching Effectiveness of TV Series. (2019). The usefulness of TV medical dramas for teaching clinical pharmacology: A content analysis of house, M.D. *Educación Médica*, 20(5), 295–303. Available from: https://doi.org/10.1016/j.edumed.2018.07.011.

Bliss, M. (1999). *William Osler: a life in medicine.* Toronto: University of Toronto Press.

Cirillo, V. J. (2014). Arthur Conan Doyle (1859–1930): Physician during the typhoid epidemic in the Anglo-Boer war (1899–1902). *Journal of Medical Biography*, 22(1), 2.

Dahms, K., Sharkova, Y., Heitland, P., Pankuweit, S., & Schaefer, J. R. (2014). Cobalt intoxication diagnosed with the help of Dr House. *Lancet*, 383(9916), 574. Available from: https://doi.org/10.1016/S0140-6736(14)60037-4.

Doctor in the House (1954). Available from: https://www.imdb.com/title/tt0046921/ [Accessed: 12 September 2022].

Grey's Anatomy (n.d.). Available from: https://www.imdb.com/title/tt0413573/ [Accessed: 15 September 2022].

Hirt, C., Wong, K., Erichsen, S., & White, J. S. (2013). Medical dramas on television: A brief guide for educators. *Medical Teacher*, 35(3), 237–242. Available from: https://doi.org/10.3109/0142159X.2012.737960.

House (n.d.). Available from: https://www.imdb.com/title/tt0412142/ [Accessed: 12 September 2022].

House Trivia. (n.d.). Available from: https://www.imdb.com/title/tt0412142/trivia/ [Accessed: 12 September 2022].

Jerrentrup, A., Mueller, T., Glowalla, U., Herder, M., Henrichs, N., Neubauer, A., & Schaefer, J. R. (2018). Teaching medicine with the help of 'Dr. House'. *PloS One*, 13(3), e0193972. Available from: https://doi.org/10.1371/journal.pone.0193972.

Kwong, K. (2013). TV medical dramas: pure entertainment or a useful teaching tool? *Healthydebate*. Available from: https://healthydebate.ca/2013/11/about-healthy-debate/opinions-about-healthy-debate/tv-medical-dramas-useful-teaching-tool/ [Accessed: 15 September 2022].

Mani, N., Slevin, N., & Hudson, A. (2011). What three wise men have to say about diagnosis. *BMJ*, 343(7837), d7769. Available from: https://doi.org/10.1136/bmj.d7769.

Mannix, K. (2017). *With the End in Mind: Dying, Death and Wisdom in an Age of Denial*. Glasgow: William Collins.

Marsh, H. (2014). *Do No Harm: Stories of Life, Death, and Brain Surgery*. London: Orion.

NHS (2017). *Multi-professional framework for advanced clinical practice in England*. England: NHS. Available from: https://advanced-practice.hee.nhs.uk/multi-professional-framework-for-advanced-clinical-practice-in-england/ [Accessed: 15 September 2022].

Pollock, L. (2021). *The Book About Getting Older*. UK: Penguin Random House.

Rudder, D. (1993). Dedication (A Praise Song) [Audio song]. Available from: https://open.spotify.com/track/5HzWV5eFVhjfuonmi8lpJC [Accessed: 15 September 2022].

Ryan, M. (2018). The Complicated Mind of Sherlock Holmes. *Line by Line: A Journal of Beginning Student Writing*, 4(2), article 4. Available from: https://ecommons.udayton.edu/lxl/vol4/iss2/4 [Accessed: 14 September 2022].

Serrone, R. O., Weinberg, J. A., Goslar, P. W., Wilkinson, E. P., Thompson, T. M., Dameworth, J. L., Dempsey, S. R., & Petersen, S. R. (2018). Grey's Anatomy effect: television portrayal of patients with trauma may cultivate unrealistic patient and family expectations after injury. *Trauma Surgery & Acute Care Open*, 3(1), e000137. Available from: https://doi.org/10.1136/tsaco-2017-000137.

Shem, S. (1978). *The House of God*. New York: Richard Marek Publishers.

Spurgeon, D. (2002). TV dramas may raise false hope of surviving heart attack. *BMJ*, 325(7361), 408. Available from: https://doi.org/10.1136/bmj.325.7361.408/f.

Thistlethwaite, J. E., Davies, D., Ekeocha, S., Kidd, J. M., MacDougall, C., Matthews, P., Purkis, J., & Clay, D. (2012). The effectiveness of case-based learning in health professional education. A BEME systematic review: BEME guide no. 23. *Medical Teacher*, 34(6), e421–e444. Available from: https://doi.org/10.3109/0142159X.2012.680939.

Van Den Berg, H. A. (2018). Occam's razor: From Ockham's *via moderna* to modern data science. *Science Progress*, 101(3), 261–272. doi.org/10.3184/003685018X15295002645082.

Verghese, A. (2011). A doctor's touch [TED Talk]. Available from: https://www.ted.com/talks/abraham_verghese_a_doctor_s_touch?language=en [Accessed: 12 September 2022].

Wicclair, M. R. (2008). The pedagogical value of house, M.D. – can a fictional unethical physician be used to teach ethics? *American Journal of Bioethics*, 8(12), 16–17. Available from: https://doi.org/10.1080/15265160802478503.

Williams, R., Evans, L., & Alshareef, N. T. (2015). Using TV dramas in medical education. *Education for Primary Care*, 26(1), 48–49. Available from: https://doi.org/10.1080/14739879.2015.11494308.

Wise, J. (2014). TV show House helped doctors spot cobalt poisoning. *BMJ* [Online], 348(feb06 9), g1424. Available from: https://doi.org/10.1136/bmj.g1424.

CHAPTER FIVE

The Pursuit of Blended Learning Intervention Strategies through Professional Collaboration – Supporting TIRI and Campus Plus Strategy

Dr Mohammed Sadiq
Assistant Teaching Professor,
Department of Accounting,
Institute of Management,
University of Bolton, UK

The Teaching Excellence Network (TEN) is a professional community of practice developed at the University of Bolton to complement the TIRI (Teaching Intensive, Research Informed) and Campus Plus strategies. The network supported education and continuing professional development programmes and philosophies with the aim of enhancing the student and teacher experience and exchanging ideas for innovative and creative blended learning methodologies. Based broadly on the local, informal pedagogical networking meetings arranged to facilitate the discussion of teaching and learning best practice, it was believed an extended format would be of considerable benefit to education professionals in the exchange of teaching and learning ideas and reduction of isolation by department or school. In its early manifestation, feedback was sought on the value of the programme to assimilation, collaboration, relationship building and promotion of the institutional ideals.

This study review indicates general satisfaction and belief in the initiative and its capacity to develop teachers and students. It is a simple programme which draws in professionals from both further and higher education to the principle of achieving improvement in teaching and learning, and in particular, blended teaching and learning practices. It fits well into the philosophies of excellence which all institutions strive to attain. The feedback was wholly positive from respondents, the primary concern being formulation for implementation of the contributions, a matter for management.

Introduction

It is a simple supposition that quality of teaching is the primary route to student achievement in learning. This is closely followed by feedback, guidance and advice. The proposition of this paper is its application to teaching in the practice of collaboration. It is professional vanity to believe that even decades of practice and teaching relieve the lecturer of the obligation to pursue personal learning through the assimilation of advice and ideas from peers, perhaps even those of less experience and status. Resources, technology, politics and personality change practice needs to suit the requirements of each intake of students in the development of their learning, expectations and ambitions. Critical thinking and academic review are not skills which can be taught without implementing their practice.

In a social environment with peers, seniors and new colleagues, it is suggested that interaction promotes discussion of ideas and methodologies of teaching, and that this results in an assimilation of good practice better achieved than by simple lecture (Santos, Figueiredo and Vieira, 2019). Indeed, in the context of the network meetings, the short presentations provide updates on current developments in HE as a guide to relatively informal discussion and exchange of views. It is of course more constructive in result to actually balance and assess before conversing. The teacher's quest must be for a level of consistency to ensure learning and student achievement. Therein lies the need for support. It is from this base that interaction with peers proves invaluable, and any planned and reflective initiative which develops skills and provides support and advice is worthy of pursuit.

Literature review: the pursuit of excellence

The purpose of this literature review is to provide a foundation of knowledge for the improvement of teaching practice, using existing studies to determine effectiveness and adapt to guide the development of the Teaching Excellence Network (Aveyard, 2018). It is not sufficient simply to take what appears a 'good idea' in formulating new relationships by network meetings; there must be value in its structure which promotes the needs and success of learners. Much of this material was considered by the author in the evolution of the TEN philosophy and practice to facilitate its introduction into educational practice at the University of Bolton. It provides a context for the programme and its aims, and synthesises 'historical' findings which guide the theoretical background to its implementation and assessment of its value to educational professionals (Boote & Beile, 2005).

Excellence in teaching and learning has its foundation in quality assessment. Greatbatch and Holland assert, however, that "studies of previous teaching quality regimes in the UK imply that assessments were influenced by universities' research reputations and other factors that were not directly linked to teaching quality" (2016: 4). The apparently formulaic path of continuous professional development and quality measurement diverts emphasis from core practice teaching strategy to fulfilment of (albeit essential) administrative roles, duties to the institution and to the regulatory authorities. No issue is taken with the need for such accountability training, but it is simply pointed out that much experiential knowledge and thought is lost when higher education lecturers have little more than a passing formal association with each other. Indeed, it is argued that quality of teaching and the improvement of student attainment and experience are somewhat of a by-product in the quest for excellence. The tutor's career passes through the stages of competency in professional standards, proficiency beyond the routine and habit, advanced proficiency and the development of seniority and academic recognition of 'expertise', distinction and leadership (Dreyfus & Dreyfus, 1986). The more conventional route of formal education and CPD lectures and programmes not only needs to be adapted and extended, but greater use of institutional knowledge and competences, tactics and strategies is to be encouraged. Professor Wind suggests that "the time has come to re-imagine higher education and to reinvent pedagogical approaches", and the farming of internal input and experience is invaluable (Pritchard, 2007; Palmer, 2008; Wind & Rangaswamy, 2001).

In what is essentially an era of consumerism in higher education and student expectation of value for their money, accentuation of return on their investment must be of primary concern to the institution (Bunce, Baird & Jones, 2017). Education has evolved into a commodity, paid for by the student–customer, subject to market competition, provided through a supply chain of individuals, teams, departments and institutions. It is shaped by a curriculum designed to accord with professional, economic, social and political needs, the product assessed by achievement of goals and learner employability. The learner perception of what constitutes excellence may differ markedly from the judgement of teaching peers and the institution, rigor and standards sacrificed for popularity and "consumer satisfaction" (Emery, Kramer & Tian, 2001). The risk in treatment of learners as consumers, encouraged by government pricing policies, and an expectation of a relatively passive investment return, threatens the purpose of higher education (Bunce, Baird & Jones, 2017). It is incumbent upon institutions to ensure that whilst student-orientated learning programmes and practices are attractive, effective and encourage self-development, standards appropriate to the level of learning are maintained and achievement improved. Students do not, in general, identify themselves as simple customers of universities, but seek the guidance to fulfil their abilities (Bunce, Baird & Jones, 2017).

In this context, albeit nearly a decade earlier, Elton (1998) suggested 'excellence', incapable of precise definition, must be measurable by outcome for the learner and more amorphous concepts of student satisfaction, peer review and respect, and personal and institutional reputation. Given the purpose of this piece is to describe and analyse a network of experience and knowledge exchange at the University of Bolton, it is beyond its scope to analyse the cultural, ethnic and multitudinous other factors which impact on the quality and assessment of teacher excellence (Howard, 2010). Here, the only criterion for assessment of pedagogical improvement is the desire to learn from others as an essential part of self-evaluation in teaching and the facilitation of quality learning to our students. Many national initiatives designed to improve access to and the results of education appear doomed to failure, particularly when accompanied with a lack of funding and oversight (Nudzor, 2013). The Teaching Intensive, Research Informed (TIRI) programme at the University of Bolton is in its fifth year, and the introduction of the TEN collaborative community of practice project, based on a relatively simple, well-used networking format, is growing. Initiatives work simply because the desire for improvement remains strong amongst those responsible for the promotion of institutional excellence.

The enhancement of skills in teaching practice, and improvement of performance and formative learning for students are essentially subjective in assessment, both personal and by peer professional observation. It depends on 'the day'; Ashwin points out that no-one can be excellent all the time (2015). This drive to improve performance can only be maintained with peer support and recognition of the value of initiatives formulated with the primary objective of teaching and learning improvement, especially in the field of blended and hybrid teaching and learning strategies.

Philosophy of the Teaching Excellence Network (TEN)

The continuing nature of skills development applies to "the process by which, alone and with others, teachers review, renew and extend their commitment as change agents to the moral purpose of teaching", according to Day (2002). It is often viewed as a formal duty, fulfilled by passive attendance at and attention to periodic lectures, a part of the job (Robinson & Sebba, 2004). As such, its effectiveness in changing behaviour and enhancing learning, it is suggested, becomes subsumed by individual choices of practice adoption rather than an interactive sharing approach to ideas and strategies for improvement. Opportunities for professional conversations and interaction, to complement peer observation and feedback, undoubtedly advance teacher self-learning. They supplement the exchange of reviews of teaching strategies such as blended models by peers and students, a support emphasis placed on CPD rather than a "top-down managerial approach" (Reynolds, 2006: 20).

This is the context in which the TEN programme began its development utilising practitioner feedback from the diverse CPD rubric. It is a model based on coaching and mentoring, promoting relationships which encourage discussion and exchange through a community of practice, a combination of knowledge. Kennedy describes CPD processes as 'transformational', facilitating professional autonomy and choice of how the teacher assimilates and uses examples of good practice (2005). The network exchange upon which this teaching improvement is based facilitates the informal peer observation programme undertaken by institutions, a forum in which ideas and practice strategies are exchanged and evaluated with authoritative feedback (Gersten, Morvant & Brengelman, 1995).

The introduction of a TEN at the University of Bolton, as an interactive, professional learning and, indeed, social programme, was an integral step in the evolution of more productive relationships between faculty colleagues and those in other departments. The sources of advice, training and continuing professional development, whilst valuable and essential per se, perhaps lose sight of the 'in-house' resource of experienced teachers and lecturers. The involvement of students will enhance the mutually beneficial and reciprocative bank of knowledge and academic discipline that is so evidently available at the University, with the Network a powerful and symbolic point of access. It facilitates enhancement of the TIRI philosophy, central to the development of University of Bolton teaching and learning.

Arrangement and networking format

Each TEN event was advertised throughout the University staff areas by way of posters, with lecturers and teaching staff, both full and part time, internal and external, notified by way of the intranet email system. A full explanation of the meeting plan was provided so attendees were aware of the nature of the function, with a stress on the informal networking value of relationship building within the University. The format was simply transferred to the education context with short presentations on teaching issues from members of staff who shared knowledge on current research, teaching and learning, and Campus Plus blended learning issues. The following are examples taken from one of the TEN sessions:

Teaching design through live engagement

> "We have been using live engagement as a vehicle for teaching Graphic Design for some years – this presentation will look at the positives and pitfalls of embedding client-driven briefs within the modular framework."

Digitising undergraduate theses at University of Bolton

> "In 2020–21 as part of approaches to support digital access to collections, the library undertook a pilot scheme with colleagues in the Faculty of Health and Wellbeing to digitise a core collection of undergraduate theses. This presentation will focus on the results of the pilot and discuss plans to roll this out across the University."

Linking teaching-informed research with research-informed teaching

> "This presentation explores details of a paper published in the Emerald High Education, Skills and Work-Based Learning Journal, by the Civil Engineering team of tutors, based on delivery of its HE6 Interdisciplinary Project module. The module positions students into groups of eight; they are given a live engineering project, and each group member is assigned a practitioner's role such as geotechnical engineer, structural engineer or project manager. Case study material is provided by industry, who also support the module with guest lectures and site visits. The research is based on an electronic survey, which extended sections of the NSS questionnaire, to capture the impact that full-time, part-time and degree apprenticeship study modes have on learning. It was found that students and apprentices with industry experience support the learning of each other, including particularly full-time students learning. Whatever

the background of students, there is extremely high positive peer influence on learning in simulated interdisciplinary team settings, and this is enhanced in groups where there is greatest diversity of work and cultural backgrounds. The paper is unique in bringing together as a team of authors, eight members of staff in civil engineering. The module is an example of best practice in Teaching Intensive, Research Informed (TIRI) delivery, though perhaps without the 'T', since the emphasis is on group work but built on learning gain on teaching. It is an example of learning that other disciplines in the University can perhaps harness and introduce into their programmes."

Acceptability of a nurse-led non-pharmacological complex intervention for knee pain

"Nurse and patient views and experiences. The overall purpose of this research programme is to develop and test the feasibility of a complex intervention for knee pain delivered by a nurse, and comprising both non-pharmacological and pharmacological interventions. In this first phase, we examined the acceptability of the non-pharmacological component of the intervention, issues faced in delivery, and resolve possible challenges."

Other contribution included the following themes:

I. Peer-discussion and inclusivity in an online seminar

II. Flexible Hybrid and Blended Online Learning with SCORM packages

III. Critical Digital Pedagogy

IV. Storyboard

V. Moodle Interactivity H5P

VI. AI – Ada Update

Over the course of the meetings held so far, the speakers would change, providing an opportunity for diversity of ideas and impressions from which peers could assess the value to their teaching.

An opportunity for post-presentation discussion is provided in a socially interactive atmosphere, with refreshments. Somewhat ironically, several tutors were able to speak to colleagues in a congenial environment for the first time. This perhaps contributed to the growth in attendance. It facilitates the connection and association of new and less-experienced teaching staff with their senior peers, thus broadening interaction within the University community as a whole. It is an opportunity to be noticed as well as to engage, discuss and promote teaching, learning and blended/hybrid teaching strategies which enhance impact on student retention, experience and outcome. The goal is teaching excellence, arguably more effectively achieved with academic professionals when not being lectured to.

Methodology of study

Whilst the increasing attendance and cross collaboration from a range of schools within the University and local colleges are gratifying for the author–organiser, feedback from attendees would promote improvement. This is not a process which was conducive to quantitative exploration but qualitative opinion. Qualitative data was therefore obtained by invitation through the use of a brief questionnaire, adopting some parameters to Bernard's 'rule': "let the informant provide information he or she thinks is important" (Bernard & Bernard, 2013).

Broadly, participants were asked for comments on: (1) the effect of the community of practice format on their sense of integration into the TIRI and Campus Plus institution and its philosophies; (2) what they personally gained from attendance; and (3) the level (1–5) of effect it had on the way they interacted with their learners in lessons. Self-assessment is complementary to the triad method of peer interaction utilised by the University to increase diversity in formal observation and the development of trust teams on teaching feedback. Additionally, each was asked if they wished to video record their feedback for presentation at the University of Bolton TIRI Conference; 12 obliged, of which seven were chosen by the author for presentation, for reasons only of time constraint.

The limitations of the questionnaire survey process are appreciated, especially given that the Likert scale is relatively simplistic in ascertaining strength of opinion on the particular issues outlined rather than the direction the study, and the programme, should take (White & McBurney, 2012). The questions then encouraged expansion on sentiment, with feedback requested on what worked well and suggestions for improvement, an evaluative expansion of the Likert process (Schraw et al., 2017). This was considered more appropriate to the informality of the event than questionnaires, and the comments were noted by the author for the purposes of this review and the tenor of future meetings. Analysis of the data returned is essentially therefore a largely personal undertaking of the researcher. This logically gives rise to issues of objectivity (Wallace & van Fleet, 2012). This became a particular concern after the evaluation process, given that the responses from those who presented, participated and attended were overwhelmingly positive. The only honest response is to acknowledge this critical point and add there is little advantage to the investment of time into a process which, like so many in education, fails (Nudzor, 2013). As an initiative, the methodology was considered appropriate to elicit early observations which would guide development. A more comprehensive study involving a more-detailed, in-depth methodology will be undertaken as the programme evolves.

Results and analysis

The response to the questionnaire was high, with 71 returned, within the specified two-week period, from the 104 sent by email. It must be noted again that this is an experimental programme and the tenor of the questions asked was intended to elicit instinctive reactions and suggestions upon which to build future plans. The Likert scale facilitated the ease of general feedback, and the opportunity to expand comments was taken up by 51 respondents, just over half. Forty-one of the more detailed answers were from teachers and lecturers at the University of Bolton, and the remaining ten from teaching staff at further education colleges who, anecdotally, were particularly enthusiastic about the framework. In brief, perceptions were sought of the degree of effect of the network format on integration, personal and career gain, and changes to interactions with colleagues and students in the formal education context.

It is accepted that the broadly positive basis of feedback is likely to be a result of the relative novelty value of the networking experience in the higher education context, but provides a basis upon which to build further learning interactions. Much of its continued success will depend on the perceived action taken in respect of outcomes. A senior colleague from the Business faculty, for example, commented that, "it was an excellent opportunity for engaging with colleagues on the business of teacher education, especially those from the university sector – this has informed our own thinking on developing teaching, learning and hybrid strategies". The emphasis of the presentations and the informal discussions stressed positivity and praise, the plan comfortably fitting within the fundamental Teaching Intensive, Research Informed framework, organically drawing out ideas on practice and excellence initiatives from the teachers.

Interaction and integration into institutional philosophies of excellence

The TEN plan was formulated to increase interaction across the Schools which incorporate the University of Bolton and reach out to other educational institutions to become involved in the regional development of excellent learning provision. The first major enquiry of the questionnaire was to ascertain the relative success of the network initiative in promoting the integration of staff and associates into the philosophies of excellence in the University education initiatives.

All respondents indicated a positivity in perception on the Likert scale, the representatives of FE colleges expressing a high level of satisfaction with the interaction process and greater understanding of what the University was striving to achieve; they each scored 5–7 on the Likert scale. The head of ESOL at Bolton College, for example, commented, "I really enjoyed attending the TEN network meetings. I've met people from Bolton University, people from Bolton and Bury colleges, and we've all been committed to sharing best possible practice between our institutions, so it's been a pleasure being involved in it". This is a positive statement from a senior member of college staff on the effect of the network format on the promotion of a sense of integration into the institution and its philosophies, coupled with the facilitation of connections to the broader network of educators.

The format of the meetings developed and expanded over quarterly sessions so far promoted effective, and enjoyable, cross-school synergies with the potential for new collaborative relationships across the post-18-year-old education sectors. The TEN process has the potential to play a key part in the continuing professional development programme, "instrumental… as dissemination of recent initiatives being fed back to our colleagues [on such improvement programmes as] the Taking a Chance on Change (TACOC) project, and blended teaching strategies such as the One-Note, Vevox and Socrative interactive presentation software". The integration of staff aids cohesion and direction for the faculty and University as a whole, particularly when conducted in an informal context of staff development, ideals, it is suggested, more effectively assimilated when discussed in a guided social environment.

Benefits to the teacher as an individual and professional learner

The teacher experience, it is suggested, is directly linked to understanding and the minimisation of a perception of academic isolation. As such, it was important to ascertain how the networking initiative promoted engagement and a sense of owning the ideals of institutional education, and the meeting participants were asked if they gained personal satisfaction from attendance and interaction. In simple terms, on a scale of 1 to 7, they were asked if they felt better, more involved, motivated, focused, appreciated. There tends to be a status division between senior professors of enviable experience and those less accomplished teachers who aspire to excellence. The TEN structure aims to effect a cultural change in promoting the equality of good, inspired thinking per se. It encourages less-experienced academics to express their teaching, assessment and student intervention plans and methods, often new and innovative, reducing the potential for academic isolation across the faculty and University. Note was taken of the assertion of Boud and Walker on the organisation and planning of meetings: "it is the learner's interaction with the learning milieu which creates the particular learning experience. While facilitators, and others, can help create the milieu, it is the learner who creates the experience" (Boud & Walker, 1990: 62).

The representative of Bradford College indicated she "particularly enjoyed the networking opportunities afforded by TEN". Amongst the University staff respondents, a lecturer in Sport Psychology enthusiastically asserted on video that "TEN provided a great opportunity to network outside of my school, meeting people from psychology and law which you don't normally do". Exposure to broader experiences can only enlighten. The meetings have also proved to be a valuable and effective induction method for welcoming new staff, and an invitation to share their best practice in an informal environment to enhance the sense of involvement in the pursuit of teaching excellence, an assimilation of experience. Diversity of teaching subject proves no bar to the effect of teaching practice, a mathematics professor commenting that the broad network of educators "provides an amazing opportunity to hear the different contributions of people and also the menu of potential teaching strategies which could be used in teaching mathematics". Other comments were brief and simple, especially from less-experienced educators and those relatively new to the institution, for one of whom it was "nice to have someone listen".

The development of new contacts and relationships through cross-school synergy enhances a sense of collaboration. This is more conducive to the success of a planned, effective and agreed strategy than imposition, particularly when experienced in small groups or teams providing observation, monitoring and support (Cordingley et al., 2005). The bottom-up exchange of methodologies and operations, and its effects on teaching quality are made available in concise and brief presentation to the informal gathering. Professionals are not lectured at. The feedback from such meetings indicates a body more receptive to new ideas; the proof of effectiveness of new plans remains with the impetus to introduce change.

Perception of effect on teaching practice and learner interaction

Evaluation of the integration purpose of the TEN required participants to be asked the final broad question of impact and effectiveness, if they thought the meetings had an impact on the way they taught and interacted with learners. Their perception of increased integration into the excellence philosophies is only of value when it has the effect of creating an ethos of continuous improvement. The only purpose of any initiative for excellence in teaching is the effect on outcomes for learners. It was particularly noted that a new member of staff said the meetings had been an invaluable "source of advice and counsel on many HE imperatives such as retention and educational gain". The value of networking amongst academics is set to continue as the higher education landscape continues to shift.

The senior lecturer in Sports at the University commented that TEN "provides a great opportunity for practising academics to share good practice across the network of the University". This is complemented by an associate of the Institute of Management adding "It was really useful for me because it has been delivered by practitioners in education". The initiative is described herein as a social programme, minimising isolation, developing relationships and exchanging ideas, but sight has not been lost of its primary purpose of achieving benefits to the experience of the learners. This point was not lost on the standards officer responsible for enhancement and learner experience: "I've enjoyed meeting people from different schools and particularly what I've been able to learn are different ideas on delivery in the classroom and different methods and tools people use which we haven't got yet, and I'm grateful for that". This encapsulates the twin purpose of networking.

The question of adaptation and change of practice, predicated on the ideas and teaching methodologies exchanged, was the only part of the perception survey to attract a significant proportion of below-average Likert-scale scores of 3. Two of those six respondents further commented that they would essentially reserve judgement and see whether it "will… change anything", one expressing a hope that it did not turn into another "talking shop". This is not simply a view shared by those respondents. Education professionals are too busy to simply chat and 'have fun' in the fulfilment of their CPD responsibilities; they want effective recognition of their contribution to the philosophy of excellence. Indeed, Professor David Hopkins, Head of Education Leadership, was concise on this point: "I think TEN is a great idea and is working really well. It fits perfectly into the TIRI philosophy. My only suggestion would be that we codify the teaching strategies that colleagues are talking about so in a sense we can produce a set of protocols that define the practice of teaching and learning inside the University, and then we can share and use them as a basis of our triad working". This recognition will enable management committees to plan for the implementation of, and monitor, pertinent improvements to university and further education teaching programmes as well as developing blended and hybrid teaching practices which further the excellence quest. It will be the subject of further study as the TEN initiative develops to examine and evaluate change as a result of collaborative, ground roots impetus and design. Whilst there is evidence from feedback of the social and interactive benefits of the programme, the true value lies action on teaching and learning improvement.

Development and integration of the TEN programme

Plans have already been made to integrate TEN into the philosophy structure of university practice and continuing teacher education. The future of this project is predicated on the successful implementation of Gibbs and colleagues' principles, which stress the development of teacher relationships with each other as a basis of improvement; adapted to this context, it is a respect and leadership structure not based simply on title and status but communication and rapport (Gibbs, Knapper & Piccinin, 2009). Credibility and trust are built through interaction and exchange, teaching problems identified and resolved through discussion. Leadership and change are not simply imposed but a teaching community is built on firm foundations of recognition and ability. The improvement of teaching relationships will enhance marketability of the department to learners, who apprise the opportunities of input and involvement in their own education, enhancing support for change and innovation in teaching, learning and research programmes.

It has been noted from the involvement and feedback of FE professionals that the value of the network initiative is not restricted to one higher education institution, but a reaching out to local stakeholders in the furtherance of added value for its student education. It must extend beyond the University structure per se into a broad regional, multi-level teacher education programme. The pursuit of a definition of excellence practice requires input from and benefit to professionals grounded in the improvement of learning. It is for this reason that the TEN is planned as the foundation for a more extensive project, a regional and potentially national integration of its socially based infrastructure into a Teaching Excellence Engagement Model being developed by the author.

What is fed into the process evidently impacts on the quality of what is produced by way of academic awareness and growth of experience and expertise. The needs of schools, colleges and the wider stakeholder community of business and political interests have to be accommodated in promoting the relevance of the style and content of the higher education process. This will enhance rather than compromise the service to the learners whose input will also be taken account of, how they wish to study and be taught. Herein lies a major benefit of the relative informality of the networking process.

The combination of academic improvement and the societal service of the University will facilitate greater retention, given the knowledge that the student voice will be heard, and improve access to differential employment options. Teaching and learning ambassadors will advertise and promote the TIRI programme externally, engage other teaching professionals, initially through the University of Bolton Group, and the wider community. An invitation has, at the time of writing, been extended to local stakeholders to address senior staff on improvement of their education service and the benefit of integration into the regional network partnership. Contact arrangements and invitations are prepared for selected business, professional and education institution representatives from high schools and FE colleges to future meetings. This will facilitate a broader exchange of knowledge of needs and solutions, placing higher education firmly as an engine for the economic advancement of learners in the changing socio-political environment.

Conclusion

In the context of the commercialisation of higher education, league tables and consumer–learner choice, universities must undertake an attractive, intelligent programme of improvement of their teaching and learning product. The university is judged by its standards and quality of teaching service to its learners, including the enhancement of employment prospects. It is, in effect, the learners who will ultimately judge the success of teaching, not simply by satisfaction with their results but the part they play in the institution and their relationships with their educators and each other. This creates the imperative of their involvement in the teaching process which can more effectively be achieved by owning the initiatives. Teachers and their students therefore have a defined mutual interest in productive communication. Standards are set to guide and push attainment; how this is brought about is of itself a collaborative exercise, and it is incumbent on TEN to encourage the involvement of the student body. It will be for future discussion to decide how this can be achieved without prejudicing the free interaction of professional commentary and ideas, which is an important aspect of the initiative.

The planning of the TEN sessions encouraging interaction and collaboration brings professional educators together in the name of teacher improvement; the aim is to create attraction rather than simply an obligation. It complements the Teaching Intensive, Research Informed (TIRI) programme, promoted by the University, with considerable scope for expansion of its principles to the broader, multi-level educational infrastructure. The focus is early intervention and student retention, transition and success through education based on the fulfilment of the academic, professional and emotional needs of the learner (University of Bolton, 2018). It is the concentration on teaching improvement which is the key to such achievement goals. As a result, the value of the TEN programme as a foundation of the engagement model has proved to be of academic interest, value and advantage to senior management, peers and junior colleagues, as evidenced by the steadily increasing attendance over the three meetings held.

It is expected that internal, University membership of the programme will increase, especially when its value to professional excellence is more widely disseminated. Beyond this, it will aid the progress of greater integration of school and college involvement with their local university, adding benefit to learner recruitment through the commitment to quality teaching. With new partners on board, from the education, business and political communities, and the involvement of students, this is a project which will become embedded as an essential part of TIRI practice. The stakeholder input is broad and its impact real for students and their society.

There is much left to evaluate as the TEN process becomes perceived as a normal activity for educators, other professionals and students. The primary assessment of its value as an integrated practice of the TIRI and TEEM programmes will be by gauging the effect of change. Future studies will seek to examine growth of diversity of involvement and the perceptions of teachers and students that the direction of their education is aimed to promote high standards of challenge and achievement, both personally and professionally. The prospects and potential of the increased opportunities of integration and collaboration in new and effective blended teaching strategies and respect are to be actively pursued.

References

Ashwin, P. (2015). Seven myths of university teaching. *Times Higher Education* (26 February). Available from: https://www.timeshighereducation.com/comment/opinion/seven-myths-of-university-teaching/2018719.article [Accessed: 14 October 2022].

Aveyard, H. (2018). *Doing a literature review in health and social care: A practical guide*.

Bernard, H. R., & Bernard, H. R. (2013). *Social research methods: Qualitative and quantitative approaches*. Sage.

Boote, D. N., & Beile, P. (2005). Scholars before researchers: On the centrality of the dissertation literature review in research preparation. *Educational Researcher*, 34(6), 3–15.

Boud, D., & Walker, D. (1990). Making the most of experience. *Studies in Continuing Education*, 12(2), 61–80.

Bunce, L., Baird, A., & Jones, S. E. (2017). The student-as-consumer approach in higher education and its effects on academic performance. *Studies in Higher Education*, 42(11), 1958–1978.

Cordingley, P., Bell, M., Thomason, S., & Firth, A. (2005). The impact of collaborative continuing professional development (CPD) on classroom teaching and learning. Review: How do collaborative and sustained CPD and sustained but not collaborative CPD affect teaching and learning.

Day, C. (2002). *Developing teachers: The challenges of lifelong learning.* Routledge.

Dreyfus, H. L., & Dreyfus, S. E. (1986). *Mind over machine: The power of human intuition and expertise in the age of the computer.* Oxford, United Kingdom: Basil Blackwell Publishing. DOI, 10, 0377-2217.

Elton, L. (1998). Dimensions of excellence in university teaching. *International Journal for Academic Development*, 3(1), 3–11.

Emery, C., Kramer, T., & Tian, R. (2001). Customers vs. products: Adopting an effective approach to business students. *Quality Assurance in Education*, 9(2): 110–115.

Gersten, R., Morvant, M., & Brengelman, S. (1995). Close to the classroom is close to the bone: Coaching as a means to translate research into classroom practice. *Exceptional Children*, 62(1), 52–66.

Gibbs, G., Knapper, C., & Piccinin, S. (2009). *Departmental Leadership of Teaching in Research-Intensive Environments* (Ser. Research and Development Series). The Higher Education Academy.

Greatbatch, D., & Holland, J. (2016). *Teaching quality in higher education: Literature review and qualitative research.* Department for Business, Innovation and Skills.

Howard, J. (2010). The value of ethnic diversity in the teaching profession: A New Zealand case study. *International Journal of Education*, 2(1), 1.

Kennedy, A. (2005). Models of continuing professional development: A framework for analysis. *Journal of In-service Education*, 31(2), 235–250.

Nudzor, H. P. (2013). The big question: Why do change initiatives in education often fail to yield desired results. *Educational Futures*, 6(1), 79–94.

Palmer, R. E. (2008). *Ultimate leadership: winning execution strategies for your situation.* Pearson Prentice Hall.

Pritchard, A. (2007). *Effective teaching with internet technologies: Pedagogy and practice.* SAGE.

Reynolds, D. (2006). Teachers' continuing professional development: A new approach. In 20th Annual World International Congress for Effectiveness and Improvement.

Robinson, C., & Sebba, J. (2004). *A review of research and evaluation to inform the development of the new postgraduate professional development programme.* TTA/University of Sussex.

Santos, J., Figueiredo, A. S., and Vieira, M. (2019). Innovative pedagogical practices in higher education: An integrative literature review. *Nurse Education Today*, 72: 12–17.

Schraw, G., Brownlee, J. L., Olafson, L., & Brye, M. V. V. (2017). *Teachers' personal epistemologies evolving models for informing practice.* IAP, Information Age Publishing, Inc.

University of Bolton. (2018). TIRI Conference 2018. University of Bolton. Available from: https://www.bolton.ac.uk/events/tiri [Accessed: 14 September 2020].

Wallace, D. P., & van Fleet, C. J. (2012). Knowledge into action: Research and evaluation in library and information science: Research and evaluation in library and information science. ABC-CLIO.

White, T. L., & McBurney, D. H. (2012). *Research methods.* Cengage Learning.

Wind, J., & Rangaswamy, A. (2001). Customerization: The next revolution in mass customization. *Journal of Interactive Marketing*, 15(1), 13–32.

CHAPTER SIX

Staff Perceptions of the Transition to Blended and Online Teaching and Learning

Professor Paul Hollins, Dr Sarah Telfer and Daniel Edmondson

Introduction

This chapter discusses the impact of the transition to blended and online teaching and learning on the teaching staff at the University of Bolton (UoB). It reports on the preliminary findings of a questionnaire which is part of an ongoing longitudinal study of staff perceptions of the support and guidance provided to them, both during the pandemic and in relation to the current implementation of the University's new strategy entitled Campus Plus. From the start of the pandemic, the University endeavoured to ensure that students were not disadvantaged in their teaching and learning experience and strived to deliver the equivalent standard of education by a digital medium, or, indeed, to enhance it (University of Bolton, 2020).

The transition had a profound and lasting effect on both staff and students, and during the initial transition to online teaching that occurred between March 2020 and March 2021, staff were exposed to the challenges posed by a sudden and fundamental transformation of their teaching, curriculum design, delivery and assessment. A radical overhaul of approaches and methods in the design and delivery was required to ensure that educational standards and student experience were maintained.

The study captured the perceptions of staff regarding the support provided to them by the University through the period of the online transition during the COVID-19 pandemic. Firstly, data was gathered on how the challenges and the support of the University impacted on academics' personnel mental health and wellbeing, and on their self-confidence in their ability to manage delivery of an effective and meaningful higher education (HE) pedagogic experience for their students. Secondly, the study examined the nature of the challenges faced by academics and the strategies that they deployed to ensure that a high-quality learning experience was maintained for students.

Whilst a number of studies have been undertaken examining student voice and student perspectives (Capranos, Dyers & Magd, 2021) there was less emphasis on research that examined the positive and negative impact of the online transition on staff. In our case, the study responded to a clear practical need for the University to understand the impact of these changes on tutors, their teaching practice, and their relationship with the institution in terms of their personal disposition and development and of the institutional support provided.

The requirements of the study were distilled into six research questions:

Research questions

1. What was the impact of the transition to online learning on the job satisfaction of University of Bolton staff?

2. What was the impact of the transition to online teaching on the personal welfare of University of Bolton staff?

3. What was the impact of the online transition on individual staff members' relationship with educational technology?

4. What was the impact of the online transition on individual staff and their interactions with peers and students?

5. What was the impact of the online transition on the teaching practice of individual staff?

6. How did individual University of Bolton staff feel they were supported by the University in making the transition to online teaching?

During the initial stages of the pandemic our perception was that there was UoB institutional intent and support, combined with resilient, flexible staff who, faced with the challenges of COVID-19 and engagement with new pedagogic practice, rapidly developed new skills, and gained experience of tools and instruments that enabled them to move beyond what was in effect an 'emergency' teaching mode to a reimagined and a new enhanced mode of blended learning.

Informed by this experience, a new model of blended learning emerged encapsulated within a new Campus Plus institutional framework for teaching and learning, underpinned by a 'four pillars approach' (University of Bolton Access and Participation Plan, 2022). This framework affords students new opportunities to engage with teaching and learning remotely accompanied by on-campus practical sessions.

The context of the study

During 2020, the COVID-19 pandemic caused a radical disruption to the work practices of academics and tutors. As a result, the institution was required to extensively re-evaluate its teaching and learning strategy and within it the purpose and application of educational technologies as a fundamental aspect of teaching. The first phase of what would emerge as an 'online transition' occurred as a direct response to the UK government's lockdown of UK institutions and we characterise this as an emergency teaching phase. Informed by the experience of the pandemic, the emergency teaching phase organically evolved into a second phase of embellishment and refinement of online pedagogic practice.

The crisis prompted HE educators internationally to reappraise their professional practice, "remote teaching roles" and beliefs (EDEN

Conference, 2021). HE teaching activities were moved online in March 2020, as part of the response to the COVID-19 regulations set out by the UK government (Gov.UK, 2021). HE policy makers, leadership and staff were required to swiftly adapt their practice and move to a new online education landscape. Some twelve months later, in March 2021, online teaching was still the predominant model in place to minimise the spread of the virus (Gov.UK, 2021). Campus access for face-to-face teaching was still not permitted unless the students were classified as key workers in areas such as teacher training and nursing (Gov.UK, 2021). The restrictions to physical access were finally lifted and face-to-face, on-campus teaching resumed in HE again in September 2021.

Mental health and wellbeing of UK university staff

Teaching and pastoral care for students during the COVID-19 pandemic were a challenge for many educators. The impact on mental health and wellbeing (MHWB) was highlighted by authors including Kim, Oxley and Asbury (2021) as an issue of great national concern, with educators comparing their brains to "browsers with a million tabs open", describing the feeling of having the "rug pulled out" from under them (Kim, Oxley & Asbury, 2021; Kim & Asbury, 2020).

The University of Victoria (2022) suggested that increased workload for staff facing the pressure of adapting to online teaching raises MHWB concerns. The University also highlighted a need for increased awareness and compassion for staff facing isolation and mental health challenges experienced in a new online teaching environment. These findings are supported by the Association for Learning Technology (ALT) 2020 annual survey on learning technology in the age of COVID-19 (Deepwell & O'Sullivan, 2020) which found that members' wellbeing had been profoundly impacted by online teaching. A report published by Durham University authored by Dougall, Weick and Vasiljevic on the mental health and wellbeing of UK university staff during the coronavirus pandemic, collected data collected in March 2021 from 1,182 staff employed across 92 UK universities. The findings of the Durham report suggested that during this period, university staff were grappling with high levels of poor mental health and wellbeing, citing issues with social inclusion, stress, high anxiety and emotional exhaustion (Dougall, Weick & Vasiljevic, 2021). During the pandemic, all UK academics were faced with the pressing challenge of transitioning all teaching delivery 'overnight' to a range of online environments to deliver both asynchronous and synchronous learning experiences. In addition to this, staff were adapting to significant new institutional policies and procedures which were created in response to COVID-19, including the management of online exam boards, the co-ordination of electronic moderation for internal and external examiners, and new assessment regulations and extensions.

An earlier meta-analysis study conducted by Faragher, Cass and Cooper (2005) demonstrated that *job satisfaction* is strongly correlated with mental/psychological health. James and Thériault (2020) discuss the challenges faced by adult education during the COVID-19 pandemic, citing "inequalities, changes, and resilience", and emphasising how educators demonstrated immense flexibility "going above and beyond" to keep adults in education and reach the most vulnerable learners. Tett (2020) suggests that in these difficult times, teachers needed more than ever to look for "resources of hope".

During the pandemic, UoB made efforts to keep staff safe and well by complying with the Coronavirus Act 2020 (Gov.UK, 2020) and adhering to the corresponding advice and regulations provided by the UK government, Public Health England, the National Health Service, the Foreign and Commonwealth Office and Bolton Council's Public Health Department (Cabinet Office, 2020; Choi, Tuel & Eltahir, 2021; University of Bolton, 2020; Williams et al., 2020). As a result of these changes, academics experienced a range of institutional challenges which contributed to pressures on their mental health and wellbeing.

Dougall, Weick and Vasiljevic (2021) highlighted that alleviating these factors fell more within the remit of HE institutions than within the remit of government and policy makers. Primarily HE academic staff were faced with the pressing challenge of suddenly transitioning their practice to an online environment. It is reasonable to assume that staff had varying degrees of digital literacy, competence and experience of accessing online platforms such as Zoom and Microsoft Teams, and of using online educational tools and technologies, and therefore that some staff were better prepared to cope with the increased pressures due to the alignment between digital skills and the demands of teaching. In addition, staff and students were unable to interact with each other in a face-to-face environment, leading to heightened stress, anxiety and insecurity through social isolation, due to the loss of a 'physical presence' and frustration at not being able to connect better with each other (Fancourt, Steptoe & Bue, 2020; University of Victoria, 2022).

It is worth noting that a significant number of the staff at the University of Bolton had, prior to the pandemic, only very limited exposure to, engagement with or experience of Technology Enhanced Learning (TEL). The profound effect of the pandemic prompted both the institution and tutors to fundamentally re-evaluate what constitutes authentic student engagement in the teaching and learning process.

Methodology

The nature of the COVID-19 pandemic, and the existential threat it presented, generated enormous risk for institutions. To mitigate that risk, agile approaches were required to produce effective guidelines and policy, both as regards health more broadly and also in terms of the impact of the pandemic on teaching and learning, and student and staff wellbeing. In this crisis management context, the UoB research team were not initially afforded the luxury of a planned and extended period of research. Consequently, a mixed methodological approach was taken, with a relatively short data collection period, and a combination of both quantitative and qualitative research methods providing robust description, evaluation and interpretation of the data. This allowed the research team to present initial findings in a relatively short space of time, and to make them available to senior management to inform policy through the established institutional process via the standing Panel for Teaching and Learning, as well as disseminating them more broadly to the wider HE sector through presentations at the Association for Learning Technology (ALT) annual conferences in 2020 and 2021.

The research provided the opportunity to undertake in-depth questioning and evaluate rich data not usually solicited through more conventional established evaluation channels such as staff surveys, departmental and faculty group meetings and general discussions. The study was focussed on gaining a deep understanding of the staff, from diverse perspectives across the institution in terms of both discipline and practice, and perceptions of the role of technology within the emergent teaching and learning environment.

The mixed methods approach that was adopted incorporated the collection of primary quantitative data, gathered through a voluntary staff online questionnaire. The data informed the development of open and closed questions to be explored by a series of self-selected focus groups, to examine the impact of the pandemic on tutors' practice and their relationship with the institution. The groups were organised within subject and school disciplines, namely the School of Art and Design and Creative Technologies, the Faculty of Professional Studies (incorporating business, accounting and law, education and psychology) and the Faculty of Health and Well-being.

This provided the research team with the opportunity to further examine any significant variance of responses within subject/school disciplines. The focus group questions were framed within the six overarching research questions detailed above. The research team adopted a phenomenological approach, one that emphasised the experiential aspects of online teaching and learning during the COVID-19 emergency. This allowed the research team to evaluate rich qualitative data almost in real time, as opposed to reflective thoughts on the experience ascribed subsequently. This part of the research provided a rich snapshot of the adaptation of staff to the COVID-19 crisis.

Online questionnaire

The appendix (see end of chapter) provides a copy of the questionnaire that was developed to examine UOB staff members' perceptions of how well they felt that they were supported by the institution, and to explore staff perceptions of the swift transition to online provision. The questionnaire was designed to provide data that would further the researchers and the University of Bolton's understanding of the factors influencing online provision. It also examined the impact of the transition on tutors' feelings of stress, anxiety and isolation, related to the practical aspects of delivering education remotely using new technology and digital skills.

The online questionnaire was distributed to all UoB staff who were invited to participate in the research, on a voluntary basis and with their informed consent. All responses to the 30 questions were anonymised and consisted of a combination of Likert scale and open questions. Likert questions were included as a method for collecting quantitative data from which preliminary conclusions were drawn. The open questions provided respondents with the opportunity to articulate issues that the research team might not have considered and to frame further detailed questioning within focus groups at a later stage.

The highest response rate was from the Faculty of Health and Well-being, which includes staff in Nursing at 36% (a rapidly expanding subject area in the University, containing high numbers of new staff with less experience of HE), followed by the Faculty of Professional Studies (which includes staff from Education). Nursing and Education studies have a high representation of female staff and during the pandemic both nurses and teachers were categorised as key workers by the government (DFE, 2021). The relatively high response rate could be attributed to the characteristics of the two faculties, as reflection is an integral part of daily professional practice in Health and Social Care, and teachers are also strongly encouraged to be critically self-reflective and responsive to engaging in research (McFadyen & Rankin, 2016).

Research focus groups

The second stage of the research project was the establishment of subject-specific focus groups, to further examine key issues raised and highlighted by respondents in the first phase of questionnaires. All three of the faculties engaged in the research were invited to participate in faculty-based focus group discussions.

The issues chosen for examination in the focus groups were as follows:

- What has lecturers' experience been of changes in university organisation and processes?

- What changes have occurred in lecturers' teaching practice?
- What is lecturers' perception of changes in students' learning?
- To what extent is there alignment between the assumptions of the strategy of the University and the perceptions of teachers?

The groups were conducted virtually over the period of a month using the Zoom video-conferencing application. Recordings of the focus-group discussions were made with consent and the group discussions were fully transcribed, whilst maintaining the anonymity of individual respondents.

Results and findings

There were 93 full questionnaire responses received across the three faculties and from this, five key themes were identified as being of interest for more detailed analysis:

- Gender aspects
- Job experience and satisfaction
- Perceptions of isolation
- Institutional support and expectations during the pandemic
- Technologies used for lesson delivery and communication.

Gender factors

Those staff that self-identified as being male and those staff that self-identified as being female are hereafter respectively referred to in this chapter as male and female.

Gender factors, whilst not a focus of the initial research brief, warranted discussion and analysis. Of those declaring a 'gender' in the survey, 57% identified as female and 40% identified as male, and this was broadly representative of the declared gender make-up of the UoB staff. However, differences between genders in the participant rate were statistically significant (with much greater than a 5% $p < 0.05$

probability of occurring by chance or through a sampling error) in the second phase of the research project, with approaching 90% of the participants self-declared as being female. This response rate variance in participation in focus groups is, however, not unprecedented, and Peterson and Smith (2019) suggest this could be due to females having more "agreeable traits" (*sic*) and greater willingness to participate in wider research. In future studies it would be interesting to investigate the reasons for this change in the participation rates for males and females in the two phases of the research.

The fact that the response rate for both questionnaires and focus groups was highest in the Faculty of Health, where a higher proportion of staff are female, could merely reflect the large cohort in the subject area; but nevertheless, this is a factor influencing the response rates. Consequently, it would be disingenuous to claim that the study is entirely representative of the gender balance in the wider workforce of the institution.

Analysis of the data revealed that female staff members who identified themselves as being 'experienced' or 'very experienced' teachers were also those who declared the highest levels of negative experience towards job satisfaction (with much greater than a 5% $p < 0.05$ probability of occurring by chance or through a sampling error). This perspective was one reinforced by the response to Q:10, where 68% of respondents indicated that they had experienced a change in job satisfaction.

Job experience and satisfaction

Of the teaching staff who responded to the research questionnaire, 75% described themselves as being experienced or as very experienced educators, with less than 10% describing themselves as inexperienced. In relation to job satisfaction, 61% of respondents declared that their job satisfaction was worse as a result of their online emergency teaching and that their satisfaction had deteriorated to varying degrees during the lockdown period. There was a significant variance in response between females and males, with females more likely to have experienced a marked deterioration in job satisfaction. Responses to Q:43 indicated that females were more likely to have experienced a deterioration in their job satisfaction, with over 50%

(54.55%) of females declaring they had experienced a downturn in job satisfaction. Comparatively, their male counterparts declared experiencing only a moderately worse level of job satisfaction. Responses to Q:11 regarding job satisfaction revealed declarations of both positive and negative factors. The positive factors declared revealed some advantages to staff in working from home as opposed to on campus, including such factors as greater working autonomy; the ability to get more work done as a result of the lack of office interruption; improved accessibility for students and colleagues working remotely; and time and money savings without the daily commute to work.

Perceptions of 'isolation'

As indicated in Table 1, some staff expressed feelings of isolation and this was identified as an issue warranting further investigation. In respect of support by the institution, those educators who declared themselves experienced were more likely to experience deteriorating job satisfaction. A lack of human interaction was identified as a contributing factor to the feelings of isolation and, as indicated in Table 1 below, those respondents identifying as female declared feeling more isolated than their male counterparts.

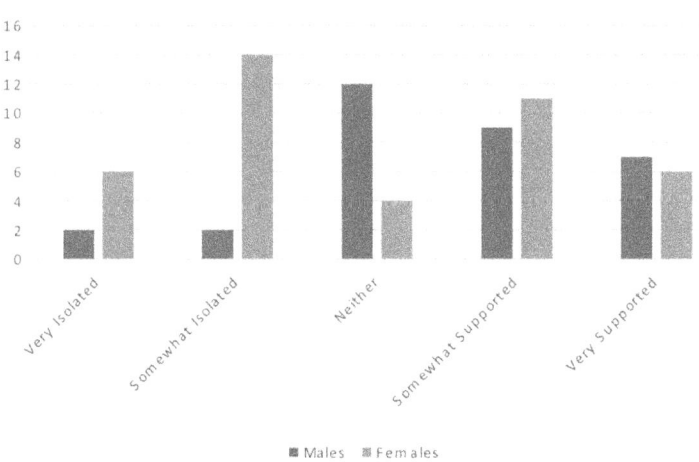

Table 1. Isolation: male vs. female

The highest rate of responses indicating feelings of isolation was from the School of Health and Well-being. This matches the results for job satisfaction, and as previously discussed, this school has a high proportion of female staff. According to the preliminary discussions with the focus groups, some staff suggested that changes to work practices prompted negative feelings amongst staff members. These were focused on feelings of isolation from colleagues, peers and students. Open questioning highlighted issues including perceptions of lack of interaction (having no face-to-face contact featured highly), and staff highlighted a lack of human interaction in the classroom and social interaction with work colleagues in both formal and informal settings.

Other comments included declarations from some staff that they missed the practical aspects of delivery which were, in their view, "more effective in a classroom setting". Conversely, staff highlighted feelings of increased pressure due to student expectations and the institution of higher levels of availability in the online environment. There was a perception of a resultant increase in workload, with higher than usual email traffic compounded by a perception of having "no time to switch off from work" whilst they were working from home.

In Table 2 below it is evident that the staff in the faculty feeling most isolated were located in the School of Health and Well-being and, as discussed above, there is a direct correlation with those staff identified as "key workers" (DFE, 2021).

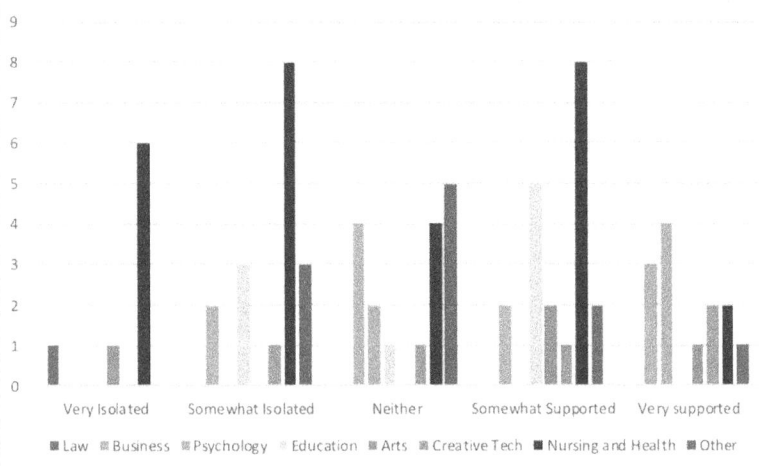

Table 2. Feelings of isolation within faculties and schools

Institutional support and expectations during the pandemic

In focus group discussion, staff expressed their belief that a critical factor in the maintenance of staff wellbeing during the pandemic was the clarity of communication and their perception of being well supported by the institution through the pandemic, and more explicitly through the emergency teaching phase. Most staff felt clear or very clear regarding the expectations of senior management in respect of the transition to online and that this had been well communicated to them.

Staff feeling of comfort with delivering online

Over 70% of all respondents declared themselves 'comfortable' with teaching online, with only 4% being uncomfortable with the experience. However, this overwhelmingly positive assertion should be treated with some caution as there may be an element of bias in the data. Despite the best efforts of the research team to reassure participants and to maintain anonymity of responses, it is acknowledged that some staff may have felt apprehension that any unfavourable responses about management might have operational repercussions.

Data from the questionnaire supported the view that staff were most concerned about increased levels of administrative tasks during the transition to online teaching and learning. The tasks highlighted by open responses in the study included compliance with requirements for registration, student attendance and student engagement. A large number of staff (45% of respondents) believed administration processes had become increasingly difficult during the lockdown period, although there was recognition by staff of the efforts of the Quality Assurance (QA) team to provide support to students and to ensure their learning experience was not compromised. Indeed 45% of respondents were neutral in terms of the impact they felt the transition had had on their students moving forward successfully with their studies. Prima facie, this may seem at odds with the earlier findings discussed relating to job satisfaction. Despite the School of Nursing and Health predominantly showing signs of isolation (tables 1 and 2), they were also the school which significantly stated they had a good level of reciprocal understanding of expectations with the University line managers. These apparent mismatches in results are an issue that warrants further study. Further analysis indicates that staff who identified themselves as 'inexperienced educators' were strongly correlated with those who described themselves as 'feeling isolated' or 'wanting support'.

Contextual factors which are unique to schools may be relevant in this regard, for example as a result of the rapid development of nursing at the University. This area is largely populated with new staff who are transitioning from being in-service NHS staff to the role of HE lecturer at the University, simultaneously balancing new online teaching with their continued professional development as a nurse during an international pandemic.

Staff response to the technologies deployed for lesson delivery and communication

A number of practical concerns and issues were highlighted in the qualitative responses to Q:11 of the questionnaire. Staff were worried about having to rely on their personal IT equipment, technology, Wi-Fi and internet connections, and declared, in open text responses, concerns over the "limited office space" at home and of health and safety issues, specifically problems relating to posture and "pains from sitting at a very small desk chair designed for occasional use".

The majority of respondents (62%) declared they enjoyed using technology within their teaching practice and only a very small percentage (1%) declared they would avoid using technology if they could. In this aspect of the research there was no significant distinction between the responses of female and male staff.

It was also suggested in open question responses that the enforced nature of lockdown had offered staff increased *time* and *creative space* to explore digital tools for education due to the compulsion to rapidly adapt and find new technologies, methods and pedagogic approaches. Staff responses also indicated that they were no longer able to avoid using IT and that *being pushed into it* had been positive.

Further, responses indicated that the staff perception of online meetings and communication between staff and teams had both improved, the number had increased with more regular contact with administration and staff meetings, and improved administrative processes online. Paradoxically, as discussed earlier in this chapter, staff viewed more meetings as both an increase in administrative burden and an improvement in institutional communication.

Some aspects of online delivery were identified as problematic by staff, and in particular 66% of respondents declared that their time in preparation had increased markedly during the online transition as compared to preparation for face-to-face teaching.

As previously highlighted, concerns also focused on increased communication, with the intensity of email traffic causing delays in staff responses and with the tone of "written communication often appearing more abrupt than spoken". Lack of access to office phones resulted in the requirement for staff to use their own mobile phones and devices, exacerbating the dissatisfaction of staff being required to use their home equipment and technologies for work. Issues relating to the digital divide and digital poverty were evident, with staff with less-sophisticated technologies and poor internet connections struggling with the expectations and assumptions of management that all staff had high-quality tools and connectivity. For some staff this was clearly not the case.

Comments from new and 'inexperienced' members of staff highlighted the challenges in declaring they were "still finding their feet". Where previously they had relied on having experienced colleagues around them to answer routine questions, they found technology-mediated communication too formal to ask experienced colleagues for their help.

This is clearly an area that requires further study. Staff observed that some students were more confident when mediated through technology, speaking up online more than in a traditional classroom setting. It was observed that students adapted to the transition and became more comfortable as sessions progressed.

Responses further indicated that staff recognised that some students preferred online learning whilst others did not, the determining factor being students' confidence in their personal digital literacy skills. Staff perceived that their younger students were notably more "tech savvy" and "comfortable with online platforms", with older students seeming "to struggle". This anecdotal evidence should, however, be regarded with some caution as there is little empirical evidence to support notions of distinctions in digital competencies by age.

Conclusions in response to the research questions

1. What was the impact of the transition to online learning on the job satisfaction of University of Bolton staff?

The transition to online teaching and learning resulted in a marked decrease in job satisfaction, particularly amongst senior lecturers and female staff. The responses indicated that this was due to (a) personal issues including a lack of technical equipment and space to work from home, (b) family commitments, especially for females such as distractions from other household members, children being home and child-care responsibilities, and being 'forced' to develop, and (c) learning new digital literacy skills for teaching online in a short amount of time.

It should be noted that there was pressure on subject areas identified by the government as training 'key workers', such as Health and Education, who were continuing to co-ordinate work and/or teaching placements for students in NHS and school/college settings. Many education settings were struggling to operate at this time and NHS hospitals were overwhelmed with coping with the pandemic. The impact of the pandemic itself on staff mental health *may* have been a significant contributing factor to levels of job satisfaction of staff within the Faculty of Health and Well-being, as indicated by the research.

2. **What was the impact of the transition to online teaching on the personal welfare of University of Bolton staff?**

As with the previous question, staff personal welfare, specifically among those identifying as female, deteriorated markedly during the lockdown and the transition to online teaching. This is consistent with other more general research undertaken with the wider population. Suffice it to say that the pressure to continue to provide a high-quality educational experience in lockdown for learners was felt intensely by staff.

3. **What was the impact of the online transition on individual staff members' relationship with educational technology?**

On the whole, both female and male staff believed that the transition to online teaching and learning had prompted them to use technology in their teaching when they may have not made the change in other circumstances. The imposition of technology prompted staff through necessity to quickly improve both their technical skills and their online pedagogical competencies, and provided a clear focus on the potential affordances of some technologies in teaching and learning. As a result, staff believed that their understanding and their relationship with technology had improved over the period.

4. **What was the impact of the online transition on individual staff and their interactions with peers and students?**

Staff indicated that in some instances interaction and engagement had improved in the online environment, with some students flourishing during the transition whilst others struggled. As highlighted above, staff suggested age as a differentiating factor, though this would require further investigation before any solid conclusions could be drawn.

5. **What was the impact of the online transition on the teaching practice of individual staff?**

A consistent pattern throughout the responses indicated that the majority staff now have a positive perspective towards the use of both blended and wholly online teaching. Exceptions to this positivity come from staff who experienced a negative impact on their own job satisfaction, though this was due to more personal and individual circumstances related to: lack of technical equipment and space to work from home; personal home circumstances such as distractions from other household members and children being home; being 'forced' to develop and to learn new digital literacy skills for teaching online in a short amount of time; and that extensive pressure on key-worker subject areas such as health and education, where staff were continuing to practise either working or co-ordinating work placements for students in NHS and school/college settings.

6. **How did individual University of Bolton staff feel they were supported by the University in making the transition to online teaching?**

It was clear that staff felt the University and their line managers have overwhelmingly provided support and clarity around the expectations of the practice of education in changed circumstances. Nevertheless, it cannot be asserted that all staff felt the same, due to a limited sample size from across the institution. Possibly the more positive people who were coping better were more inclined to spend time doing a questionnaire…

It must be acknowledged that the sample size does currently reflect a good representation of the current demographic of the University in relation to the gender split and staff-to-student ratio in each school. Data indicates that inexperienced staff felt more isolated and so moving forward they would require more support in online teaching, whereas 'experienced' teachers were positive about the digital skills they had learnt and about using blended learning in the future. This finding is supported by Carrillo and Flore's 2020 review of online teaching, suggesting a comprehensive review of the pedagogy of online education to utilise technology more effectively to support remote teaching and learning structured institutional processes to support and train new and 'inexperienced' staff on remote teaching delivery and digital literacy skills.

Future recommendations

The research findings informed the following recommendations moving forward:

- Reflection upon the role that online and distance education will play moving forward, learning from the best practices which emerged from lockdown learning.

- The possible evolution of 'hybrid' blended models of teaching delivery creating a new prototype of HE, requiring new 'digital citizenship' skills.

- Institutional inclusion procedures to combat 'digital poverty', thereby promoting social inclusion, equality and diversity.

- Continued exploration of more online non-traditional assessment methods and procedures.

- Consideration of how to implement best practice and resilience in affective factors such as mental health and wellbeing, and promoting positive behaviour online for both teachers and students.

The initial research has been followed by a second series of focus groups, the responses to which are currently being analysed.

In summary, the preliminary findings of the study concluded that although the move to online teaching had led to a negative impact on the mental health and wellbeing of some tutors, the majority of tutors, who participated in the study, felt well supported by the institution during the transition to online teaching and learning. However, several concerns were identified and highlighted as being problematic, and these included a perception by some tutors of a lack of institutional support and explicitly in the provision of appropriate hardware and software. Tutors reported instances where they were required to use personal technologies, including mobile phones, laptops and desktop computers, which resulted in increased levels of anxiety and in incurring additional expense for upgrading their home broadband speed and in buying new equipment such as computer screens.

The new Campus Plus model at UoB provides a more flexible blended learning approach for staff, combining face-to-face, asynchronous and synchronous teaching and learning, to benefit mental health. However, new challenges are on the horizon, with a government focus on ecological sustainability, and the shift to online education which we have discussed here can make a contribution to this. Although the blended online teaching environment is seen an improvement in reducing staff's carbon footprint (Arora, Bhaukhandi & Mishra, 2020; Nižetić, 2020), issues of the cost of living and 'fuel poverty' (i.e. heating and powering 'offices at home') present new challenges and financial pressures for staff working from home.

Appendix – Educational Technology and COVID Impact Questionnaire.

Q1 What is your gender?

Q2 In which Department/School do you mainly teach? Please choose one.

Q3 How would you describe your relationship with the internet and computer technology (ICT)?

Q4 Would you have answered this question differently before the lockdown?

Q5 If your answer would have been different, can you briefly say in what way you have changed?

Q6 Can you give any examples of the changes (if any)?

Q7 Has your job satisfaction changed since the lockdown?

Q8 If so, in what way has it changed?

Q9 Can you give any examples of the changes (if any)?

Q10 In your online teaching, have you felt isolated from the University or supported by it?

Q11   Can you give any examples of valuable support that you have received, or support that you would have liked to receive?

Q12   In your online teaching since the lockdown, has it been easy or difficult to maintain the University's academic administration and quality processes?

Q13   Can you give any examples of aspects that went surprisingly smoothly, or which caused unexpected difficulties?

Q14   To what extent has the shift to online teaching been supported by the University since the lockdown?

Q15   Can you give some examples of necessary changes (if any) in areas such as management, quality control and academic administration?

Q16   In moving to online teaching, has it been clear to you what the University and your line manager expect from you?

Q17   How comfortable do you feel with delivering online lectures, tutorials and seminars?

Q18   What makes you feel uneasy (if anything)?

Q19   What makes you feel comfortable (if anything)?

Q20   Has the quantity or quality of your interactions with students changed since the move to online teaching?

Q21   Can you give any examples?

Q22   Having moved to online teaching, do you feel that you have a more or a less accurate picture of how your students are moving forward in their studies?

Q23   Can you give any examples?

Q24   How much have you had to do to adapt your face-to-face teaching to the online environment?

Q25   If you have made adaptations, can you give examples?

Q26 Do you find that you need to plan more, or less, for online classes?

Q27 Why do you think there is a difference (if there is one)? Can you give some examples?

Q28 In the move to online teaching, do you feel that you are solving your own problems yourself, or that you making changes as part of a coordinated and shared process?

Q29 Can you give any examples?

Q30 Do you feel you require more training and online technical support?

Q31 What do you need (if anything)?

Q32 Which technologies have you used to deliver lectures and communicate with students?

Q33 Why do you use the ones that you have chosen?

Q34 In your experience, how comfortable do your students feel accessing and participating in online lectures, tutorials and seminars?

Q35 Can you give any examples of what makes students feel comfortable or uncomfortable?

Q36 In your experience, do students find the support services made available to them by the University valuable in their participation in online classes?

Q37 Can you give any examples of support which is of no value (if any)?

Q38 Can you give any examples of valuable support (if any)?

Q39 Do you think that your students would benefit from more training in the use of technology, and online technical support?

Q40 What training or support do you think they need (if any)?

Q41 Do you have any other comments that you would like to add?

Q42   We are also looking for participants who are willing to be interviewed on this topic. If you would be willing to take part in an interview or focus group, please leave your contact email here.

References

Arora, S., Bhaukhandi, K., & Mishra, P. (2020). Coronavirus lockdown helped the environment to bounce back. *The Science of the Total Environment*, 742, 140573–140573.

Cabinet Office (2020). [Online]. Available from: https://www.gov.uk/government/organisations/cabinet-office [Accessed: 18 July 2020].

Capranos, D., Dyers, L., & Magd, A. J. (2021). *Voice of the online learner 2021: Amplifying Student Voices in Extraordinary Times*. A Wiley Education services Project [Online]. Available from: https://universityservices.wiley.com/voice-of-the-online-learner-2021 [Accessed: 18 July 2022].

Carrillo, C., & Assunção Flores, M. (2020). COVID-19 and teacher education: a literature review of online teaching and learning practices. *European Journal of Teacher Education*, 43:4, 466–487 [Online]. Available from: DOI: 10.1080/02619768.2020.1821184 [Accessed: 18 July 2022].

Choi, Y.-W., Tuel, A., & Eltahir, E. A. B. (2021). On the environmental determinants of COVID-19 seasonality. GeoHealth, 5, e2021GH000413 [Online]. Available from: https:// doi.org/10.1029/2021GH000413 [Accessed: 18 July 2021].

Deepwell, M., & O'Sullivan, H. (2020). *Learning Technology in the age of COVID-19: Key findings from the 2020 Annual Survey*. Association for Learning Technology (ALT) 2020 Survey. Available from: https://www.alt.ac.uk/news/all_news/key-findings-our-annual-survey-202021 [Accessed: 20 July 2022].

DFE (2021). Covid Guidelines Coronavirus (COVID-19) DfE 2021 qualifications funding: form guidance [Online]. Available from: https://www.gov.uk/government/publications/dfe-exam-support-service-claiming-costs/coronavirus-covid-19-dfe-2021-qualifications-funding-form-guidance [Accessed: 18 July 2022].

Dougall, I., Weick, M., & Vasiljevic, M. (2021). Inside UK Universities: Staff mental health and wellbeing during the coronavirus pandemic. Project Report. Durham University.

EDEN Conference (2021). [Online]. Available from: https://eden-europe.eu/eden-2021-annual-conference [Accessed: 24 November 2022].

Fancourt, D., Steptoe, A., & Bu, F. (2020). *Trajectories of anxiety and depressive symptoms during enforced isolation due to COVID-19 in England: a longitudinal observational study* [Online]. Available from: https://discovery.ucl.ac.uk/id/eprint/10117860/. [Accessed: 21 July 2022].

Faragher, E. B., Cass, M., & Cooper, C. (2005). The Relationship between Job Satisfaction and Health: A Meta-Analysis. *Journal of Occupational Environmental Medicine*, 62, 105–112 [Online]. Available from: http://dx.doi.org/10.1136/oem.2002.006734 [Accessed: 21 July 2022].

Gov.UK (2020). Coronavirus Act 2020 [Online]. Available from: legislation.gov.uk [Accessed: 13 July 2022].

Gov.UK (2021). Critical workers and vulnerable children who can access schools or educational settings – GOV.UK [Online]. Available from: [Withdrawn] www.gov.uk [Accessed: 13 July 2022].

James, N., & Thériault, V. (2020). Adult education in times of the COVID-19 pandemic: Inequalities, changes, and resilience. *Studies in the Education of Adults*, 52(2020): 129–133

[Online]. Available from: https://www.tandfonline.com/doi/full/10.1080/02660830.2020.1811474 [Accessed: 13 July 2022].

Kim, L. E., & Asbury, K. (2020). 'Like a rug had been pulled from under you': The impact of COVID-19 on teachers in England during the first six weeks of the UK lockdown. *British Journal of Educational Psychology*, 90(4), 1062–1083. https://doi.org/10.1111/bjep.12381 [Accessed: 11 June 2022].

Kim, L. E., Oxley, L., & Asbury, K. (2021). 'My brain feels like a browser with 100 tabs open': A longitudinal study of teachers' mental health and well-being during the COVID-19 pandemic. *Br J Educ Psychol*, 92(1), 299–318. doi: 10.1111/bjep.12450. Epub 2021 Aug 1. PMID: 34337737; PMCID: PMC8420299 [Accessed: 11 June 2022].

McFadyen, J., & Rankin, J. (2016). The Role of Gatekeepers in Research: Learning from Reflexivity and Reflection. *GSTF Journal of Nursing and Health Care*, 4(1), 82–88 [Online]. Available from: http://dl6.globalstf.org/index.php/jnhc/article/view/1745 [Accessed: 12 November 2022].

Nižeti, S. (2020). Impact of coronavirus (COVID-19) pandemic on air transport mobility, energy, and environment: A case study. *International Journal of Energy Research*, 44(13), 10953–10961.

Peterson, S. J., & Smith, G. T. (2019). Impulsigenic personality: Is urgency an example of the jangle fallacy? *Psychological Assessment*, 31(9), 1135–1144 [Online]. Available from: https://doi.org/10.1037/pas0000740 [Accessed: 2 November 2022].

Tett, L. (2020). A response to Vol. 11, supplementary issue, 2020. *Concept*, 11(2), 1–3 [Online]. Available from: http://concept.lib.ed.ac.uk/article/view/4459/6043 [Google Scholar] [Accessed: 22 November 2022].

University of Bolton (2020). Coronavirus [Online]. Available from: https://www.bolton.ac.uk/coronavirus/ [Accessed: 24 November 2022].

University of Bolton Access and Participation Plan (2022). [Online]. Available from: Access and Participation | University of Bolton [Accessed: 12 June 2022].

University of Victoria (2022). [Online]. Available from: https://www.uvic.ca [Accessed: 13 June 2022].

Williams, S. N., Armitage, C. J., Tampe, T., & Dienes, K. (2020). Public perceptions and experiences of social distancing and social isolation during the COVID-19 pandemic: a UK-based focus group study. *BMJ Open*, 10(7): e039334. doi: 10.1136/bmjopen-2020-039334. PMID: 32690752; PMCID: PMC7387310. Available from: https://pubmed.ncbi.nlm.nih.gov/32690752/ [Accessed: 13 June 2022].

CHAPTER SEVEN

Blended Learning: Authentic Assessment and Clinical Supervision

Dr Nick Wadsworth and Mel Greenhalgh

This chapter outlines two case studies from two postgraduate programmes delivered at the University of Bolton: Applied Sport and Exercise Psychology (MSc) and Cognitive Behavioural Psychotherapies (MSc/PGDip). Both programmes utilised core principles from the University's new Campus Plus framework to support students throughout the pandemic. On the Applied Sport and Exercise Psychology (MSc) the Campus Plus model and the GAME+ framework were both used to create authentic assessments, in line with the changing landscape of applied sport and exercise psychology, to improve the employability skills of students. On the Cognitive Behavioural Psychotherapies (MSc/PGDip) programmes, blended learning was used to refine the delivery of clinical supervision and lectures in a way that would enhance student self-determination and experience.

Case Study 1: Applied Sport and Exercise Psychology (MSc)
Authentic assessment and employability

Authentic assessments are designed to create a closer alignment between academic expectations and industry standards (Villarroel et al., 2018). This alignment can enhance theoretical learning and promote application of this theoretical knowledge within professional contexts (Bloxham, 2015). Authentic assessments have been found to improve the quality and depth of student learning (Dochy & McDowell, 1997); to enhance autonomy (Raymond et al., 2013); to develop higher-order cognitive skills (Ashford-Rowe, Herrington & Brown, 2014); to facilitate motivation (Nicol, Thomson & Breslin, 2014); and to stimulate reflection and meta-cognition (Vanaki & Memarian, 2009). Furthermore, the alignment of academic assessments with professional standards places greater emphasis on employability skills (Sambell, McDowell & Montgomery, 2013) or Graduate Attributes (GA; Crammer, 2006), which helps foster the development of competent students as future employees (Gulikers et al., 2004). GA (*"achievement of skills, understanding, and personal attributes that make graduates more likely to secure employment and be successful in their chosen occupations"* – Yorke & Knight, 2006: 8) are integral when considering the holistic development of students and so should be embedded throughout degree programmes (Oliver & Jorre de St Jorre, 2018). These attributes move beyond discipline-specific knowledge and focus on vital transferrable skills such as communication, reflective thinking and confidence (Oliver, 2011). This is essential, given that many employers believe graduates to be lacking these basic skills (Singh, Thambusamy & Ramly, 2014). Hence, authentic assessments might be one of the ways higher education institutions can enhance employability rates (Villarroel et al., 2018) and better prepare students to find meaningful work following graduation (Oliver, 2015; Yorke & Knight, 2006).

However, whilst there is some evidence that GA can (and have) been developed over the course of a degree programme (Treleaven & Voola, 2008), the employability skills of students are still regarded as the lowest measure in relation to employer satisfaction, especially within the context of the field of psychology (Senekal & Smith, 2022). This might be because academics are often not engaged with the integration of GA within their modules (Radloff et al., 2009) and can be resistant to integrating GA in their assessments, as they deem the technical content to be a priority or have practical difficulties in delivering these attributes (large class sizes, lack of time, etc.; Jones, 2009a). Furthermore, some academics may perceive this as an added burden to their already busy schedules (Brush & Saye, 2008; Jafari, 2004). Academics within a higher education context have never been busier than during the COVID-19 pandemic, which according to a recent survey, conducted by the British Psychological Society (BPS), left psychology staff feeling overworked and under-supported (BPS, 2022). In addition to this lack of time, research has also demonstrated that academics generally do not fully understand how GA should be integrated alongside the technical content (Davenport, Spath & Blauvelt, 2009) and as a result GA are not made explicit to the students (Jorre de St Jorre & Oliver, 2018). In order for students to develop these GA, it is essential that they are first and foremost aware of these skills (Bowden et al., 2000), allowing them to take responsibility for their development and ensuring they are more marketable to potential employers (Sullivan & Baruch, 2009). Academics then must consistently reinforce these GA throughout their teaching and ensure they are made explicit within assessment (Hughes & Barrie, 2010).

It has been found that academics that successfully achieve this are deemed to "care more than most" by their students (Jorre de St Jorre & Oliver, 2018). This is important, because the development of strong relationships between teachers and students is one of the most important factors in the learning process (Aregbeyen, 2010). Hence, by focusing on the integration of GA within curriculum design and aligning it to assessments, there is the potential that the learning experience will be more meaningful, employability rates will be improved and a supportive environment can be created. One of the ways that GA can be integrated within an authentic assessment is through principles of constructive alignment (Biggs, 2014). Constructive alignment is an approach to teaching that considers the intended outcomes of a programme prior to teaching taking place (starting with the end in mind). The learning outcomes are clearly stated, and teaching, assessment and feedback are all aligned to successfully achieve these outcomes (Biggs, 2014).

GA should be integrated as part of the outcomes of degree programmes (Biggs, 2014) and embedded within assessment criteria to ensure assessments are authentic and best preparing students for employment (Oliver & Jorre de St Jorre, 2018). However, this approach to curriculum design can be extremely challenging as it requires consideration of the assessment criteria, involvement of key stakeholders, a detailed implementation strategy, quality assurance and staff development, whilst placing the student at the centre of the entire process (Hughes & Barrie, 2010). Furthermore, students often feel as though the emphasis placed on GA is too generic for them to be meaningful and for that reason decide to focus their attention on the learning outcomes of the assessment rather than development of these employability skills (Jorre de St Jorre & Oliver, 2018). To achieve this, employability must be viewed holistically. Generic GA alone are not sufficient when preparing students for the world of work (Bridgstock, 2009). Bridgstock (2009) critically argues that a student experiencing the transition from education to work needs to be familiar with their chosen industry, identify the best opportunities for advancement, know how to develop personal and professional relationships, and be competent in obtaining and progressing within a given role. This would suggest that the development of GA is dependent on the context in which they are delivered (Knight & Page, 2007) and so it is essential that the culture is critically considered (Jones, 2009b; Jones, 2013) when designing and implementing authentic assessments. Furthermore, learning has been found to be most effective when knowledge is obtained within the context in which it will be used (Kwan, 2000).

Graduate Attributes Matrix for Employability (GAME) and the Campus Plus model

The University of Bolton places great importance on the holistic development of the student population. The Graduate Attributes Matrix for Employability (GAME; undergraduate provision) and GAME Plus (GAME+; postgraduate provision) were developed by a panel of senior staff within the University, in consultation with potential employers. Based on internal discussions and feedback from external stakeholders, ten of the most important GA were identified and developed into the following framework (see Figure 1 and Figure 2).

Figure 1. The University of Bolton's Graduate Attributes Matrix for Employability

Graduate Attribute	Definition
Self-Aware	To have a clear perception of your personality, strengths, weaknesses, thoughts, beliefs, motivations and emotions and how these can affect your subsequent decisions and behaviors through self-reflection
Resilient	To utilise effective coping strategies to withstand, learn from or recover quickly from difficult, stressful and challenging situations.
Problem Solver	To use a range of techniques and consider a number of options in a systematic manner, to find positive solutions to challenging problems posed
Effective Communication	To actively listen, share information, provide direction and express ideas and feelings effectively through a range of different forms (verbally, visually and written) so that the intended message is successfully delivered, received, understood and responded to
Global Citizen	To understand, respect and embrace diversity, different cultures and different ways of working, and to recognise the global issues that affect us
Enterprising	To demonstrate creativity, innovation, initiative and resourcefulness, and be ready to act as opportunities present themselves
Adaptable	To be flexible and responsive to change in any given situation or work environment, or in response to the needs, wishes or demands of others
Collaborative	To develop a purposeful relationship/team with two or more people to constructively explore ideas and achieve shared goals
Confident	To be able to demonstrate a firm belief in yourself and your abilities
Lifelong Learner	To evaluate personal performance and independently seek and act upon means of improvement to allow for the advancement of skills and knowledge for personal and professional reasons

Figure 2. Definitions of the ten Graduate Attributes included in GAME

The GAME framework was initially developed for undergraduate programmes, and soon after, the GAME+ framework was developed for postgraduate courses. The GAME+ framework focuses on five core themes: *influence and impact*; *critical self-management*; *creativity and innovation*; *professional identity*; and *skills mastery*. In addition to the GAME frameworks and in response to the COVID-19 pandemic, the University of Bolton also created the Campus Plus model (see Figure 3).

1	The University is a **teaching-led** institution and as such places a particular emphasis on effective teaching, individualised learning and on student achievement that leads to positive outcomes.
2	The University's **Teaching Intensive, Research Informed** philosophy is the heart of what we do.
3	The University is campus-based with **face-to-face teaching** the principal delivery strategy.
4	**Educational technology** which promotes flexibility, individualisation, empowerment, and fun is a core component of our delivery.
5	Face-to-face **in person** scheduled teaching (approximately 70%) is **supported by online** scheduled learning (approximately 30%) and directed learning.
6	Programmes adopt effective delivery strategies **using local solutions** supported by central professional services.
7	**A central learning support** infrastructure, including specialist support, library and IT services are crucial to student success.
8	The success of the Campus Plus model is measured by our **student outcomes** particularly in relation to academic engagement, retention, success, and employment.
9	The blended learning experience for students benefits from **a solid foundation established at the outset of the academic semester and year through campus-based** induction, teaching sessions and other learning activities.
10	Academic staff are **supported to develop creative and flexible delivery** mechanisms.
11	The University is committed to the development of creative, innovative, inclusive, collaborative learning opportunities recognising **the need to timetable scheduled session and allocate resources effectively.**
12	**Attendance and engagement are essential for successful learning.** Though our supportive attendance policy, we make expectations clear about attendance and engagement requirements.

Figure 3. Twelve principles underpinning the University of Bolton's Campus Plus model

The development of the Campus Plus model, post COVID-19, has been an excellent example of how the landscape of HE has changed, with a movement towards more blended learning approaches. Research does demonstrate positive correlation between attendance and academic achievement within a higher education (HE) context (Büchele,

2021), and this connection between attendance and performance extends to sporting degree programmes (Gough, Duffell & Eustace, 2021). However, very little is understood about the impact blended learning environments have on the relationship between attendance and performance (Finlay, Simpson & Tinnion, 2022). Interestingly, new research is beginning to suggest that engagement in online learning activities might have a more significant positive impact on student learning and achievement than face-to-face attendance (Finlay, Simpson & Tinnion, 2022). This might suggest that face-to-face lectures alone are slowly losing their relevance as academics utilise technological advancements to create collaborative online learning environments (Moore, 2020). Undoubtedly, the HE context has changed significantly due to the COVID-19 pandemic and, therefore, so has the landscape of sport and exercise psychology – especially when considering the professional contexts of elite sport (Schinke et al., 2020a; Schinke et al., 2020b).

Applied Sport and Exercise Psychology (MSc)

The Applied Sport and Exercise Psychology (MSc) programme is dual accredited by the British Psychological Society (BPS) and the British Association of Sport and Exercise Sciences (BASES). Both of these accrediting bodies have clear competency frameworks that accredited programmes must align to. Successfully achieving dual accreditation requires programmes to deliver contemporary topics in sport and exercise psychology, which mirror the ever-changing landscapes of professional contexts. Hence, it was vital to consider the impact of COVID-19 on professional practice within the programme delivery. This was achieved through adapting the '40-minute practice skills assessment' on one of the Semester 1 modules: *Individual Support: Person and Performer (SEP7004)*. Students were provided with a case synopsis of a real client that one of the teaching staff had encountered in their work as applied practitioners during the pandemic. Students were tasked with conducting an intake interview and needs analysis with this particular client (within simulated role-play scenarios). The GA associated with this assessment was Skills Mastery, with emphasis placed on the students' ability to communicate (ask open questions, engage in active listening, demonstrate counselling skills such as paraphrasing, etc.) effectively. To match the changing landscape of applied sport and exercise psychology, formative assessments were utilised, to allow the students a chance to practise these core skills, through Zoom and in person. Working with athletes online became commonplace during the pandemic (Reel, 2020) and is much more common now after the pandemic (Price, Wagstaff & Thelwell, 2022), and so to create a truly authentic assessment, it was important to provide our students with a chance to practise these unique skills.

Case Study 2: Cognitive Behavioural Psychotherapies (MSc/PGDip)
CBT Clinical Supervision and Training

Clinical supervision can be defined as "an intervention provided by a more senior member of a profession to a more junior colleague or colleagues who typically (but not always) are members of the same profession" (Bernard & Goodyear, 2013: 8). In Cognitive Behavioural Therapy (CBT), clinical supervision takes the form of a contractual agreement whereby the CBT therapist agrees to share their clinical practice with openness and honesty in a way which provides the clinical supervisor with insight into the quality of clinical work provided (Turpin & Wheeler, 2011). Supervisors use similar strategies in clinical supervision to those used in training in order to assist the supervisee to develop competence in CBT delivery including pre-reading, didactic advice, modelling of skills, role-play, and visual or audio-recording review (Milne, 2009; Bennett-Levy et al., 2009a). The personal and professional development field provides the essential toolkit for learning, including experiential learning (e.g., Kolb, 1984; Ravitz & Silver, 2004) and reflective practice (e.g., Schön, 1983; Bennett-Levy et al., 2009b).

There are simultaneous benefits to the development of a therapist's competence through the use of clinical supervision. Firstly, clinical supervision enhances therapeutic experience for the client through the oversight of clinical cases, the focus on the quality of interventions provided and the promotion of safe clinical practice. Further, the professional development of the supervisee is also enhanced, developing and embedding clinical skills that are an essential ingredient in the recipe of a successful treatment (Turpin & Wheeler,

2011). In university settings where CBT training occurs, clinical supervision also serves the function of ensuring fitness to practise, "serving as a gatekeeper for those who are to enter the particular profession" (Bernard & Goodyear, 2013: 8).

Clinical supervision is valued by recipients of its benefits. Rabinowitz, Heppner and Roehlke (1986) found that 45 CBT trainee therapists, at different stages in their CBT training program, valued their competence as a therapist as the most important outcome of completing their training. They established that trainees also valued the "supporting, reassuring and nurturing" nature of the supervisor as the most important process of clinical supervision.

Feedback is an essential part of the shift between declarative and procedural knowledge acquisition in CBT, moving the supervisee from 'knows' to 'knows how', and it may be most powerful when provided following role-plays or observing a patient recording with a supervisee (Sudak et al., 2016). Törnquist and colleagues (2018) highlight the importance of positive feedback and support as an integral part of CBT training from the perspective of supervisees. Positive feedback and support play an important inhibitory role in mitigating secondary traumatisation from the content of client cases, and also serve to prevent burnout (Pulido, 2012), a problem that is of high risk for professionals working in mental health settings (Valenti et al., 2014).

Supervisee satisfaction with their clinical supervision is important if supervisees are to feel confident in the delivery of their interventions and their competence. Ben-Porat and Itzhaky (2011) established a significant correlation between supervisees' satisfaction with clinical supervisory experiences and confidence in their own competence. Negative supervisory experiences can indeed have long-lasting implications for supervisees, some of whom have found themselves leaving the profession because of problems within the supervisory relationship (Ramos-Sánchez et al., 2002).

Geographical distance between supervisee and supervisor can have a substantial impact on available time, with traveling for clinical supervision using valuable time that could be more fruitfully utilised. In the past, telephone supervision could be offered as an alternative delivery mode but, although it reduces the need to travel, this had mixed results, with supervisees reporting a disconnect with their clinical supervisor, plagued by a lack of perceptual cues (Wetchler et al., 1993). One way of mitigating this before the coronavirus pandemic was to form the supervisory relationship prior to telephone supervision commencing, in order to develop the supervisory alliance (Wetchler et al., 1993).

This system of remotely delivering clinical supervision and services by audio-visual technology on the internet, such as via Zoom, or by telephone has proven robust for working through the coronavirus pandemic (Cromarty, Gallagher & Watson, 2020) when delivery methods were forced to adapt to ensure CBT treatment was still made available. Delivering CBT training and supervision remotely by audio-visual technology requires the use of a webcam, microphone, speakers and a good internet connection (Cromarty, Gallagher & Watson, 2020), with telephone audio used in the event of connection problems as a back-up (Sudak et al., 2016). This technology may enhance the use of perceptual cues in remotely accessed clinical supervision in comparison with telephone delivery (Bennett-Levy et al., 2012; Cromarty, Gallagher & Watson, 2020). Cromarty, Gallagher and Watson (2020) recommend the use of Zoom as an online platform that offers the facilities of screen sharing, video calling and session recording. Other recommendations included slowing the pace of discussions, muting sound when not speaking, and using built-in chat to type messages and screen sharing to enhance communication in online training and supervision sessions.

Remote clinical supervision allows focus on the individual and their caseload, and although there is a paucity in the research literature concerning remote clinical supervision in CBT (Cromarty, Gallagher & Watson, 2020), there is some preliminary evidence of effectiveness of telephone- and videoconference-based clinical supervision in CBT for problem gambling (Oakes et al., 2007) as well as anxiety and depression (Cromarty et al., 2016; Koivu, Saarinen & Hyrkas, 2012).

There is an emerging theoretical and empirical base for CBT training and supervision (Bennett-Levy et al., 2009b). Trainers of CBT can draw on an evidence base of training or supervision methods for the development and achievement of CBT competencies. An example of this can be found in the declarative, procedural and reflective (DPR) model of therapist skill development (Bennett-Levy, 2006), which is widely adopted and has its origins in information processing theory (Kuyken, Padesky & Dudley, 2009). The model posits three major information processing systems (declarative, procedural and reflective) to describe how therapists learn therapeutic skills. The declarative system forms the repository of knowledge about therapy developed from lectures and reading. The procedural system is known as the storehouse of therapy skills (Bennett-Levy, 2006) whereby declarative knowledge is translated into clinical practice (skills-in-action). The final, reflective, system of the model is the reflective system which explores the implications of knowledge and procedural practice to consolidate or modify existing knowledge and contribute to new learning (Bennett-Levy et al., 2009b).

In remote methods of CBT delivery, trainees' declarative knowledge is developed through case discussion and observation of their peers' clinical skills through viewing clinical recordings in small groups. Role-plays are utilised for procedural learning as a whole group or in individual breakout facilities on the online platform. Reflective feedback from trainees is sought immediately after role-plays or reviewing of clinical recordings, where they are asked for their own reviews of what went well and what they would consider changing (Sudak et al., 2016). The supervisee then also benefits from the feedback of the supervisor as well as peer trainees. Procedural 'experiential' role-plays allow deeper reflections than feedback after the declarative lectures (Bennett-Levy, 2006).

Remote clinical and case management supervision in CBT can be audio visual or by telephone. The same platform as CBT training can be used but remote supervision delivered on a one-to-one basis allows focus on the individual and their caseload (Cromarty, Gallagher & Watson, 2020). Remote supervision has good fit with existing CBT supervision models of delivery, such as the Cakestand model (Armstrong & Freeston, 2006) and evidence-based clinical supervision (EBCS) principles (Milne, 2009).

Cognitive Behavioural Psychotherapies (MSc/PGDip)

The Cognitive Behavioural Psychotherapies (MSc/PGDip) programme is accredited by the British Association of Behavioural and Cognitive Psychotherapists (BABCP). The accrediting body has clear guidelines for delivery of CBT training for accredited programmes, and with the advent of the coronavirus pandemic it was critical that programmes find ways to minimise disruption to patient care provided by trainee CBT therapists and to ensure that CBT training was able to continue. Online delivery of clinical supervision and lectures became an acceptable, substitute mode of training delivery during the pandemic to limit the disruption caused to clinical practice by the absence of face-to-face teaching. Post-pandemic, the benefits of online delivery were realised and whilst lectures returned to the classroom on campus, clinical supervision provision remained online as part of the blended learning model. Having resonance with Self-Determination Theory (Ryan & Deci, 2000), when the CBT students were invited to provide feedback about the new blended learning format, it became clear that the students' psychological needs of competence, autonomy and relatedness were satisfied by the refined format, providing some of the essential nutrients that are required for optimal functioning, growth and wellbeing.

> "You don't need to wait around on campus until it is supervision time, you can use this time more effectively."

With respect to autonomy, the need to feel ownership of and self-govern one's behaviour, students reported experiences of enjoying the flexibility to look after their wellbeing and eat lunch at home, as well as the wellbeing of others (for example, by being able to pick children up from school due to the reduced need to remain on campus). Online supervision removed the geographical limitations and obstacles that face-to-face supervision once caused. Optimal functioning was supported here where students reported having volition to dedicate extra time to study instead of wasting time waiting on campus for the next class. Students reported having autonomy to work and to manage other commitments concurrently.

> "I think having teaching in person is great for the natural exploration of topics, and working with peers to consolidate learning."

In relation to competence, the need to produce desired outcomes and to experience mastery, students expressed that they valued having dedicated lecture time to role-play key therapy skills and that being able to do this aspect of learning face-to-face on campus gave them a greater sense of competence. They discussed the fruits of having more time to organise themselves and manage their time more efficiently, enhancing their feelings of competence. With respect to online clinical supervision though, students commented on the helpfulness of being able to write up supervision notes immediately after the session, which they had found more difficult to do when supervision was delivered face-to-face on campus prior to the pandemic, and they noted that this gave rise to feelings of competence.

> "There are many more opportunities to engage with one another. Being in the same room makes it easier to comment, ask questions and even share a joke. Break times during online lectures in the pandemic were spent alone, while on campus we sit together and chat now."

Finally, concerning relatedness, the need to feel connected to others, students enjoyed the face-to-face aspect of blended learning that allowed time to connect with other students, to chat and have coffee, to share ideas and have in-depth discussion. Students talked of the comfort they felt when asking questions of tutors when the students are sat together in class, which they commented felt less comfortable online. They pointed out that humour made a welcome return when face-to-face classes resumed, which enhanced a sense of connectedness too, a characteristic of connection with others that the students reported had faded away in online delivery.

Given that social contexts that support students' autonomy, competence and relatedness promote intrinsic motivation (Liu et al., 2014; Wang, 2017), it is hoped that as these three psychological needs are met by the blended learning model, balancing online clinical supervision with face-to-face lectures and workshops, intrinsic motivation will likely increase. Student motivation is critical:

when they are highly motivated, they tend to stay engaged and acquire knowledge in a more coherent form, apply their knowledge more frequently and achieve greater academic performance (Deci & Ryan, 2012; Reeve, 2009). The blended learning model adopted into the programme will greatly benefit student experience and the achievement of our students.

References

Aregbeyen, O. (2010). Students' perceptions of effective teaching and effective lecturer characteristics at the University of Ibadan, Nigeria. *Pakistan Journal of Social Sciences*, 7(2), 62–69.

Armstrong, P., & Freeston, M. (2006). Conceptualising and formulating cognitive therapy supervision. In N. Tarrier (ed.), *Case Formulation in Cognitive Behaviour Therapy* (349–371). London: Routledge.

Ashford-Rowe, K., Herrington, J., & Brown, C. (2014). Establishing the critical elements that determine authentic assessment. *Assessment & Evaluation in Higher Education*, 39(2), 205–222. doi:10.1080/02602938.2013.819566.

Bennett-Levy, J. (2006). Therapist skills: a cognitive model of their acquisition and refinement. *Behavioural and Cognitive Psychotherapy*, 34, 57–78.

Bennett-Levy, J., McManus, F., Westling, B. E., & Fennell, M. (2009a). Acquiring and refining CBT skills and competencies: Which training methods are perceived to be most effective? *Behavioural and Cognitive Psychotherapy*, 37(5), 571–583.

Bennett-Levy, J., Thwaites, R., Chaddock, A., & Davis, M. (2009b). Reflective Practice in Cognitive Behavioural Therapy: The Engine of Lifelong Learning. In R. Dallos & J. Stedmon (eds.), *Reflective Practice in Psychotherapy and Counselling* (115–135). New York: Open University Press.

Bennett-Levy, J., Hawkins, R., Perry, H., Cromarty, P., & Mills, J. (2012). Online cognitive behavioural therapy (CBT) training for therapists: outcomes, acceptability, and impact of support. *Australian Psychologist*, 47, 174–182.

Ben-Porat, A., & Itzhaky, H. (2011). The contribution of training and supervision to perceived role competence, secondary traumatization, and burnout among domestic violence therapists. *Clinical Supervisor*, 30(1), 95–108.

Bernard, J. M., & Goodyear, R. K. (2013). *Fundamentals of Clinical Supervision* (5th ed.). Boston, MA: Pearson Education.

Biggs, J. (2014). Constructive alignment in university teaching. *HERDSA Review of Higher Education* (Vol. 1).

Bloxham, S. (2015). Assessing Assessment: New Developments in Assessment Design, Feedback Practices and Marking in Higher Education. In H. Fry, S. Ketteridge & S. Marshall (eds.), *A Handbook for Teaching and Learning in Higher Education* (4th ed.; 107–122). Abingdon: Routledge.

Bowden, J., Hart, G., King, B., Trigwell, K., & Watts, O. (2000). *Generic capabilities of ATN university graduates*. Canberra: Australian Government Department of Education, Training and Youth Affairs.

BPS (2022). https://www.bps.org.uk/news/psychology-staff-overworked-and-under-supported-light-covid-19-reveals-new-findings.

Bridgstock, R. (2009). The graduate attributes we've overlooked: Enhancing graduate employability through career management skills. *Higher Education Research & Development*, 28(1), 31–44.

Brush, T., & Saye, J. (2008). The effects of multimedia-supported problem-based inquiry on student engagement, empathy, and assumptions about history. *Interdisciplinary Journal of Problem-Based Learning*, 2(1), 21–56.

Büchele, S. (2021). Evaluating the link between attendance and performance in higher education: The role of classroom engagement dimensions. *Assessment & Evaluation in Higher Education*, 46(1), 132–150.

Crammer, S. (2006). Enhancing graduate employability: Best intentions and mixed outcomes. *Studies in Higher Education*, 31(2), 169–184.

Cromarty, P., Drummond, A., Francis, T., Watson, J., & Battersby, M. (2016). NewAccess for depression and anxiety: Adapting the UK Improving Access to Psychological Therapies Program across Australia. *Australasian Psychiatry*, 24(5), 489–492.

Cromarty, P., Gallagher, D., & Watson, J. (2020). Remote delivery of CBT training, clinical supervision and services: In times of crisis or business as usual. *The Cognitive Behaviour Therapist*, 13.

Davenport, N. C., Spath, M. L., & Blauvelt, M. J. (2009). A step-by-step approach to curriculum review. *Nurse Educator*, 34(4), 181–185.

Deci, E. L., & Ryan, R. M. (2012). Motivation, personality, and development within embedded social contexts: An overview of self-determination theory. In R. M. Ryan (ed.), *Oxford Handbook of Human Motivation* (85–107). Oxford, UK: Oxford University Press.

Dochy, F., & McDowell, L. (1997). Assessment as a Tool for Learning. *Studies in Educational Evaluation*, 23(4), 279–298. doi:10.1016/S0191-491X(97)86211-6.

Finlay, M. J., Simpson, T., & Tinnion, D. J. (2022). Association between attendance, online course activity time, and grades: Analysis of undergraduate sport science cohorts during the COVID-19 pandemic. *Journal of Hospitality, Leisure, Sport & Tourism Education*, 31, 100397.

Gough, L. A., Duffell, T., & Eustace, S. J. (2021). The impact of student attendance on assessment specific performance in sport degree programs. *Journal of Hospitality, Leisure, Sport & Tourism Education*, 29, Article 100323.

Gulikers, J. T., Bastiaens, T. J., & Kirschner, P. A. (2004). A five-dimensional framework for authentic assessment. *Educational technology research and development*, 52(3), 67–86.

Hughes, C., & Barrie, S. (2010). Influences on the assessment of graduate attributes in higher education. *Assessment & Evaluation in Higher Education*, 35(3), 325–334.

Jafari, A. (2004). The 'sticky' ePortfolio system: Tackling challenges and identifying attribute. *EDUCAUSE Review*, 39(4), 38–49.

Jones, A. (2009a). Generic attributes as espoused theory: The importance of context. *Higher Education*, 58(2), 175–191.

Jones, A. (2009b). Re-disciplining generic attributes: The disciplinary context in focus. *Studies in Higher Education*, 34(1), 85–100.

Jones, A. (2013). There is nothing generic about graduate attributes: unpacking the scope of context. *Journal of Further and Higher Education*, 37(5), 591–605.

Jorre de St Jorre, T., & Oliver, B. (2018). Want students to engage? Contextualise graduate learning outcomes and assess for employability. *Higher Education Research & Development*, 37(1), 44–57.

Knight, P., & Page, A. (2007). The assessment of 'wicked' competences: A report to the practice-based professional learning centre for excellence in teaching and learning in the Open University. Available from: http://www.open.ac.uk/cetl-workspace/cetlcontent/documents/46od21bd645f8.pdf [Accessed: 22 February 2009].

Koivu, A., Saarinen, P. I., & Hyrkas, K. (2012). Who benefits from clinical supervision and how? The association between clinical supervision and the work-related well-being of female hospital nurses. *Journal of Clinical Nursing*, 21(17–18), 2567–2578.

Kolb, D. A. (1984). *Experiential Learning: Experience as the Source of Learning and Development*. Englewood Cliffs, NJ: Prentice Hall.

Kuyken, W., Padesky, C. A., & Dudley, R. (2009). *Collaborative Case Conceptualization: Working Effectively with Clients in Cognitive-Behavioral Therapy*. New York: Guilford.

Kwan, A. (2009). Problem-based learning. In *The Routledge International Handbook of Higher Education* (91–107).

Liu, W. C., Wang, C. K. J., Kee, Y. H., Koh, C., Lim, B. S. C., & Chua, L. L. (2014). College students' motivation and learning strategies profiles and academic achievement: a self-determination theory approach. *Educational Psychology*, 34(3), 338–353.

Milne, D. (2009). *Evidence-based Clinical Supervision: Principles and Practice* (1st ed.). Oxford: Blackwell.

Moore, A. (2020). Evaluating factors for student success in a flipped classroom approach. *EAI Endorsed Transactions on e-learning*, 18(3), 1–11. Available from: https://doi.org/10.4108/eai.3-12-2020.167293.

Nicol, D., Thomson, A., & Breslin, C. (2014). Rethinking Feedback Practices in Higher Education: A Peer Review Perspective. *Assessment & Evaluation in Higher Education*, 39(1): 102–122. doi:10.1080/02602938.2013.795518.

Oakes, J., Battersby, M., Pols, R., & Cromarty, P. (2007). Exposure therapy for problem gambling via videoconferencing. *Journal of Gambling Studies*, 24, 107–118.

Oliver, B. (2011). *Assuring graduate outcomes good practice report*. Sydney: Australian Learning and Teaching Council.

Oliver, B. (2015). *Assuring graduate capabilities: Evidencing levels of achievement for graduate employability*. Sydney: Office for Learning and Teaching.

Oliver, B., & Jorre de St Jorre, T. (2018). Graduate attributes for 2020 and beyond: recommendations for Australian higher education providers. *Higher Education Research & Development*, 1–16.

Price, D., Wagstaff, C. R., & Thelwell, R. C. (2022). Opportunities and considerations of new media and technology in sport psychology service delivery. *Journal of Sport Psychology in Action*, 13(1), 4–15.

Pulido, M. L. (2012). The ripple effect: Lessons learned about secondary traumatic stress among clinicians responding to the September 11th terrorist attacks. *Clinical Social Work Journal*, 40(3), 307–315.

Rabinowitz, F. E., Heppner, P. P., & Roehlke, H. J. (1986). Descriptive study of process and outcome variables of supervision over time. *Journal of Counselling Psychology*, 33(3), 292–300.

Radloff, A., de la Harpe, B., Scoufis, M., Dalton, H., Thomas, J., Lawson, A., ... Girardi, A. (2009). *The B factor project: Understanding academic staff beliefs about graduate attributes.* Melbourne: ALTC.

Ramos-Sánchez, L., Esnil, E., Goodwin, A., Riggs, S., Touster, L. O., Wright, L. K., & Rodolfa, E. (2002). Negative supervisory events: Effects on supervision satisfaction and supervisory alliance. *Professional Psychology: Research and Practice*, 33(2), 197–202.

Ravitz, P., & Silver, I. (2004). Advances in psychotherapy education. *Canadian Journal of Psychiatry*, 49(4), 230–237.

Raymond, J., Homer, C., Smith, R., & Gray, J. (2013). Learning through Authentic Assessment. An Evaluation of a New Development in the Undergraduate Midwifery Curriculum. *Nurse Education in Practice*, 13(5): 471–476. doi:10.1016/j.nepr.2012.10.006.

Reel, J. J. (2020). Leading During a Pandemic: Lessons Gleaned from Sport Psychology. *Journal of Clinical Sport Psychology*, 14(4), 325–329.

Reeve, J. (2009). Why teachers adopt a controlling motivating style toward students and how they can become more autonomy supportive. *Educational Psychology*, 44, 159–178.

Ryan, R. M., & Deci, E. L. (2000). Self-determination theory and the facilitation of intrinsic motivation, social development and wellbeing. *American Psychologist*, 55(1), 68–78.

Sambell, K., McDowell, L., & Montgomery, C. (2013). *Assessment for Learning in Higher Education*. London: Routledge.

Schinke, R., Papaioannou, A., Henriksen, K., Si, G., Zhang, L., & Haberl, P. (2020a). Sport psychology services to high performance athletes during COVID-19. *International Journal of Sport and Exercise Psychology*, 18(3), 269–272.

Schinke, R., Papaioannou, A., Maher, C., Parham, W. D., Larsen, C. H., Gordin, R., & Cotterill, S. (2020b). Sport psychology services to professional athletes: working through COVID-19. *International Journal of Sport and Exercise Psychology*, 18(4), 409–413.

Schön, D. (1983). *The Reflective Practitioner: How Professionals Think in Action*. New York: Basic Books.

Senekal, J. S., & Smith, M. R. (2022). Assessing the employability and employment destinations of professional psychology alumni. *South African Journal of Psychology*, 52(1), 11–22.

Singh, P., Thambusamy, R., & Ramly, M. (2014). Fit or Unfit? Perspectives of Employers and University Instructors of Graduates' Generic Skills. *Social and Behavioral Sciences*, 123, 315–324. doi:10.1016/j.sbspro.2014.01.1429.

Sudak, D. M., Codd, R. T., III, Ludgate, J., Sokol, L., Fox, M. G., Reiser, R., & Milne, D. L. (2016). *Teaching and supervising cognitive behavioral therapy*. Hoboken, NJ: John Wiley & Sons.

Sullivan, S. E., & Baruch, Y. (2009). Advances in career theory and research: A critical review and agenda for future exploration. *Journal of Management*, 35(6), 1542–1571.

Törnquist, A., Rakovshik, S., Carlsson, J., & Norberg, J. (2018). How supervisees on a foundation course in CBT perceive a supervision session and what they bring forward to the next therapy session. *Behavioural and Cognitive Psychotherapy*, 46(3), 302.

Treleaven, L., & Voola, R. (2008). Integrating the development of graduate attributes through constructive alignment. *Journal of Marketing Education*, 30(2), 160–173.

Turpin, G., & Wheeler, S. (2011). *Supervision Guidance*. Department of Health: London.

Valenti, M., La Malfa, G., Tomassini, A., Masedu, F., Tiberti, S., & Sorge, G. (2014). Burnout among therapists working with persons with autism after the 2009 earthquake in L'aquila, Italy: A longitudinal comparative study. *Journal of Psychiatric and Mental Health Nursing*, 21(3), 234–240.

Vanaki, Z., & Memarian, R. (2009). Professional Ethics: Beyond the Clinical Competency. *Journal of Professional Nursing*, 25, 285–291. doi:10.1016/j.profnurs.2009.01.009.

Villarroel, V., Bloxham, S., Bruna, D., Bruna, C., & Herrera-Seda, C. (2018). Authentic assessment: creating a blueprint for course design. *Assessment & Evaluation in Higher Education*, 43(5), 840–854.

Wang, A. K. J. (2017). The joy of learning: what is it and how to achieve it. *Exchange*, 1, 7–11.

Wetchler, J. L., Trepper, T. S., McCollum, E. E., & Nelson, T. S. (1993). Videotape supervision via long-distance telephone. *American Journal of Family Therapy*, 21(3), 242–247.

Yorke, M., & Knight, P. T. (2006). *Embedding Employability into the Curriculum*. Heslington, York: The Higher Education Academy.

CHAPTER EIGHT

Combining E-Learning and Face-to-Face Teaching in the Law School – The Digitally Enhanced Flipped Classroom for Teaching and Learning the Law

Dr Alicia Danielsson

In contrast to many other disciplines, law has been slow to implement innovative teaching strategies. There are many contributing factors. One significant factor can be found in the seemingly insurmountable quantity of information that needs to be conveyed in each lecture, often at the expense of practical skills training. Flipped classroom strategies are a convenient form of blended learning, whereby the content-heavy learning elements are provided via reading tasks which are to be completed by students before they attend their lectures, thereby freeing up valuable face-to-face class time for live problem-solving activities. In theory, this approach presents an ideal solution to assist law teachers with the balancing of content and practical skills development and increased student engagement. However, this approach only works effectively if all students complete their reading. Yet, the past decades have witnessed a reduction of reading being undertaken in education – a trend which often is attributed to an increased usage of electronic devices. In the School of Law within the University of Bolton, the COVID-19 pandemic demonstrated how the popularity of devices such as laptops, tablet PCs and smartphones could be utilised to integrate more interactive digitally enhanced blended learning formats into structured legal learning environments. With this transition, the flipped classroom (FC) allowed for the effective combining of e-learning and face-to-face teaching components. Tools, such as the H5P Moodle plugin or SCORM packages have enabled the School of Law to digitally enhance our flipped classroom strategies to increase student engagement by offering more interactive methods of knowledge acquisition than the traditional reading lists.

The challenges of traditional law school pedagogy

The traditional approach to teaching in law schools has been characterised by hyper-individualised and passive listen-and-learn approaches to learning (Fortin Lalonde, 2022; Silver & Ballakrishnen, 2022; van Klink & de Vries, 2016). This, combined with the highly competitive employment environment within the legal sectors, forces students early on not only to prioritise grades above learning but also to focus strongly on their performance in comparison to their peers (Sturm & Guinier, 2007; Espeland, Sauder & Espeland, 2016). When recalling the traditional approach to law teaching, many a lawyer will look back on hundreds of pages of reading each week in preparation for class, trying to memorise all of the details in case the lecturer called on them in classes in which one was being lectured at, trying to jot down every word in preparation for quizzes, all the while missing the wider context of the subject matter, as one was focussed on absorbing details rather than actively engaging with the learning (Evans, 2021; Law Vicissitudes, 2013). Despite decades of calls for change to the teaching practices in law schools, and a growing body of academic literature calling for more engaging and innovative teaching practices within them, the transition has been slow. Legal educators are well known for teaching their modules the same way they have previously been taught because "that's just the way it's always been done" (Mahavongtrakul, 2020). In the following chapter, some of the key features of digitally enhancing flipped classrooms within law schools will be showcased, followed by an autoethnographic recount of the implementation of some of these tools within an exemplary module on the master's of law programme at the University of Bolton. The intention is to demonstrate how many of the current trends relating to blended learning and the post-COVID-19 literature on the transition to innovative teaching were implemented in this example of teaching practices, and to set out the observations that were made in the process.

The COVID-19 pandemic and the much-needed catalyst for teaching innovation in law schools

Despite the previously mentioned rigid approaches to legal education, scholars and legal educators as well as law students had been increasingly calling for educators within law schools to implement and utilise more innovative teaching approaches, designs and delivery, including a stronger focus on practical employability skills and the use of innovative teaching technologies, even before the COVID-19 pandemic (Keyes & Johnstone, 2004; Rubin, 2007; Glesner, 1990; Spencer, 2012). The COVID-19 pandemic and the national lockdowns that were put in place across the globe placed higher education institutions in a situation in which traditional methods of teaching and learning were not possible (Mishra, Gupta & Shree, 2020; Ali, 2020; Pokhrel & Chhetri, 2021). One of the consequences was that blended learning increased in popularity and almost became an expectation within higher education teaching provisions (Jones & Ravishankar, 2021; Singh, Steele & Singh, 2021; Turnbull, Chugh & Luck, 2021). However, despite the long-awaited changes to teaching practice, trends are also emerging within higher education pedagogy whereby a significant amount of law educators are reverting back to their traditional pre-2020 approaches to teaching (Rapanta et al., 2021; Gladwin-Geoghegan & Thompson, 2021). As such, it is vital to capture and promote the innovative changes that had emerged within law education to ensure that the gains from the COVID-19 pandemic are not lost, but rather foster long-term innovation to teaching practices.

As has already been explained in previous chapters of this book, blended learning encompasses teaching in which the delivery combines different learning and teaching formats, mostly in reference to the combination of face-to-face settings as well as virtual and online setting (Buhl-Wiggers, Kjærgaard & Munk, 2022; van Caenegem & Mundy, 2021). It is also a term which has become practically omnipresent within the literature relating to higher education since the COVID-19 pandemic (Kaplarević-Mališić et al., 2022; Nikitaki, Papadima-Sophocleous & Nicolaou, 2022).

The experiences of higher education teaching during the COVID-19 pandemic demonstrated that a mix of in-person and online activities is excellent for encouraging students' active participation in learning, which may be a reason why blended learning is frequently linked to active learning (Zheng, Ma & Lin, 2021; Mali & Lim, 2021; Li, Li & Han, 2021; Nurwakhidah & Suganda, 2022). One form of blended learning, which combines different formats of teaching, is 'flipped' learning, which is often also referred to as flipped classroom teaching (Low et al., 2021; Wolff & Chan, 2016). A flipped classroom, or flipped learning, is a form of teaching design whereby students are instructed to work independently through a series of preparatory activities prior to taking part in the scheduled face-to-face sessions (Tomas et al., 2019; Pardo et al., 2018; Cifuentes, 2021). This way, the content learnt during the activities can then be applied under the guidance and supervision of the instructor, who will in most cases be the subject-matter specialist (Rehman & Lakhan, 2021). This flipping of tasks sees traditional lectures replaced by independent knowledge-gathering activities, and the valuable in-person face-to-face sessions take the shape of workshops or tutorials rather than the traditional teacher-centred lectures (Khayat & Osama, 2022; Tabassum, 2021). This means that the valuable time students have with the subject-matter specialist is not used merely for fact distribution, which is an activity that could be achieved through various other means, such as reading, watching videos, completing interactive online learning activities, and many other facilities. This frees up the face-to-face teaching time of the subject-matter specialist to demonstrate, illustrate, train and monitor students' practical application skills, which are less easily completed by other means.

'Active learning', 'blended learning' and 'flipping the classroom' – key terms that have amalgamated with digital technology

With active learning, the student becomes the centre of attention rather than the instructor, who instead serves as the subject-matter expert. In the past, almost exclusively up until the COVID-19 pandemic, the majority of legal education was characterised by teacher-centred approaches. As such, these teacher- or instructor-centred teaching approaches meant that the instructor was primarily responsible for imparting the factual components of their subject-matter knowledge through lectures in which students were required to listen to what was said and document these facts in their notes (Valz, 2022; Mahavongtrakul, 2020).

As was explained in the introductory section of this chapter, the conventional approach within legal education in law schools had been under increased scrutiny and opposition since the 1990s. It is now widely accepted within academic literature relating to higher education pedagogy that active engagement and active involvement of students in the activities undertaken in lectures increases learning (Hess, 1999). In order to promote students' active involvement in learning, improvements have been made to the way face-to-face classes were designed and delivered. However, the increase in popularity of so-called 'blended learning' and the development of specific blended learning strategies bear the potential to enrich and enhance active engagement and participation in class activities within higher education teaching and learning.

Blended learning' is just a term for combining various delivery methods; however, this concept expanded in popularity during a time of national remote teaching and learning in which the delivery of higher education teaching was heavily reliant on technological advancements (Divjak et al., 2022; Oliveira et al., 2021). As such, blended learning as a term comes preloaded with an unspoken understanding that the combination of various delivery methods will in most cases involve a combination of in-person instruction and technologically enhanced activities (Watson, 2008; Serrano et al., 2019). Blended learning's goal is to improve student learning by utilising resources that promote an active learning style. In fact, some scholars within academic literature relating to pedagogy claim that blended learning courses require active learning (Kirpalani, Grimmer & Peebles, 2020; Kerns, 2019; Hess, 1999).

It has been our experience within the University of Bolton that blended learning combined with a flipped classroom approach allowed for a richer learning experience for students. Yet, it was not only the students who benefited from this approach, but also the instructors. Being a research-informed, teaching-intensive university, the University of Bolton places a strong emphasis on innovative teaching practices which are assessed through various means, including teaching observations and student satisfaction results in national surveys. When applying a more traditional teacher-centred approach to legal education, it could be challenging to cover all the required knowledge of the law relating to an area within a three-hour lecture while maintaining student interest and student engagement, and ensuring classes are sufficiently interactive to achieve practical skills development in addition to the, at times, vast quantities of factual knowledge that need to be conveyed within a single lecture. Previous scholarly studies into the use of blended learning within legal education had already found that this kind of approach could "free up class time to discuss the economic, political, and social contexts in which the law operates" (Lo, 2014: 14). Furthermore, Hewitt (2015) found that the use of technology could enable a more in-depth examination of material than may be possible in face-to-face classes. The move to a blended learning approach combined with a flipped classroom brings together both traditional and non-traditional components (Slomanson, 2014; Towfigh, Keesen & Ulrich, 2022; Vargiu, 2022). It is traditional in that the instructor continues to be in charge of ensuring that the students are receiving subject-matter knowledge. However, it differs from traditional education in that students access and receive knowledge online rather than through in-person lectures. The instructor lectures to the class as part of the conventional style of legal education (Vargiu, 2022; Keyes & Johnstone, 2004; Balsam, 2019). In order to build, improve and refine their own, in-depth grasp of those subjects, the instructor would find, compile, describe, synthesise and analyse pertinent materials, particularly primary legal text, in order to prepare for lectures. What was previously considered the standard practice involved law students first hearing the outcomes of the content-heavy preparation undertaken by the subject-matter expert. The presumption that merely by hearing this information, students would learn the content of the lecture was generally unrealistic, and students would often find that they needed to catch up on the majority of content in their own time by reading over the relevant subject materials in textbooks following the lectures (Burns et al., 2017).

The move towards the use of blended learning in the form of flipped classroom teaching involved students being required to complete assignments and study materials outside of scheduled class times while using the flipped learning approach. Flipped learning is distinct from merely giving students a two-hour lecture tape. Flipped courses often take the form of modules that cover each of the individual subjects that make up the course. As such, the materials the students would be required to engage with in their preparation for face-to-face lectures included interactive online learning tasks, often facilitated with H5P integration facilities within the learning management system, Moodle. Examples of these learning activities included interactive videos in which quizzes, fill-in-the-blank exercises, reading activities, external links and numerous other interactive components had been embedded within short videos in which the lecturer or instructor had outlined the key concepts of the specific topics to be covered. These were interspersed with additional primary sources and links to further materials from third parties, as well as additional synchronous or asynchronous activities (Watson, 2008; James, Chin & Williams, 2014; Wehling et al., 2021). In a way, the difference between a flipped classroom and the traditional teacher-centred lecture is less noticeable for students in law schools than in many other subject areas – in particular, because legal education often expects students to finish extensive reading outside of class time (Lane, 2015; Smith, 2020). Flipping the classroom merely involves shifting the reading materials and other learning activities to before each class rather than after each class. However, at the same time, students benefit from more explicit and systematic instructions on how to approach and finish the independent, pre-lecture learning activities. Nevertheless, this concept comes with additional preparatory requirements for instructors, who are required to develop all the pre-lecture learning activities.

Although there were of course challenges, in particular in relation to ensuring that all students had completed the mandatory learning activities prior to the face-to-face sessions, the experience revealed additional benefits besides merely freeing up time in the classroom for more practical exercises and skills training. In particular, the fact that students were expected to undertake the online learning activities independently within their spare time allowed them to adjust their schedule flexibly to accommodate their individual circumstances. The blended learning, flipped classroom approach also enhanced differentiation practices, as students could progress through the learning activities at their own individual pace. This meant that students were more in control of their own knowledge acquisition, which in turn allowed for the in-person lectures to commence on a more equitable level of knowledge amongst all the learners. In other words, the face-to-face time would resemble what was traditionally referred to as workshops or tutorials, in which there are much higher levels of student participation.

The aim is that, after finishing the module, a student should have learned about the subject at a comparable level using the pre-class preparation materials as would have been the case had they attended a more traditional physical, in-person lecture. Students attend and engage in face-to-face sessions where they apply what they have learnt after being given this information. These lessons may resemble the sorts of workshops or tutorials utilised in the conventional teaching approach, but with a higher focus on student participation. From this viewpoint, flipping the law classroom could nevertheless be described as a more traditional practice, in the sense that instructors plan and lead in-person classes that students are expected to attend. Flipped learning differs from entirely online courses in that it places a high priority on the interactions that take place within a face-to-face interactive lecture session amongst students and instructors. In particular, a vital benefit of a digitally flipped classroom for student learning is that students learn more via collaboration with peers and with instructor feedback and assistance than they do from traditional lectures (Burns et al., 2017).

Practical advantages and disadvantages of a digitally enhanced flipped law classroom

The previous section of this chapter explained some of the fundamental concepts and dynamics which undergird the implementation of a digitally enhanced flipped classroom in law-school lectures. However, it is clear that a pragmatic approach needs to underly the endeavour. In order to be able to implement a version of a digitally enhanced flipped classroom within a law school, it is vital to understand the benefits as well as the weaknesses of this experience in order to develop a holistic version that meets the needs of particular cohorts and subject areas.

It has already been explained in some depth in this book that blended learning and, in particular, a flipped classroom resemble workshops or tutorials more than traditional teacher-centred lectures, which due to the nature of their setup are often more engaging for students than other educational tools.

In terms of some of the advantages a digitally enhanced flipped classroom brings with it, in contrast to either an online lecture or a face-to-face lecture, a blended learning delivery approach has more potential for active student engagement, which in turn may result in improved learning results amongst the students (Chen, Wang & Chen, 2014; Buhl-Wiggers, Kjærgaard & Munk, 2022; Ma & Lee, 2021). In this regard, the minor shift in emphasis, whereby the emphasis of instruction is relocated to the students' active learning (Angadi et al., 2019; Kay, MacDonald & DiGiuseppe, 2019), sees students being encouraged more to actively participate in synthesising and analysing information as opposed to just listening, writing and comprehending, as in a standard lecture. This, in turn, can facilitate, encourage and empower students to participate in an elevated degree of cognitive activity. It enables customisation to meet various learning styles, in that students may go through the information at their own pace (Zhampeiis et al., 2022; Howell, 2021). Students willingly rewrite any portions of the course that they find demanding or difficult. Both students and instructors could experience improved efficiency, understanding and engagement with the learnt knowledge, which will increase happiness and enjoyment as a result. It is also a better way to utilise instructors' time with the students (Jia et al., 2022; Zain & Sailin, 2020).

Blended learning also allows for a strong connection to other current issues in higher education, which can then be tackled more efficiently. For example, it bears the potential for increased flexibility, especially for students or instructors who may have atypical schedules or other life circumstances, in particular by providing improved accessibility. As such, students who may have struggled with the more traditional approach to lecturing, due to challenges affecting their ability to attend lectures at set times (for instance, work or caring responsibilities), are able to adjust their learning schedule around their life circumstances, thereby creating a more equitable and inclusive learning offering (Tashiro & Hebeler, 2019; Van der Werf et al., 2021). Despite there being no appreciable differences in the results of the learning between either entirely physical, in-person or completely remote, online class deliveries, a growing number of meta-studies in this area are consistently showing that blended learning is the more efficient delivery option (Means et al., 2009; Hess, 1999). These results have been linked to active student involvement with the resources (Means et al., 2009; Vaughan, 2014; Jeffrey et al., 2014). The chance for students to create their own knowledge motivates them. It has been demonstrated that active learning is beneficial in getting students to think critically about law and legal issues (Burns et al., 2017; Boyle, 2003; Alexander, 2018). In situations when there is still active engagement with lecturers and distinct assessment criteria, students respond well to the use of technology. Instead of better learning outcomes, however, there are indications that these results are more closely related to improvements in student satisfaction (Alexander, 2018; Şahin & Kurban, 2019).

When students are aware of the rationale for using technology and how it will help them accomplish their academic goals, they will be inspired to utilise it (Al-Kumaim et al., 2021; Zainuddin et al., 2019). The experiences and knowledge taken away from the COVID-19 pandemic relating specifically to flipped learning in legal education confirm many of the findings found in the growing body of academic literature in this area of pedagogy. It was generally perceived that when using flipped learning techniques in law classes at the University of Bolton, students showed up to their lectures well prepared and with a much better comprehension of the relevant subject matter, which meant that there was more time available for instructors to focus on the application of the content being taught, thereby being able to provide more formative feedback to students and enhance employability skills. This not only improved students' learning and skills, but also contributed to a more confident cohort of students.

Nevertheless, despite the obvious advantages, a flipped classroom may also pose certain difficulties for instructors and learners. When examining the literature, an often-mentioned disadvantage relates to the workload instructors have to complete. Flipped learning differs significantly from traditional learning in many ways, and instructors must not only rethink their materials, modules and programmes, and their roles as educators, but also learn new technical skills (Zawilinski, Shattuck & Hansen, 2020; Aidoo et al., 2022; Birgili & Demir, 2022). Studies have shown that the sudden move to more technologically advanced teaching components has the potential to make instructors feel unqualified, unconfident or inadequately prepared to create flipped-mode courses for delivery (Salvador et al., 2022; Lukas & Yunus, 2021; Javier, 2020). This, in turn, combined with internal institutional demands and expectations around the utilisation of new, innovative technologies to enhance online teaching and learning, can cause stress amongst instructors, particularly when they do not feel adequately supported with available technology or training facilities specifically for the endeavour of creating flipped online course components. Moreover, some instructors might worry about how course modifications and student opposition to them would affect their student ratings. Finally, a small percentage of educators may oppose any novel method (Burns et al., 2017).

Students' participation in and opposition to blended and flipped learning may also be a problem. Particularly if they are inexperienced with flipped courses, students may worry that they are expected to comprehend the subject without sufficient instructor guidance. In that situation, it is critical to explain to students in straightforward terms how flipped courses operate, what is expected of them, how to engage with the teacher, and how to take advantage of discussion and consulting possibilities (Chao, Chen & Chuang, 2015; Bailey & Lee, 2020; Roehling, 2017).

In particular, the acknowledgment that there could be challenges in the implementation of a flipped learning approach is vital. Such challenges include obstacles to students' active participation, a lack of student motivation to prepare adequately, and technical skills difficulties for instructors seeking to implement flipped classroom components within their law teaching. In terms of expectations of learning from a more transmissive, teacher-centred task to a student-focussed, technology-enhanced, active learning experience, the COVID-19 pandemic shifted legal education for all involved into a sudden transitional phase. However, the question still remains: how will the transition continue? As indicated earlier, this transition could be the beginning of a radical innovative change to legal education, or a temporary transition that is slowly shifting back to more traditional teaching. The key to ensuring that the long-term outcomes resemble the former option is to document experiences, both positive and negative, and to advocate for the bigger picture in this respect. Every transitional period comes with new and uncomfortable components, and it is easy to let these experiences overshadow the many positive elements. Thus, the following will present an exemplary case study from a module within the University of Bolton's School of Law not only to bring the growing body of theoretical knowledge to life, but also to document the holistic implementation of a technologically enhanced flipped classroom in legal education.

The use of blended learning combined with flipped learning, an exemplary case study – a postgraduate module in Public International Law

This case study was motivated in part by the University of Bolton's institutional mandates to embrace blended learning as part of their Campus Plus agenda. This section discusses how a module was transformed over the COVID-19 pandemic, to incorporate flipped and other blended learning strategies which were digitally enhanced to facilitate teaching and learning. The module chosen was Public International Law, an HE7 level, postgraduate law module. This module was chosen specifically, due to various characteristics that allowed the instructor to think about flipped classroom techniques and explore different technological tools in different settings, while not risking any negative impact on student learning. The cohort in question comprised approximately 15 postgraduate law students, of which more than half were international students. As such, the majority of students already had a solid educational foundation in law, but had not previously engaged in flipped classroom learning. The module was worth 20 credits and ran for 15 weeks, which involved 13 weeks of one three-hour lecture per week, one reading week for assessment preparation purposes and one week for the final assessment. In particular, this showcase was intended to develop best practices which could be distributed throughout the School of Law and the wider

University to improve efficiency and enhance the learning experiences of students at the University of Bolton.

This case study is based on the instructor's own experiences and observations utilising autoethnography. It is acknowledged that this approach comes with an element of subjectivity, but at the same time, this is intentional. The generalisability is in part mitigated through the comparison with academic literature on the subject. As such, as will be demonstrated in this section, many of the experiences recorded in this case study resemble what is found in academic scholarship. At the same time, the subjectivity of the case study also highlights the individual nature of teaching and learning. In line with the underpinning views of hermeneutics and dialectics from philosophical scholars such as Hegel and Gadamer (Gadamer, 1976; Hegel, 1874; Hegel, 1991; Hegel, Burbidge & Dickey, 1993), teaching and learning and the engagement with the subject matter of law are not things that can be separated from the people who are actively engaged with them. As such, things such as a person's character, previous experiences, assumptions of the world and abilities cannot be separated from their experiences, perceptions and understandings of teaching and learning, thereby resulting in subjective experiential findings and conclusions.

In light of the findings from the literature, as well as key themes that emerged during the experience of the instructor in this endeavour, the following key focal themes have been focussed on:

- The setting up of digitally enhanced flipped classroom activities
- The implementation and application of digitally enhanced flipped classroom activities within the Public International Law module
- Experiences of student engagement and student learning

In the following, each of these themes will be explored in turn on the basis of the instructor's experiences and observations. In line with the autoethnographic method used for this purpose, the narrative tone will change in the following, whereby a first-person narrative will be used.

The setting up of digitally enhanced flipped classroom activities

Based on the findings from the literature, it did not come as a surprise to me, as the instructor on the module Public International Law, that the initial workload was significantly increased. All the lecture content from the previous years of the course needed to be reworked and rethought. I chose this module as an example to test the digitally enhanced flipped classroom in legal education due to the nature of the module as well as the characteristics of the cohort. As such, public international law as a subject can be content heavy and abstract, especially when trying to convey the way this unique legal system operates between traditional legal principles and novel political, social, economic and cultural dynamics that differ significantly from most national legal systems. It was my experience, both from being a law student in law school myself and studying public international law, and from teaching the subject to the next generation of law students, that public international law as a subject is difficult to grasp in the early stages. At the same time, it is a subject matter that heavily relies on context and discussions and links strongly to contemporary international politics that students are exposed to frequently in the media. Unfortunately, trying to provide enough technical legal knowledge to allow for in-depth contemporary discussions is not always an easy task.

To give an example, it is difficult to discuss enforcement issues and the lack of possible legal sanctions in relation to violations of international law, without understanding the basic concepts of personality, statehood and state recognition. Similarly, a class will struggle to discuss prevention or prosecution provisions for human rights violations without an understanding about the vertical nature of human rights law more generally. It was clear that there was a significant scope for improvement; however, the form this would ultimately take was the most challenging decision. Previous attempts to flip the learning in the classroom had not resulted in the desired outcomes. In particular, similar to the findings in the literature referred to in the previous section, providing students with reading activities before the class often resulted in a confusing and inefficient lecture, due to discrepancies in completion rates of the provided tasks. It was often found that only a small number of students had completed all the reading, with even fewer students having undertaken further research to facilitate their own findings. I would then find myself in the awkward position whereby I had a few options, none of which were particularly useful for effective teaching or learning. One option would be to continue with the in-class exercises or discussions, in which only a small number of students would actively engage, with many other students continuously interrupting the discussions to ask questions. An alternative option often involved trying to rush through the content of the reading in a slightly superficial and shorter teacher-centred lecture style, which was superfluous for the students who had already done the work, and too superficial for the students who had not, which was less effective than continuing with the traditional lecture method I was trying to move away from. The third option would be just to revert back to my previous lecture, which was beneficial for the students who had not engaged with the pre-class reading materials, but demotivating for the students who had prepared properly for the class.

Based on these prior experiences, I was keen to develop a way for students to engage with their weekly class preparations, while mitigating the diverse completion rates. This was where technological developments have significantly enhanced what is possible in terms of providing flipped learning activities. In the early stages of the transition of the module, I created a series of videos. This was easier than I had expected. As the content of the module was already finalised and readily available from the previous year, I recorded myself giving my traditional in-class lectures. As there were no interruptions for questions, in-class discussions, exercises or breaks, what would usually be a two-to-three-hour lecture could easily become a 45-to-50-minute video of all the factual information needed. As such, the preparation of the video took only a little longer than the length of the video. It took approximately five minutes to add soft, concentration-enhancing music to the video using any video editing software that was available on whichever PC I was using, and an additional ten minutes to convert the video into the desired format and save it to my computer. Adding the interactive components of the activity was also much easier than I expected. The H5P Moodle integration tool already had all the functionalities required to convert my recorded lecture into an interactive video. I merely needed to upload the video into the designated space, click on the specific locations in the timeline of the video and add the interactive exercises I wished to add. In particular, exercises that I found particularly useful included multiple-choice questions, fill-in-the-blank exercises (either ones in which words needed to be typed and those in which words needed to be dragged and dropped), external links to legislation or other documents, and activities involving hotspots.

The ease of use of the H5P Moodle integration was a significant surprise. At the same time, the more I used it, the more forms of activities I found, which were mostly easier and faster to create than the initial series of videos. Over the course of the semester, a structure started to emerge in relation to the pre-class activities that I was preparing for the students. The videos I was recording became shorter. I would create shorter three-to-six-minute videos on each of the subjects, which had still been taken from my original course materials. However, I would then start to alternate formats, thereby adding more differentiation to the activities. As such, videos would often be followed by short reading activities, quizzes, chat forums for online student discussions and interactive workbooks. In particular within the workbooks, reflective activities were easy to implement, yet highly effective tools. Although outside of the scope of this case study, the reflective log activities could be the subject of further investigations, as they generated the highest rates of engagement, and the questions the students were given to reflect on were referred to frequently in the lectures, demonstrating a lasting impact on the students.

The key takeaway from my experience in setting up the digitally enhanced flipped classroom activities was that it was much easier and faster than I had been made to believe from the current available literature. The efficiency of my teaching has been increased not only by the fact that any video, text, image or audio can be converted into an engaging online activity in mere minutes, but also through the long-term potential of the created activities, which could be used repeatedly, on-demand by the students and by myself in future lectures.

The implementation and application of digitally enhanced flipped classroom activities within the Public International Law module

The first time I implemented the technologically enhanced flipped classroom in the Public International Law module, I received mixed responses from the students. The majority were positively surprised. It was expressed that they had not come across similar activities before, which reminded them of other online training courses. In particular, the fact that the students were able to go over any part of the lecture more than once, in the event that they had not understood something, was expressed as a welcome advantage. Some students were confused at times with the quizzes in the videos – especially when they thought the answer to a question was different to the one that was provided. However, this was beneficial, as when the in-class session commenced, they were able to raise the question, which allowed me to take the time to explain the correct answer to them and how they could have found this.

Some students initially shared that they had struggled with the exercises. However, the most common issue was finding the exercise on the Moodle page. Once the buttons had been demonstrated to the students, though, these issues were quickly resolved for the remainder of the module.

Once all the materials had been created and students had been introduced to the functionalities and expectations, the implementation encountered very few difficulties, if any. In fact, the time that was saved within the face-to-face lectures proved more useful than initially expected as well. Suddenly, I had all the time I had previously only wished I could have with my students to elevate their practical application of the learnt knowledge. The learning journey undertaken by the students into the subject matter of Public International Law was now able to place a greater emphasis on contemporary discussions, run simulations (such as model UN activities), carry out mock assessments to prepare students for their final assessments, invite guest speakers who are prominent actors within the specialist legal field, and generally run more practical tutorials in which students were able to apply their learning to hypothetical scenarios and problem questions.

Initially, one of my concerns had been that using all my previous lecture materials for the pre-class sessions would leave me without activities to carry out in the face-to-face lecture time. However, the opposite was the case. As students were coming to the classes with already-existing knowledge, the activities almost ran themselves. As such, the classroom had been truly flipped – not only in terms of the content and design of the module delivery (whereby the reading is undertaken prior to the class and the practical application is then trained during the scheduled face-to-face sessions) but the in-class dynamic, which became flipped as well. Now, although I was the person suggesting, promoting and facilitating the in-class activities, it was the students who lead the majority of the class. This meant that the preparation for the face-to-face lectures also became increasingly easier and faster. At times, a short video sketch relating to a topic, or even a court judgement, poster or reading activity would be sufficient to prompt an entire lecture full of discussions and debates.

Experiences of student engagement and student learning

All in all, the observations and experiences with transitioning to a blended learning model that utilised an enhanced flipped classroom for the postgraduate LLM module Public International Law exceeded expectations in relation to student engagement and student learning. Even while writing about the implementation of the module design, it was challenging to refrain from delving too much into the experienced increases in student engagement, although there were, at first, similarly to my previous experiences with pre-class reading activities, a few students who had not engaged with the material. However, there also seemed to be a strong sense in the class that students appreciated how much work had been undertaken by me, their instructor, to create the interactive learning materials. This resulted in peer pressure and shaming amongst students within the cohort to undertake the pre-sessional activities. A significant contributor to student engagement with the online materials is also presumed to be closely linked with the functionality on Moodle to check the completion logs for the activities. Thus, students were more likely to complete the provided tasks because they knew that the tutors and/or instructors could monitor their online activity on the virtual learning environment. As students became increasingly aware that I was able to see if they had in fact completed their weekly tasks, the engagement on the module's Moodle page increased.

I found a similar trend in relation to the activities that required student contributions, such as reflective logs and written answers to questions. The fact that students needed to input text into a text-box made the pre-class activities resemble school homework more, and the completion of the activities became more tangible. It surprises me to this day how even postgraduate students often showcase attitudes towards learning that view this as something that is done to please the instructor rather than for their own benefit. Regardless of the reasons behind this, however, the important point I am trying to make here is that the activities that required a form of input by the students generated higher engagement rates.

One criticism that has been raised in similar circumstances by some students on undergraduate programmes during the early stages of seeking to introduce flipped classroom activities was that, in being provided with online self-directed teaching, they felt they were not getting what they had paid for. Despite the in-person, face-to-face contact time for lectures being unchanged, it almost seemed as though the students had an expectation that the purpose of the lecture was to provide them with the skills and knowledge they needed to excel, without much individual work by the students. The same complaints were not raised within the postgraduate cohort. Instead, comments were made about how much they appreciated the activities that had been created for them. Many students expressed views that were based on the comparison of this teaching and learning approach with their previous experiences of studying on more traditionally designed undergraduate courses. This meant that the postgraduate students were aware of the expectations in traditional law lectures and were able to compare their learning experiences. Moreover, the different demographic on the postgraduate law programmes, which consists of a higher proportion of mature students than is the case on undergraduate programmes, could have contributed to an increased appreciation for the teaching approach and, in turn, to significantly more in-class engagement. The student demographic on LLM programmes is characterised by larger proportions of students with other responsibilities outside of their studies, including employment commitments, caring and parental responsibilities. The increased flexibility in relation to the time and location at which students carried out their pre-class preparation activities made the learning processes more inclusive for all students, regardless of their personal circumstances.

A particularly evident change I observed in the classes was an increase in confidence levels. Unless a student had not completed their weekly in-class activities, it was witnessed how students were able to share their thoughts in the lecture and discuss their concerns and related ideas with the rest of the class. The enhanced confidence was also reflected in their participation and performance, even in summative assessments. As such, increased confidence in the subject matter also resulted in a more confident approach to exams, in-class presentations and mock negotiations. It is still to be seen if the increased confidence in these areas will result in better performance in employment. However, my initial observation is that the positive experiences and successes students had in their lectures, due to the better preparation before classes, has boosted overall confidence exhibited by the students in relation to their abilities.

It was also noted during the in-class exercises that the more equitable starting point of the lecture, in relation to knowledge and understanding, contributed to increased and improved collaboration between peers during the lecture. Students were not as focussed on trying to demonstrate their abilities to the instructor in the class in competition with their peers, but rather, sought active collaboration in areas they were passionate about. Removing the 'race' of knowledge acquisition during the class allowed students to engage with the actual subject matter and contemporary issues at hand. Students were not solely focussed on their own learning and trying to memorise as much as possible in the shortest time possible, but rather on discussing some of the more pressing questions of public international law in general. This, in turn, will have had a positive effect on a wide range of professional, academic and employability skills of the students, including teamwork and collaborative skills, the ability to show initiative and independence of thought, creative problem-solving skills, communication and public-speaking skills, understanding people/interpersonal skills, attention to detail, research and preparation skills, and global citizenship.

Apart from the experiential observations I made in the actual lectures, the Moodle page logs from the students also demonstrated a significant increase in engagement. As such, in previous years it was not uncommon to see very little engagement from students on the VLE pages for modules. Students would log on approximately once a week to download the lecture slides. In the event that an announcement was sent out from one of the news fora, student engagement on the online platform would spike slightly, as students would visit the page to read the posted update. However, engagement with the online learning platform was mostly characterised by an 'as little as possible and as much as necessary' approach. However, with the use of a digitally enhanced flipped classroom approach, the student engagement on the VLE was significantly greater. Students were visiting the VLE several times a week, not only working through the provided materials, but also checking other areas, once they had logged onto the platform, including other tiles I had added to the page with potentially interesting information for students, such as further reading materials, employability information relating to skills and job opportunities, online social spaces where students could exchange information and even recommended social events or activities, such as lists of recommended movies to watch, that may have themes related to the subject of the module. It seemed that once students were encouraged to engage with the VLE, they started to actively engage more with it, beyond what they were required to do. The increased engagement also had other unintended consequences. Apart from engagement with the subject matter in the module itself, students showcased a disproportionately strong interest in the subject matter, even after the module had concluded. In this respect, more than half of the cohort later chose to write their final course projects on topics relating to the area of public international law. Three students progressed into doctoral research in areas of public international law following the completion of their master's degree course. Although this may be a coincidence, it is also not unrealistic to presume that the increased engagement with the content of the module due to the shift in the approach to content delivery and teaching and learning resulted in the development of interest in and passion for this specific area of law.

Findings, summary and conclusions

The experience of applying a flipped classroom approach supported by interactive digital online activities for postgraduate legal education has been positive. Despite an initially increased workload, it was found that setting up and implementing flipped learning activities involved much less input from instructors than expected. As such, the VLE platform used (in this case Moodle) already utilises integration tools which are easy to use for instructors and in fact save a lot of time in contrast to writing full, teacher-centred lectures. Nevertheless, it is also advised that instructors take some time in the earlier weeks of a semester or term to get students familiarised with the digital technology. Management of student expectations in the initial stages of a module is vital – especially as the students will have diverse views on their expected learning processes, instructor directions and the value placed on face-to-face teaching, as well as different personal circumstances that will impact their ability to engage with pre-class preparation materials or face-to-face lectures.

Flipped classroom techniques were particularly useful for postgraduate law students, who already had substantial legal knowledge and possessed the necessary skills to undertake independent learning activities relating to law. Yet, it was still vital to provide students with guidance on how to complete the pre-class tasks. However, once the initial technical limitations had been overcome, the teaching approach not only enhanced the engagement of students with the subject matter, improved student understanding and satisfaction, and freed up more time for the instructor to focus more on the practical application of the learnt knowledge, but also resulted in increased collaboration amongst students, improved confidence levels and enthusiasm for the law.

In particular, the technological enhancement of the flipped learning approach contributed significantly to the increased engagement from the students with the subject matter. The most significant improvement to engagement with pre-class activities was a component of contribution from the students. As such, if students were required to write open text answers to certain questions, it was more likely that the students would complete the activities. It is presumed that this will have related, at least in part, to the threat of being caught out by the instructor for not having completed the activities.

Postgraduate students in law may have more autonomous learning styles, be more skilled and confident using technology to support learning, and be less reliant on in-person instruction. In terms of improving access to learning for students who often have trouble attending and accessing conventional modes of legal learning and teaching, namely live lectures and tutorials, the adoption of flipped, blended learning models with considerable technological assistance has shown great promise. The approaches trialled in this case study within the Public International Law module at the University of Bolton may also serve as an exemplary model for other instructors seeking to design new, or enhance existing, curricula and learning experiences that could serve large groups of diverse students with the differentiation they require to accommodate the varying degrees of previous knowledge and learning requirements. Nevertheless, within all these developments, the student voice remains vital. The entire endeavour would not have been possible without the regular feedback from students, both verbal and written, as well as the evident increase in active student engagement within the lectures and with the flipped classroom activities and the students' dedication to learning. As such, in modules that have a significantly higher student number than the number in the case study of this chapter, it would be advisable to incorporate regular surveys throughout the transitional run of the module, to ensure any designs developed are suitable for the learning needs of the cohort.

Nevertheless, much like the vast majority of our students, we found flipped learning to be immensely beneficial. Generally speaking, we relished the difficulties brought on by conceptualising our instruction in a totally new manner. The next steps for the School of Law within the University of Bolton will be to look into flipped learning's potential beyond the parameters of this study, in other classes, and particularly at other levels. Sharing these experiences within the University's Blended Learning showcase has allowed the wider University teaching community to come together for the purpose of building internal expertise across departments and disciplines. In particular, experiences like the one showcased in this chapter will counter the fear of the unknown amongst legal educators, and will ideally provide the much-needed support and encouragement law teachers require.

References

Aidoo, B., Macdonald, M. A., Vesterinen, V. M., Pétursdóttir, S., & Gísladóttir, B. (2022). Transforming Teaching with ICT Using the Flipped Classroom Approach: Dealing with COVID-19 Pandemic. *Education Sciences*, 12(6), 421.

Alexander, M. M. (2018). The flipped classroom: Engaging the student in active learning. *J. Legal Stud. Educ.*, 35, 277.

Ali, W. (2020). Online and remote learning in higher education institutes: A necessity in light of COVID-19 pandemic. *Higher education studies*, 10(3), 16–25.

Al-Kumaim, N. H., Alhazmi, A. K., Mohammed, F., Gazem, N. A., Shabbir, M. S., & Fazea, Y. (2021). Exploring the impact of the COVID-19 pandemic on university students' learning life: An integrated conceptual motivational model for sustainable and healthy online learning. *Sustainability*, 13(5), 2546.

Angadi, N. B., Kavi, A., Shetty, K., & Hashilkar, N. K. (2019). Effectiveness of flipped classroom as a teaching–learning method among undergraduate medical students–An interventional study. *Journal of Education and Health Promotion*, 8.

Bailey, D. R., & Lee, A. R. (2020). Learning from experience in the midst of COVID-19: Benefits, challenges, and strategies in online teaching. *Computer-Assisted Language Learning Electronic Journal*, 21(2), 178–198.

Balsam, J. S. (2019). Teaming up to Learn in the Doctrinal Classroom. *Journal of Legal Education*, 68(2), 261–283.

Birgili, B., & Demir, Ö. (2022). An explanatory sequential mixed-method research on the full-scale implementation of flipped learning in the first years of the world's first fully flipped university: Departmental differences. *Computers & Education*, 176, 104352.

Boyle, R. A. (2003). Employing active-learning techniques and metacognition in law school: Shifting energy from professor to student. *U. Det. Mercy L. Rev.*, 81, 1.

Buhl-Wiggers, J., Kjærgaard, A., & Munk, K. (2022). A scoping review of experimental evidence on face-to-face components of blended learning in higher education. *Studies in Higher Education*, 1–23.

Burns, K., Keyes, M., Wilson, T., & Stagg-Taylor, J. (2017). Active learning in law by flipping the classroom: An enquiry into effectiveness and engagement. *Legal Education Review*, 27(1), 6100.

Chao, C. Y., Chen, Y. T., & Chuang, K. Y. (2015). Exploring students' learning attitude and achievement in flipped learning supported computer aided design curriculum: A study in high school engineering education. *Computer Applications in Engineering Education*, 23(4), 514–526.

Chen, Y., Wang, Y., & Chen, N. S. (2014). Is FLIP enough? Or should we use the FLIPPED model instead?. *Computers & Education*, 79, 16–27.

Cifuentes, L. (2021). Course designs for distance teaching and learning. In *A Guide to Administering Distance Learning* (174–205). Brill.

Divjak, B., Rienties, B., Iniesto, F., Vondra, P., & Žižak, M. (2022). Flipped classrooms in higher education during the COVID-19 pandemic: findings and future research recommendations. *International Journal of Educational Technology in Higher Education*, 19(1), 1–24.

Espeland, W. N., Sauder, M., & Espeland, W. (2016). *Engines of Anxiety: Academic Rankings, Reputation, and Accountability*. Russell Sage Foundation.

Evans, G. (2021, 10 January). How I memorised everything in law school: Digestible notes. Available from: https://digestiblenotes.com/law/legal_guides/memorise_everything_law_school.php [Accessed: 12 October 2022].

Fortin Lalonde, C. L. (2022). Educating for Meaningful Citizenship: A Critical Corpus Analysis of Public Education Policy in Canada (Doctoral dissertation, Carleton University).

Gadamer, H. G. (1976). *Hegel's Dialectic: Five Hermeneutical Studies*. Yale University Press.

Gladwin-Geoghegan, R., & Thompson, C. (2021). Legacy of Lockdown: Exploring the Opportunities for Development in Legal Education as a Consequence of the COVID-19 Pandemic. *Journal of Ethics and Legal Technologies*, 3(1).

Glesner, B. A. (1990). Fear and loathing in the law schools. *Conn. L. Rev.*, 23, 627.

Hegel, G. W. F. (1874). *The Logic of Hegel*. Clarendon Press.

Hegel, G. W. F. (1991). *Hegel: Elements of the Philosophy of Right*. Cambridge University Press.

Hegel, G. W. F., Burbidge, J., & Dickey, L. (1993). *The Cambridge Companion to Hegel*. Cambridge University Press.

Hess, G. F. (1999). Principle 3: Good practice encourages active learning. *Journal of Legal Education*, 49(3), 401–417.

Hewitt, A. (2015). Can you learn to lawyer online? A blended learning environment case study. *Law Teacher*, 49(1), 92–121.

Howell, R. A. (2021). Engaging students in education for sustainable development: The benefits of active learning, reflective practices and flipped classroom pedagogies. *Journal of Cleaner Production*, 325, 129318.

James, A. J., Chin, C. K., & Williams, B. R. (2014). Using the flipped classroom to improve student engagement and to prepare graduates to meet maritime industry requirements: a focus on maritime education. *WMU Journal of Maritime Affairs*, 13(2), 331–343.

Javier, C. (2020). The shift towards new teaching modality: Examining the attitude and technological competence among language teachers teaching Filipino. *Asian ESP*, 16(2.1), 210–244.

Jeffrey, L. M., Milne, J., Suddaby, G., & Higgins, A. (2014). Blended learning: How teachers balance the blend of online and classroom components. *Journal of Information Technology Education*, 13.

Jia, C., Hew, K. F., Bai, S., & Huang, W. (2022). Adaptation of a conventional flipped course to an online flipped format during the Covid-19 pandemic: Student learning performance and engagement. *Journal of Research on Technology in Education*, 54(2), 281–301.

Jones, K. A., & Ravishankar, S. (2021). *Higher Education 4.0: The Digital Transformation of Classroom Lectures to Blended Learning*. Springer Nature.

Kaplarević-Mališić, A., Dimitrijević, S., Radojevic, I., & Kovačević, M. (2022). Developing Teaching Competencies for Implementing Blended Learning in Higher Education: Experiences of Faculty of Science, University of Kragujevac. In *Proceedings TIE 2022 9th International Scientific Conference Technics and Informatics in Education*. University of Kragujevac, Faculty of Technical Sciences, Čačak.

Kay, R., MacDonald, T., & DiGiuseppe, M. (2019). A comparison of lecture-based, active, and flipped classroom teaching approaches in higher education. *Journal of Computing in Higher Education*, 31(3), 449–471.

Kerns, B. R. (2019). A case study of a flipped curriculum using collaborative and active learning with an adaptive learning system (Doctoral dissertation, Indiana State University).

Keyes, M., & Johnstone, R. (2004). Changing legal education: rhetoric, realty, and prospects for the future. *Sydney L. Rev.*, 26, 537.

Khayat, D., & Osama, S. (2022). The impact of using flipped mobile learning in continuing professional development to develop electronic lecture skills among female university teachers in the kingdom of Saudi Arabia (Doctoral dissertation, University of Southampton).

Kirpalani, A., Grimmer, J., & Peebles, E. R. (2020). A Blended Model of Case-Based Learning in a Paediatric Clerkship Program. *Medical Science Educator*, 30(1), 23–24.

Lane, S. (2015). Information Age to Interaction Age in Legal Education: How Far Have We Progressed?. *American Journal of Educational Research*, 3(12), 1511–1518.

Law Vicissitudes. (2013). Ten things I wish I'd known before becoming a law student. *Guardian* (25 July).

Li, Q., Li, Z., & Han, J. (2021). A hybrid learning pedagogy for surmounting the challenges of the COVID-19 pandemic in the performing arts education. *Education and Information Technologies*, 26(6), 7635–7655.

Lo, V. I. (2014). A Transnational Law Subject in the Australian Law Curriculum. *Bond L. Rev.*, 26, 53.

Low, M. C., Lee, C. K., Sidhu, M. S., Lim, S. P., Hasan, Z., & Lim, S. C. (2021). Blended learning to enhanced engineering education using flipped classroom approach: An overview. *Electronic Journal of Computer Science and Information Technology*, 7(1).

Lukas, B. A., & Yunus, M. M. (2021). ESL Teachers' Challenges in Implementing E-learning during COVID-19. *International Journal of Learning, Teaching and Educational Research*, 20(2), 330–348.

Ma, L., & Lee, C. S. (2021). Evaluating the effectiveness of blended learning using the ARCS model. *Journal of Computer Assisted Learning*, 37(5), 1397–1408.

Mahavongtrakul, M. (2020, March 5). *Implementing Flipped Classrooms into Law School Pedagogy*. Available from: https://dtei.uci.edu/2020/03/05/implementing-flipped-classrooms-into-law-school-pedagogy/ [Accessed: 13 October 2022].

Mali, D., & Lim, H. (2021). How do students perceive face-to-face/blended learning as a result of the Covid-19 pandemic?. *International Journal of Management Education*, 19(3), 100552.

Means, B., Toyama, Y., Murphy, R., Bakia, M., & Jones, K. (2009). Evaluation of evidence-based practices in online learning: A meta-analysis and review of online learning studies.

Mishra, L., Gupta, T., & Shree, A. (2020). Online teaching-learning in higher education during lockdown period of COVID-19 pandemic. *International Journal of Educational Research Open*, 1, 100012.

Murray, I., Cianfrini, M., Clements, J., & Wilson-Rogers, N. (2019). Taxation, innovation and education: Reflections on a flipped lecture room. *J. Australasian Tax Tchrs. Ass'n*, 14, 122.

Nikitaki, S., Papadima-Sophocleous, S., & Nicolaou, A. (2022). From Face-to-face to Online Foreign Language Teaching: Capitalising on Lessons Learned During COVID-19. In *English as a Foreign Language in a New-Found Post-Pandemic World* (1–28). IGI Global.

Nurwakhidah, A., & Suganda, A. D. (2022). Capacity Building in an Effort of Improving Blended Learning-Based Teacher Competence during Covid-19 Pandemic. *Tarbawi: Jurnal Keilmuan Manajemen Pendidikan*, 8(01), 121–128.

Oliveira, G., Grenha Teixeira, J., Torres, A., & Morais, C. (2021). An exploratory study on the emergency remote education experience of higher education students and teachers during the COVID-19 pandemic. *British Journal of Educational Technology*, 52(4), 1357–1376.

Pardo, A., Gašević, D., Jovanovic, J., Dawson, S., & Mirriahi, N. (2018). Exploring student interactions with preparation activities in a flipped classroom experience. *IEEE Transactions on Learning Technologies*, 12(3), 333–346.

Pokhrel, S., & Chhetri, R. (2021). A literature review on impact of COVID-19 pandemic on teaching and learning. *Higher Education for the Future*, 8(1), 133–141.

Rapanta, C., Botturi, L., Goodyear, P., Guàrdia, L., & Koole, M. (2021). Balancing technology, pedagogy and the new normal: Post-pandemic challenges for higher education. *Postdigital Science and Education*, 3(3), 715–742.

Rehman, U., & Lakhan, M. A. S. A. (2021). A review on state of the art in flipped classroom technology a blended e-learning. *Int. J*, 9.

Roehling, P. V. (2017). *Flipping the College Classroom: An Evidence-based Guide*. Springer.

Rubin, E. (2007). What's Wrong with Langdell's Method, and What to Do About It. *Vand. L. Rev.*, 60, 609.

Şahin, M., & Kurban, C. F. (2019). *The New University Model: Flipped, Adaptive, Digital and Active Learning (FADAL)*. FL Global Publishing.

Salvador, R., Limon, M., Borromeo, C. M., Parinas, M. A., Manrique, L., de la Cruz, L., & Dalere, J. M. (2022). Exploring Technical-Vocational Education Teachers' Challenges and Adaptation Strategies in Teaching Courses Outside their Specializations. *Journal of Technical Education and Training*, 14(2), 34–48.

Serrano, D. R., Dea-Ayuela, M. A., Gonzalez-Burgos, E., Serrano-Gil, A., & Lalatsa, A. (2019). Technology-enhanced learning in higher education: How to enhance student engagement through blended learning. *European Journal of Education*, 54(2), 273–286.

Silver, C., & Ballakrishnen, S. S. (2022). Where Do We Go from Here? International Students, Post-Pandemic Law Schools, and the Possibilities of Universal Design. *Can. J. Comp. & Contemp. L.*, 8, 313.

Singh, J., Steele, K., & Singh, L. (2021). Combining the Best of Online and Face-to-Face Learning: Hybrid and Blended Learning Approach for COVID-19, Post Vaccine, & Post-Pandemic World. *Journal of Educational Technology Systems*, 50(2), 140–171.

Slomanson, W. R. (2014). Blended learning: A flipped classroom experiment. *J. Legal Educ.*, 64, 93.

Smith, M. (2020). Integrating technology in contemporary legal education. *Law Teacher*, 54(2), 209–221.

Spencer, A. B. (2012). The law school critique in historical perspective. *Wash. & Lee L. Rev.*, 69, 1949.

Sturm, S., & Guinier, L. (2007). The law school matrix: Reforming legal education in a culture of competition and conformity. *Vand. L. Rev.*, 60, 515.

Tabassum, A. (2021). A Comparative Analysis of Traditional Flipping Versus Virtual Flipping. *Journal of English Language Teaching and Applied Linguistics*, 3(4), 57–62.

Tashiro, J., & Hebeler, A. (2019, July). An adaptive blended learning health education model for families of a parent with serious medical problems. In *International Conference on Blended Learning* (59–71). Springer, Cham.

Tomas, L., Evans, N. S., Doyle, T., & Skamp, K. (2019). Are first year students ready for a flipped classroom? A case for a flipped learning continuum. *International Journal of Educational Technology in Higher Education*, 16(1), 1–22.

Towfigh, E. V., Keesen, J., & Ulrich, J. (2022). Blended Learning und Flipped Classroom in der grundständigen Lehre. *ZDRW Zeitschrift für Didaktik der Rechtswissenschaft*, 9(2), 87–111.

Turnbull, D., Chugh, R., & Luck, J. (2021). Transitioning to E-Learning during the COVID-19 Pandemic: How Have Higher Education Institutions Responded to the Challenge?. *Education and Information Technologies*, 26(5), 6401–6419.

Valz, J. (2022). An Examination of Pandemic Challenges Faced by Professors at Two Universities and the Need for Improved Technology Integration in Pre-service Teacher Preparation Programs (Doctoral dissertation, Texas Wesleyan University).

van Caenegem, W. A., & Mundy, T. (2021). Special Report on Online Legal Education in Australia. Available from: SSRN 3951659.

Van der Werf, W. M., Slot, P. L., Kenis, P. N., & Leseman, P. P. M. (2021). Inclusive practice and quality of education and care in the Dutch hybrid early childhood education and care system. *International Journal of Child Care and Education Policy*, 15(1), 1–29.

van Klink, B., & de Vries, U. (eds.) (2016). *Academic Learning in Law: Theoretical Positions, Teaching Experiments and Learning Experiences*. Edward Elgar Publishing.

Vargiu, P. (2022). Downsizing Teaching: The Case for Seminars as the Backbone of Law Degrees. *Asian Journal of Legal Education*, 9(1), 114–123.

Vaughan, N. (2014). Student engagement and blended learning: Making the assessment connection. *Education Sciences*, 4(4), 247–264.

Watson, J. (2008). Blended Learning: The Convergence of Online and Face-to-Face Education. Promising Practices in Online Learning. North American Council for Online Learning.

Wehling, J., Volkenstein, S., Dazert, S., Wrobel, C., van Ackeren, K., Johannsen, K., & Dombrowski, T. (2021). Fast-track flipping: flipped classroom framework development with open-source H5P interactive tools. *BMC Medical Education*, 21(1), 1–10.

Wolff, L. C., & Chan, J. (2016). *Flipped Classrooms for Legal Education* (Vol. 13). New York: Springer.

Zain, F. M., & Sailin, S. N. (2020). Students' experience with flipped learning approach in higher education. *Universal Journal of Educational Research*, 8(10), 4946–4958.

Zainuddin, Z., Habiburrahim, H., Muluk, S., & Keumala, C. M. (2019). How do students become self-directed learners in the EFL flipped-class pedagogy? A study in higher education. *Indonesian Journal of Applied Linguistics*, 8(3), 678–690.

Zawilinski, L., Shattuck, J., & Hansen, D. (2020). Professional development to promote active learning in the flipped classroom: A faculty perspective. *College Teaching*, 68(2), 87–102.

Zhampeiis, K., Assanova, G., Toishybaeva, G., Saparbaeva, A., Orazbaeva, A., & Manapova, G. (2022). Academic Lectures: Communicative Approaches to Interactive Lectures in Today's Classroom. *Journal of Positive School Psychology*, 7545–7555.

Zheng, W., Ma, Y. Y., & Lin, H. L. (2021). Research on blended learning in physical education during the covid-19 pandemic: A case study of Chinese students. *SAGE Open*, 11(4), 21582440211058196.

CHAPTER NINE

Lessons of How to Support Students Working on the Front-Line during the COVID-19 Pandemic – Blended Learning Support Strategies

Dr Joanne Smith

The COVID-19 pandemic was described as unprecedented in our time, as we faced a situation where the UK population was 'locked down' to restrict people coming together to avoid infection. From an HE and university perspective, this meant an end to face-to-face, classroom-based teaching. From March 2020, teaching staff found themselves teaching online, which was a significant transition: for many staff this was not usual practice, as we had previously been classroom focused. Hence this method, previously only undertaken in exceptional circumstances, became a new norm. Teaching became embedded within the home, which was further altered as teachers and learners facilitated parallel activity, with their children at home. This required careful negotiation of time and space to allow for the facilitation of the different activities and commitments.

I have been teaching for over 25 years and have experienced many changes, but nothing so rapid. The pandemic might be seen as a watershed. Here I would like to share some of what happened and depict some of the adaptions which might be able to show us the potential for change. In times of crisis there is innovation and transformation – people think outside of the box as they move forward. The commitment to students and wish for them to have a good experience is at the heart of the change process: teaching and learning were seen to be the important priority. This chapter is based upon experiences of the support available to the team, my own teaching and learning / TIRI walks and teaching observations alongside evaluation and programme-leader feedback.

In supporting those who are delivering teaching and learning in this new environment, it became obvious that many were out of their comfort zone, and questioning the new methods and their own ability. The classroom as a physical space is dynamic and has several dimensions which support learning, which can be difficult to replicate in an online space. We connect through eye contact, body language, even the clothes we wear, which all give out messages of who we are and how we are feeling. Almost overnight we find ourselves in a 'flatter space', where we might struggle to make ourselves heard, or to check understanding. Some tutors were concerned that students did not put on cameras and that they did not know if learners were engaged or not. This was a challenge as many learners struggled with confidence, hence the blank screens; or alternatively, being in the home meant students were responding to children, who might be close at hand, and so the camera was off for privacy. This all contributed to potential barriers in communication. Solutions to these barriers required diverse solutions and activities which included looking at the different ways in which students wanted to learn and providing flexibility to try and support people in their development.

Some groups showed real confidence and chatted, commented and joined in the sessions, some used chat during the classes and others used forums after the sessions. A lack of participation was challenging and pairing up of tutors was sometimes helpful. At other times, breakout rooms or preparation before sessions were useful. The aim was to be encouraging without pressuring. As time went on, confidence grew. Technology proved essential.

The words 'you are on mute' became a motto for 2020 and we found out the problems with our equipment and broadband – sometimes when we began to teach. We were forgiven when things went wrong – mostly – because we cared and tried our best. What has been considered so far might be applicable to any students – but as if this was not enough, the students here were involved in front-line services, so they were not only trying to manage their studies and their family, they were also working in a sector what had been transformed.

Challenges of supporting students who were on the front-line

The obvious challenge of having students working on the front-line was that they were going through challenges outside of education. Front-line workers were defined as those who needed to work during the pandemic and often face to face with the public. Some had to change work patterns at short notice as other staff went off sick, which meant they needed to be flexible to workplace demands. Some of the students changed their job role to prioritise the needs of the pandemic, which for some meant getting close to COVID-19 – and thus facing the risk of the unknown and infection. As students increased their likely contact with COVID, concerns grew that they might bring infection back to their family. This meant that there was increased stress for some and disruption. This employment was obviously a priority, but the students were also learners, aiming to be better at what they were able to offer and looking to improve their own future careers. So their tutors needed to be very supportive, understanding and flexible, and to give professional guidance which would help them. Technology was part of the solution, as recordings of sessions were provided, meaning learning could take place at a time that suited the student.

The feedback from students was that although there were many challenges, their learning remained essential and important to them. For some, whilst domestic and work demands increased in their life, their study was a place that was about them, that gave them a focus outside of the pandemic. Hence students were committed and this was mirrored by the lecturers.

Taking a student-centred approach from a classroom to a virtual space required significant adaptation: remaining thoughtful in terms of tone and manner; conveying information in a similar way to classroom teaching, despite the new environment; being reassuring, structured, engaging and welcoming. There was also a requirement for tutors to be understanding, giving consideration to the whole experience of the student. This involved understanding that there might be times when the load was too much, assessing when the pace needed to be altered or deadlines extended. Keeping student centred: recognising that we were human beings living, working and learning within a crisis situation.

There were a number of strategies to ensure students were able to progress:

- *Change and the importance of being holistic and flexible*

  Flexibility within learning was key. This included flexible thinking. How could our excellent practices and engagement in university (in the classroom) be brought into a virtual space, through visuals and the use of a variety of methods? When we recorded sessions, we did not want to become just a voice; we wanted to be the tutors that students already knew. This involved still being human: "if we were in the University now, I would probably say 'have a bit is a break', 'Take a minute', 'have a walk about' or 'refresh your brain'"; "If you don't understand any of this, rewind and start again"; "I have included a paper with some more information"; "There is this video…"; "Join me on the chat after the session"; "Drop me a line". All these phrases can be used to reflect commitment and accessibility, showing the students that you still care about them. Being on a screen should not make us any less human.

- *Creating connections*

  We modified our teaching to meet the needs of the new situation, for example using groups or breakout rooms, or getting together just to chat or ask questions. There were quizzes to revise for examinations and observations.

- *Assessment*

  There was an acceptance that things were not the same and there might need to be changes, which had rigour whilst reflecting the new situation: this was applied to the ways in which people were assessed and the amount of assessment there was. Part of the education process is of course centred on assessment – checking that learning has taken place and the students have the knowledge and skills they need. There were clearly some areas which were much improved, including the ways in which they were able to use technology. But there was acceptance that some things would need to be tested in a more flexible way: student exams online; recorded presentations/ reflections which might normally be about placement on case studies; some simulation in terms of considering practice situation.

Whilst changes made during the pandemic might have been viewed as temporary measures which would come to an end once the situation became normal, in fact there could be no putting the toothpaste back in the tube. It was now out there and it was far from all bad – in fact, a lot of what was seen was really positive and showed a potential to create a new blended approach. This was associated with flexibility, which can create an eclectic and responsive approach that engages learners by drawing from positives and using a broader range of more holistic and student-centred practice. There are many benefits in terms of academic stretch, but this also increases support options and scaffolding, which were so important for those who were experiencing many issues.

Below are some of the adaptions made by teams.

School of Health and Society & working at the front-line – case studies

Health and social care

The students in health and social care included those working in a sector which might be seen to be increasingly stretched during the pandemic, as the workforce was required to do more whilst the staff were affected by COVID. This included examples where learners employed in the care-home sector faced rapid change, with legislation changing regularly as the situation and knowledge moved on. Hence their learning journey incorporated the rapidly changing situation. Education in health and social care incorporates reflection, knowledge of process and practice, yet there was a significant amount that was unknown. Hence, as we are expected to be the experts, there was a degree of the unknown, which required significant flexible thinking and/or problem-based learning and regular updates. It remained important to offer reassurance and support but this was a dynamic situation. This meant that there was stress for students at times, as they might be asked to come out of their comfort zone or do additional shifts as the workforce was inevitably struck down by COVID. A student went from a community setting into ICU, working with people with COVID. There was an increased death rate in many health and social care settings, creating additional pressures in the workplace.

This situation needed to be managed well to ensure there was recognition of the change and adaptions and support being provided. Flexibility was so important. Tutors supporting students in practice used virtual meeting spaces to provide supervision and space to share concerns and problem solve. There were close links with mentors and managers, which also required a flexible and responsive approach as they too were under pressure. There were increased considerations of what could be offered out of hours or when students were available, which might be out of the usual time. Some of this was technology based, all was personable – giving tutorials and supervision, giving time to talk about other things.

The group was critical in terms of support; time to chat became as important as the class content. Peer support is often important at university and is increasingly recognised as important to student success. Bohannon and Bohannon (2015) associated peer mentoring with the creation of a safe space that allowed the mentee to grow in confidence, through guidance and role modelling. This can be even more important where there are additional pressures from the practice area. Lewis and Cardwell (2018: 1233) found peer support important for students on professional courses as they experienced similar stresses to other students, such as academic workload and financial pressure, but also from the effects of 'death and suffering'. Peer support is associated with creating a situation in which students feel they are able to succeed and a sense that they have a common identity with their fellow students. Peer learning is used widely across the University and includes sharing work experiences and talking through cases in areas like health and social care, which support learning through connecting theory and practice but also based on a shared understanding in the group. During the lockdown this was difficult to achieve as face-to-face meeting was no more – yet this was probably needed more than ever, not only for learning, but also for wellbeing. Hence the formal structure and sessions facilitated needed to be more open, giving times to drop in and have a chat, even at times without the lecturer being there. The chat might be about the learning and there were lots of times when it was, but sometimes it was just about what work was like or what it was like educating your children whilst learning yourself. Tutors tried to gude on managing time; we looked at people who might be on their own and feeling different pressures. The key seemed to be creating a support network replicating the atmosphere of the University and giving reassurance through a safe/shared space, transferring an ethos from a classroom into a virtual space, including care and support and confidence building.

Example: Have a go / Learning together

Some aspects of health and social care are very practical; they might be about the human body. In a session I observed, I saw practical demonstrations of walking aids, consideration of gait and how we walk, inviting the students to get up on their feet and walk a few steps. Think about how we do that. What is it like? This reflected creative engagement which allowed the students to link theory and practice in a meaningful way.

Organising Time: three-hour online lesson in manageable chunks, based on student feedback (from Health and Social Care Programme Leader):

- 1pm. 'Check in and chat' (live Zoom students given check-in code, etc. then just some time chatting, catching up and socialising – along with any Q&As from previous week – they missed campus and each other and I wanted to recreate the 'classroom' as best as I could).
- 1.30–2.30. Send them away to watch or listen to a recorded lecture (this would have places to pause, make notes and

answer posed questions, and there could be video clips, etc. on Moodle to access when directed as well; I would keep Zoom in the background in case of any issues, etc.).

- 2.30–2.45. Stretch legs and take a break.
- 2.45–3.30/3.45. Back to live Zoom for discussion/feedback/ summary. Revisit the questions and/or points for discussion in the recording. (I would record this live class and add it to Moodle later.)

Benefits identified:

- Definitely the use of pre-recorded lectures – particularly for information giving, essay guidance, etc.
- Zoom has been excellent for tutorials and dissertation supervision so this will stay, I think – though students have been given a choice as some still prefer to come on campus. Blended learning works well in this way.
- Greater use of online tools – interactive whiteboard, kahoot, etc.
- These experiences and skills will also enhance a student's employability.

What we have learned and how we have changed:

- Increases in resilience and adaptability.
- Technology can support students. Some placements could not go ahead and students experienced virtual cases, which helped them discuss and develop problem-solving approaches.
- The barriers present when using technology need to be considered.
- There is a need to listen to students and show a 'humanistic' approach to teaching and learning.

Social work

Social-work students undertake significant placement experiences as part of their programme and much of their learning and assessment is linked to this. Linking theory with practice is an essential ethos to ensure that the students are ready to become social workers. A quick transformation was again required, which once more involved increased communication through digital means. The skills needed for this change required developing good levels of engagement, initially between the groups and between tutors and students, but as this developed it became obvious that what was being undertaken in the University (i.e. online) could also be transferred into practice. Hence the digital skills which social-work students developed were two-fold: being needed for the purpose of teaching and learning, but also to offer practice. The use of distance methods of working with service users was an important move forward during this time. There was once again a sense that there would be some additional pressures to manage, which meant that alternative methods of communication were required.

Important skills to be developed in social work are communication and interpersonal, which are used to engage with people accessing services and the teams. This is of course about gaining and sharing clear information. In the learning environment, whilst the subject matter is important so are the skills which are role modelled that will become essential to the social-work role. What is taught is not always about the subject matter but the skills alongside the knowledge. In some ways, educators can take this for granted. In terms of areas like social work, this is essential to practise and understand. So doing this online created a pressure on both sides.

It was important to understand the camera and the ways it can be used to communicate, particularly in terms of eye contact, pace, tone of voice and body language. This was role modelled by staff and identified as a transferable skill. Clarity of information is also important. The use of staff working in pairs was valuable here to create a dialogue, so students might then feel confident to join in with an existing discussion.

The challenge of staff being role models when they might feel like novices was significant as we moved quickly to delivering online. Students look to lecturers to be the expert in the room, but this was not always the case. Specialist IT services were at the heart of the approach, as was sharing experiences and knowledge. A team approach.

Placements were different than before. Some continued to work 'in the office' but many did not. These placements would be making calls or using technology, and when this was essential it needed to be fully risk assessed in line with the government guidance.

An innovative development was the 'garden visit', where students from the social-work centre might meet in someone's garden. Whilst this had first to be carefully considered in terms of confidentiality, it proved to be a compromise which was well received.

Working through COVID has been an important opportunity for reflection and students have probably moved ahead much more with technology in this time than they would have before. Once more, challenges were met with a flexible approach and a problem-solving attitude.

- Remote social work
- Virtual placements
- Working in the community in new ways
- Working as social-work teams were going through changes
- Alternative methods included 'garden visits' and 'sign-ups', amongst others

Early childhood studies

Early childhood studies included students working in the early years sector, such as nurseries, pre-schools, primary schools and child minders, amongst others. The students included those undertaking a UG degree who would normally complete a placement in each year of study, which would form the basis of significant parts of their programme, and foundation degree students who were in the workplace and as such connected their learning with their work. In the initial stages of the pandemic, early years was not always recognised as being as essential, although as time progressed this was re-evaluated as this work is essential to key workers with your children.

There were two aspects to this work and the students involved: firstly, those undertaking the more traditional (UG) academic pathway were faced with not being able to come into university, which created issues as discussed above; but they were also not able to undertake placements, which were essential to their learning. Hence the use of simulation. This was scenario based and helped the students to consider the situations they might find themselves in through reviewing interactions, space and location, and problems which might arise in the space. This was beneficial in ensuring that the students could give consideration to the situations they might encounter, allowing them to take a problem-based approach. This was well received and seen to ensure that students progressed both through individual work and group-based activities.

Simulated placements were an important resource, aligning the student with the area of practice that they would need to achieve and thus being an important step into practice. This might not be a perfect fit as a substitute, but it had value in skills development (often scenario based) and allowed students to align their knowledge with practice expectations. They include: risk assessment, professional skills, planning EYs curriculum, looking at wider issues associated with safeguarding and child wellbeing. This offers a real range in terms of role-play. The opportunities of the simulated placement are not as an absolute substitute for in-person placement, but offer a viable alternative.

Those in practice on work-based learning programmes found themselves essential – when the lockdown took place, there was care for essential workers. This was a challenge in terms of working with children who did not understand the pandemic and its requirements for hand washing and especially social distancing. The students reflected on initiatives they brought into the workplace around education around hand washing and other precautions, once more showing some unique opportunities for learning. There was increased concern at times amongst the group of students as they wanted to remain in the workplace but also to keep their families safe. The staff created initiatives that included time to chat, flexible resources and regular updates. There was also increased use of recordings of classes, when there were times that we were back in the classroom; but the students wanted to avoid going into situations where there might be risks that could then create cross infections. The staff team showed excellence in being flexible and responsive, making excellent use of a variety of technological solutions.

Early years:

- Supporting families to continue working
- Minimising risk and supporting change in nurseries schools

Community development and youth work

The role of the community worker became essential during the pandemic, including activity around support for isolating people who might not getting the supplies they needed, and community interventions that represented a lifeline often in terms of reaching out to people who might be lonely. Yet many traditional community settings were closed, under restrictions. Furthermore, youth work became recognised as essential after a while as young people became socially isolated from each other, as households could not mix, and schools and other facilities were closed. Changes in the delivery of courses were seen and student placements were either cancelled of adapted to meet the new situation. In terms of teaching and learning in this area, working in and with groups is essential, as communication and interpersonal skills are essential. The important place of virtual connections became evident once more: as the group was essential, the creativity of the students was embraced with clear guidance from the tutors. Breakout rooms were used and observations showed a high level of focus on use of alternative ways to engage: engaging with the practical in a different way, looking at what community hubs needed, and providing understanding of what young people were managing. Also working with networks and professional bodies. There is always a balance to be maintained when the student is on a professional programme which relates to them having sufficient experience to go into the practice domain.

The inclusion of work experience is fundamentally linked with the place of experiential learning, which is associated with learning from lived, real-life experiences (Kolb, 2015). During the pandemic, professional bodies offered some flexibility as a temporary measure which was helpful in keeping the students on programme and stopping them feeling they were being left behind. In the example of youth work, reducing hours and looking at alternative ways to show competence were important, but this needed to be balanced with students wanting to participate in practice, as this helped them to forge links between theory and practice. During the pandemic the role of those working with young people did change as they were seen to be 'key workers', which showed the importance of this group – but also meant that there needed to be close working and guidance.

Youth work online:

- The importance of young people's experiences became increasingly evident in terms of wellbeing

- Many youth-work facilities did not initially function, and then changed in terms of doing community outreach and online sessions

- This meant becoming skilled at a distance to ensure the care and support of young people was a priority

The effects of change and some lessons learnt

Communications were essential in all the cases shown. The students need to develop interpersonal skills and become confident as they will need to communicate with the people who use their services, their team and the wider group delivering the services. There were countless restrictions to interaction during the pandemic and the new situation required creative solutions that changed the ways we work.

Problem solving from teaching staff, students and practice areas showed creative and flexible approaches. The students were able to reflect and learn, and for many this was a unique situation. There was a light shone on human services during the pandemic. Appreciation of roles was evident and there were inspirational stories as students made valued contributions and were supported by tutors to maintain their role whilst also engaging with education.

There were many challenges around non-engagement of students including blank screens and non- responsiveness. This was associated with a lack of confidence, which teams worked hard to overcome – practice makes perfect.

In education and especially HE we assume that the lecturer/tutor is an expert. There is a sense that they will 'know everything'. However, when we went into a new situation, this was not the case and there were gaps in knowledge and skills at this time. There was a need to be authentic, focusing on the shared experience of learning together and supporting one another. Learners are of course looking to those in charge of their education to steer, but when the new norm emerged there was a shared learning.

As we are increasingly concerned with the 'co-creation' of teaching and learning in terms of experiences and space, there is increased focus on what students would like to find within their education, and how they would like to learn and even be assessed. This is a significant shift and shows a new way of considering educational relationships. Innovation often comes through necessity. Here was a point where change needed to happen – and the voice of the student became the grounds for this change. What would work for them? What new skills did they need? How would they want to proceed? The partnership was vital to success and feedback was generally positive in terms of students feeling they were listened to.

Merging spheres: The lockdown meant the closure of the University but also schools and other child-care facilities; moreover, many people found themselves working from home. This meant that there was an overlap of the domestic, employment and learning spheres. The effect of this meant that teaching and learning had to be respectful of this additional pressure, and as they went into the home space, due consideration had to be given to form and contents. Sometimes the opportunity to learn at the time of delivery was not possible

– hence the importance of flexible delivery matched to individual circumstances.

New normal and blended learning

So, as we move back into the normal situation, what is clear is that there is a 'new normal', which should be positive in terms of keeping the best of what we have learned. The academic areas discussed here are linked with 'practice', with people skills at the forefront (interpersonal, communication, practical, etc.). Meeting in real spaces such as a classroom is highly valued; however, the other virtual or simulated learning environments are now more fully understood, as are the opportunities they offer.

So, whilst the benefits of students being alongside one another and working together are probably now more fully appreciated, other spaces have become part of the blend. There are some clear benefits, including student joint group projects being easier to co-ordinate, as there had previously been challenges when meeting together outside of the timetable. One-to-one support, such as tutorials and supervisions, is increasingly flexible and often better received as students are increasingly confident in using technology as part of their learning. There are also aids, such as recordings of sessions, which allow students to learn at their own pace and check if they are not clear about an area. Hence, blending in-class and online creates increased flexibility around ways of learning and opportunities.

The blended ways in which competences might be achieved became clear. This does not mean that we don't need practice, as immersion in an environment will ensure the development of skills. But it does mean that there are many viable alternatives that can be used, including simulation and use of virtual means.

Pedagogy: In a multi-disciplinary team, which spans a number of academic areas and practice specialisms, there is one thing that connects us and might be seen to be the basis of our collaborative approach. This is that we are all concerned with people – be they at different places across the lifespan and with different needs and circumstances. There is increased focus on the role of students as empowered participants who have a voice and should be heard and responded to (Scott, 2015). Whatever the discipline might be, we would want our students to be person centred and have an understanding that how they practice should be inclusive and can be life changing. If this is an ethos then the pedagogy that relates to it is influenced by a humanistic approach:

> humanism refers to the ability of each unique human personality to act as a subject of one's own life and activities (and not an object of any plans, programs and curricula), as well as to the fact that it is the human nature as a whole that takes part in learning, creativity, activity – and not just the mind, not only the rational side of personality. (Mielkov et al., 2021)

A humanistic approach can be connected to seeing learners as human individuals with their own experiences and expectations. Much benefit is derived from this approach not least because throughout the learning a key attribute is the empathetic approach of the individual. This is important for the delivery of human services, so if education and those delivering teaching and learning are able to do anything to support this development, then they should be able to role model this. This is always important, but more so at the time of the pandemic when a number of pressures came together.

Summary

This workforce was identified as offering essential services, the absence of which would have detrimental effects upon the wellbeing of community. Front-line workers were given priority during the pandemic, because they were offering essential services. There was recognition that they were experiencing pressure in the workplace associated with there being greater demand on aspects of the services, paralleled with staff shortages due to increased sickness in the workforce. There were also changes throughout the workplace – which meant that there was redevelopment of staff.

During COVID...

- Employment changed in the sector
- Some roles changed
- Some sector priorities changed
- Remote working came into youth and social work
- New approaches included accommodating and protecting from COVID-19

Home changed:

- Children were at home (home schooling)
- Other care responsibilities required management, in the face of some restrictions in service
- Some could access children in school, but not all (and students who did have children in school had concerns about infection risks)
- Home became a place of study

Foundation Health and Social Care Degree, March 2020

- Over two weeks, this went from being classroom based to remotely taught
- Staff wanted to be flexible and supportive, as this was an area where students changed work and were working in the most demanding situations
- Including moving from community team into ICU
- Including working in care homes where the death rate increased
- Concerns about threat of infection needed to be addressed

What the teams did

- Blended and flexible approaches
- Listening to students to get a sense of what was required
- Used Zoom, Teams and Moodle
- Used team approaches
- Shared ideas

Listening and being holistic

- Personal tutoring pages
- Working with the wider university team
- Recognising the pressure of being on the front-line and creating virtual spaces
- Social-work quiz
- Service-user sessions online
- Drop ins
- Chat at the beginning of sessions
- Sessions about managing the new situation, focussing on wellbeing and work–life balance

Keeping student centred

- There were students who had not been in the University so the teams needed to create the environment
- The Early Years students showed a split: some were concerned about coming into University and then going into EY settings due to their responsibility to children and families and reducing risk of infections, whilst others wanted to be in uni and missed this
- Consequently, a blended approach of some on campus and some studying at home was adopted (EYs PL)
- Creating a positive environment online (HSC PL)

References

Bohannon, R. L., & Bohannon, S. M. (2015). Mentoring: A decade of effort and personal impact. *Teacher Leadership in Nonsupervisory Roles*, 81(2), 31–36.

Kolb, D. A. (1984). *Experiential Learning: Experience as the Source of Learning and Development*. Englewood Cliffs, NJ: Prentice Hall.

Lewis, E. G., & Cardwell, J. M. (2019). A comparative study of mental health and wellbeing among UK students on professional degree programmes. *Journal of Further and Higher Education*, 43(9), 1226–1238. DOI: 10.1080/0309877X.2018.1471125.

Mielkov, Y., Bakhov, I., Bilyakovska, O., Kostenko, L., & Nych, T. (2021). Higher education strategies for the 21st century: philosophical foundations and the humanist approach. *Revista Tempos e Espaços em Educação*, 14(33), e15524. Available from: http://dx.doi.org/10.20952/revtee.v14i33.15524.

Scott, C. L. (2015). THE FUTURES of LEARNING 3: What kind of pedagogies for the 21st century? UNESCO Education Research and Foresight, Paris. [ERF Working Papers Series, No. 15].

CHAPTER TEN

Using Peer-Led Online Community Groups to Foster Connectedness during COVID-19

Dr Tara Chandler and Jo Luckhurst

Campus connectedness was first referred to by Lee and Robbins in 1995 by applying the theory of social connectedness to the university context (or 'college', given the concept was first developed in the US). Social connectedness is the sense of belonging people feel within the society in which they are embedded. When people perceive themselves to be socially connected, they feel a sense of value, of being trusted, have a sense of trust in others, and feel integrated within the group (Whitlock, Wyman & Barreira, 2012). Having a sense of belonging can apply to social groups beyond family relationships, for example to organisations or geographic locations in which the individual is embedded (Whitlock, Whyman & Berreira, 2012). Having a strong sense of connectedness within an organisation means the individual closely identifies with the values and culture of the organisation itself and experiences a sense of pride to be part of that establishment. For example, an individual may feel a sense of connectedness to the company for which they work (Huynh, 2012) or to an educational institution such as a university or college (Tinto, 2005). Within the university setting, campus connectedness considers both social factors, such as having a close bond and sense of togetherness with peers, social integration, assimilation and engagement (Brooman & Darwent, 2014; Sollitto, Johnson & Myers, 2013; Flynn, 2014), and organisational factors, such as feeling connected to campus life, fitting in and having a sense of academic integration (Tinto, 1998). Campus connectedness, therefore, can be described as the perception of belonginess, relatedness and affiliation that a student experiences within the university setting (Lee & Robbins, 1995).

Social connectedness has consistently been shown to have implications for both psychological and physical health and wellbeing. In psychological terms, those who are more connected are more likely to experience positive mental health and cope more effectively with life challenges (Arslan, 2021), demonstrating a greater sense of resilience when faced with difficulties. The evidence suggests that a strong sense of connectedness acts as a protective factor against negative impacts of adversity, with individuals having access to a greater pool of resources to drawn upon in times of difficulty (Kiely et al., 2021). When people have a greater sense of belonging, they are more likely to utilise the support of others within the group, whether emotional or practical advice and guidance (Kiely et al., 2021). The impact of this social support opportunity is positively associated with an increased level of physical health and, ultimately, lifespan (Kramer, 2017; Whitlock, Wyman & Barreira, 2012; Frisby, Hosek & Beck, 2020). Yet when individuals are socially disconnected, the impact has shown to be an increased sense of isolation and loneliness. This sense of loneliness and isolation is associated with an increased mental and physical ill-health which has the potential to impact mortality (Beller & Wagner, 2018).

Having a strong sense of connectedness has been linked to increased health and wellbeing amongst the student population (Arslan, 2021). A greater feeling of campus connectedness has been associated with increased rates of retention, which is influenced by higher levels of engagement in academic activities. Furthermore, a greater sense of campus connectedness is associated with an increased likelihood of accessing support services within the university and increased engagement with tutors and peer support. These positive associations with campus connectedness have been shown to lead to better academic outcomes and ultimately are predictors of successful graduate employment outcomes (Bridgstock & Tippett, 2019).

Clearly, building a sense of connectedness within the university setting is important for a positive student experience, and these positive social connections can occur prior to the student arriving at the university. Research has demonstrated that, alongside motivation (college commitment), having strong social connectedness before transitioning to university has a direct effect on students staying once they get there (Allen et al., 2008). So, prior social connectedness is influential in supporting the transition to campus; however, once on campus it is evident that building campus connectedness is essential to students' experience, and their sense of resilience continues as they face further academic challenges (Kwan, 2022).

To help students develop their perceptions of connectedness, universities have a range of methods to encourage participation in campus life within and beyond the course being studied. Within the subject groups, tutors will utilise 'getting to know you' activities, group work and class discussions to help the group get to know each other. These methods are designed to create a shared identity amongst the school or faculty, and ultimately a peer community. Social-media communication channels, such as WhatsApp groups, which occur outside the formal university channels, can be excellent tools to support students to connect with their course mates and engage in learning and social activities (Thomas, Orme & Kerrigan, 2020). Universities may encourage students to become peer mentors or student ambassadors, and to become involved in societies to enhance connectedness with the wider university population, also considered civic engagement (Fink, 2014), and to create a sense of identity that aligns with the institution. From a service-user perspective, more formal buddying and peer mentoring systems for students who need additional support have also been shown to have positive impact on student wellbeing and retention, further impacting on their sense of connectedness (Lucas & James, 2018).

In March 2020 due to the COVID-19 lockdown, educational establishments were required to quickly transition to an online learning model of delivery (Aristovnik et al., 2020). The use of digital technologies such as Microsoft Teams and Zoom became ubiquitous with academics and students having to adjust to this new learning environment (Aristovnik et al., 2020). Whilst most universities and colleges had some experience of online provision, utilising virtual learning environments (VLEs) such as Moodle and Blackboard to supplement face-to-face delivery, during the pandemic the need to substitute all in-person teaching with online methods was a huge shift in the teaching and learning experience (Aristovnik et al., 2020). Transitioning to a remote delivery model had implications for the student experience, greatly affecting their sense of connectedness to campus (Arslan, 2021). During the lockdowns, students reported an increased sense of isolation from their university and their peers, which was shown to have a negative effect on student engagement with live lectures delivered online, and with independent learning tasks; with students reporting having 'Zoom fatigue' (Wiederhold, 2020). Subsequently, students described feelings of psychological distance, loneliness and disconnection from peers and educational institutions (Arslan, 2021). This experienced physical and psychological distance was linked to increased anxiety related to academic performance, a reduced sense of academic self-efficacy and an increase in mental health problems (Alemany-Arrebola et al., 2020; Sahu, 2020).

These factors in turn resulted in reduced student motivation, engagement and ultimately retention, which some research suggests is a result of perceived breaches in the student–instructor–university psychological contract by moving from a face-to-face delivery model to blended or distance learning (Gazica, Leto & Irish, 2022). As a result of lower academic self-efficacy, universities saw a reduction in student assignment submissions and an increase in the number of students who required additional learning support, such as study plans and extended deadlines. Research has shown that connectedness can moderate the effects of isolation and loneliness (Arslan, 2021) and encourage student psychological health and wellbeing, and so during the COVID-19 pandemic and social-distancing guidelines, it was important for universities to encourage connectedness via alternative means. For example, finding a way to utilise digital platforms to build student perceptions of connectedness in the absence of the traditional face-to-face interactions.

Historically, remote or online learning is shown to jeopardise the learner experience. Moreover, online learning impedes the student's experiences of connectedness within the learning environment, the peer group, the organisation and the faculty (Barbarick, 2013;

Laux, Luse & Mennecke, 2016). For example, Zhao (2002) identified a greater negative impact on connectedness amongst online learning communities. Students studying an online course were less likely to be engaged in the education process due to barriers to connectedness, and the pedagogical choices were limited and less effectively received in remote environments (Zhao, 2002). In addition to this, student-to-student and student-to-faculty relationships are impacted due to communication limitations. The remote learning environment effects subtle visual cues that aid relationship development such as body language, personality, emotion responses, as well as verbal communication that can be broken or disjointed due to technical failure (Zhao, 2002). Connectedness is key to learner success in higher education, and students who feel a greater sense of connectedness have reduced feelings of isolation and achieve better academic outcomes (Jamison & Bolliger, 2020). Lambrinidis (2014) explains that effective online education should combine academic content and social aspects of learning that aid the online community. Jamison and Bolliger (2020) explain that a lack of sense of community in remote learning courses is the key reason for connectedness issues in online learning. Students with greater social interactions in online learning environments have higher perceived learning outcomes and course satisfaction. Not only this, but social interaction is also particularly important amongst vulnerable student populations such as non-traditional students and first-year higher education students who are transitioning to the HE environment. Vulnerable groups are shown to thrive in social environments when feelings of connectedness within the peer group and wider organisation are strong (Melkun, 2012; Lambrinidis, 2014).

There is evidence to show that digital resources can develop connectedness in students over an extended period when the remote learning focuses on developing the peer-to-peer and peer-to-faculty communities. Therefore, establishing an online community is integral to feeling connected in online or remote learning courses (Jamison & Bolliger, 2020). Community learning can be defined as a learning approach that reflects social constructivism and facilitates learning via a knowledge exchange and negotiating meanings within a cohort (Laux, Luse & Mennecke, 2016). The community learning approach encourages faculty and students to reflect on and recognise individual strengths. When individual strengths are combined, all members of the cohort collaborate in the learning process where each member of the group offers a unique perspective that enhances discussion (Stahl, 2013). In a community learning approach, students and faculty can share experiences and knowledge through social interaction such as discussion or conversation (Cai & Zhu, 2012). It is essential that discussion is facilitated in order to control the process, diffuse conflict and encourage the contribution of ideas across all members of the group (Dewiyanti et al., 2007). Due to the importance of community in online learning environments, Jamison and Bolliger (2020) explain that teaching staff must make additional effort to create learning resources and pedagogy that encourage peers and faculty to make connections. Online courses that foster a sense of community encourage interaction and collaboration between peers and faculty (Barnard, Paton & Rose, 2007). Students with a greater sense of community are more likely to work together to complete assignments or projects and to share information. Community-based teaching methods that inspire collaboration are shown to increase student satisfaction and retention (O'Keeffe, 2020). To ensure student persistence through their online courses, online programmes should offer collaborative learning communities that allow interaction between students and reflect a face-to-face learning community (Laux, Luse & Mennecke, 2016). A collaborative online learning community in higher education is encouraged as student engagement and the student experience are shown to be improved (Maina, Wagacha & Oboko, 2017). Not only this, Laux, Luse and Mennecke (2016) discuss the impact of collaborative or community-based online learning and that it assists student employability profiles whereby students develop collaborative skills in critical thinking, problem solving and effective communication on online and digital platforms that are evolving in the workplace.

There are a range of digital methods to aid in collaborative online learning. Discussion boards or discussion forums and chatrooms are used to facilitate a dialogue interaction within student groups that are working on a shared task, for example assessment (Melkun, 2012; Kuong, 2015). There are some limitations to discussion boards if a host does not facilitate critical appraisal of learning resources and some students have expressed issues with discussion boards that are used only to submit assessment and therefore limit collaboration and interaction (Lambrinidis, 2014). The live virtual classroom, when delivered as an activity-orientated device, is shown to mimic the face-to-face classroom well, and to facilitate collaboration and peer-to-peer and peer-to-faculty interaction. Teaching staff using the virtual classroom are encouraged to segment teaching sessions into short time frames allowing regular reflection and interaction between peers (Zhao, 2002; Kuong, 2015). Faculty should facilitate peer-to-peer collaboration using a multi-media approach, for example activities that involve chats or discussion, role-play activities and simulators (Kuong, 2015). As previously stated, informal communication channels, such as WhatsApp messaging groups, were already being used by students before the pandemic as a way of increasing their sense of connectedness. During the lockdowns and social-distancing guidelines during the pandemic, the use of alternative communication channels, therefore, was implemented to help students maintain (if current students) and develop (if new students) their sense of connectedness. The identification of additional online platforms to connect students with their peers and tutors was essential in giving student cohorts a sense of control over their socialisation, learning and assessments, as well as creating a shared identity amongst the cohort. It is clear, therefore, that using appropriate technologies with a clear purpose within the university setting can promote the development of connectedness amongst the student population, thereby encouraging increased academic self-efficacy and engagement, and thus increased academic achievement.

Whether online or face-to-face teaching, the design of collaborative learning is essential to successful learning outcomes and experiences. The authors of the current chapter identified a face-to-face method of pedagogy that was shown to have a significant influence on the sense of connectedness amongst peer groups (Van der Meer & Scott, 2009): Peer Assisted Study Support (PASS). PASS is a method of group study sessions that are facilitated by trained students studying in higher year groups (PASS Leaders). The aims of PASS sessions are to provide a safe community for students to discuss ideas, resolve questions and solve problems with academic or study-skills content (Sole et al., 2012). Therefore, PASS sessions should run separately from, but concurrently with the curriculum so that students can negotiate session themes or topics that will support academic achievement. Furthermore, PASS aims to promote collaboration between peers, building a sense of connectedness (Van der Meer & Scott, 2009).

Prior to the COVID-19 pandemic, the authors of the current chapter had successfully run the PASS scheme within their organisation. PASS was shown to build student connectedness and in turn assist in desirable academic outcomes and student experiences. Therefore, the authors identified an opportunity to maintain student connectedness under COVID-19 remote learning, by shifting the PASS scheme from face-to-face, in-person sessions, to peer-led online community groups using the PASS ethos. The peer-led online community groups ran once a week using Zoom as the virtual classroom. The authors recruited leaders from senior years to facilitate the online community groups and the cohort identified themes or topics to discuss in session. Leaders were encouraged to write a bio alongside their session Zoom links so that students could choose to attend a community group that reflected their learner needs. For example, a range of leader profiles were recruited based on ensuring a range of gender, age and student profiles (traditional/non-traditional) were available to learners. Palloff and Pratt (2007) highlight that there are limitations to implementing effective methods of delivery from face-to-face to online situations. Therefore, the authors reviewed the effectiveness of the peer-led community groups at weekly intervals by conducting focus groups with the peer-led community group leaders. Themes across the focus groups were: 1) community group leader identity is important when building connections, 2) presenteeism is important when building connections, 3) autonomy has implications for attendance, 4) usability and accessibility mediate the perception of community, and 5) students long for face-to-face interactions despite access to an online community.

The peer-led community group leaders consistently gained positive feedback from students when the cohort identified with the leader's student identity. The organisation in which the community groups were conducted consists of a diverse range of learner experiences including first-time university attendees, mature learners, learners with additional needs and learners with work, family and/or carer commitments. Students reported a positive experience and a feeling of connectedness when they identified a shared characteristic or experience with the group leader. Group leaders reported that this experience of shared identity resulted in increased academic self-efficacy amongst the cohort. It is recommended that students can opt into sessions where the leader biography matches their personal experiences in an attempt to facilitate connections. Tadal and Marino (2022) highlight that matching occurs when students recognise "shared similarities or commonalities", and further, that matching students increases feelings of belongingness or connectedness, in turn leading to a greater sense of wellbeing and academic achievement (Rubin & Guth, 2022).

Presenteeism, described by the online peer-led community group leaders, is defined as being both verbally and visually present in the online sessions. Leaders identified that when students were absent in term of their audio or video presence, other students reported feelings of disconnection (i.e. feeling isolated in group discussions when some students attended with their cameras off or engaged in discussions via the chat feature as opposed to the audio feature). The peer-led online community group leaders encouraged students to attend with their camera and audio features on, yet some students explained feelings of heightened social anxiety and understandably opted to maintain attendance without audio and video presence. This approach to attendance was reported as having implications for how connected students were to one another and therefore problematic to building student connectedness. Peper and colleagues (2021) identified in their research that students often attend Zoom sessions by appearing unresponsive (e.g. without an active video and audio feature); the implications of this impact the nonverbal cues that are required to develop interactions between students. Body language, facial expressions and movement are essential visual feedback that encourage interaction; when their absence is coupled with an absence of auditory feedback, students experience academic and personal disconnect (Peper et al., 2021).

The peer-led online community groups ran concurrently with the curriculum, outside of scheduled classes. Therefore, students could choose to opt in or out of the community group sessions. This autonomy led to a low uptake as many students were unable to attend due to work and family commitments. Due to this attendance issue, it is recommended that community groups are embedded within timetabled sessions as a value-added curriculum resource. Goulas, Griselda and Megalokonomou (2021) identified that when high-achieving students were given autonomy over their attendance, their performance increased. In addition, Ma and colleagues (2020) highlight that giving students an option to attend structured sessions promotes autonomous learning ability. Yet, when students were given autonomy, their attendance subsequently dipped and the opportunity to develop connections was missed.

The peer-led online community groups were administered to students at the start of the COVID-19 pandemic lockdown, so to many students the concept of Zoom was still novel. Subsequently, navigation of the interaction between Moodle and Zoom was complex for some students, which in turn impacted the accessibility of the group sessions. Not only this, personal internet connections were at times limited, again impacting access to the sessions. Findings from the current review identified consistency with previous research that suggests many students will have experienced online learning for the first time under COVID-19 lockdown regulations, suggesting that competencies and accessibility were low for many students. When students are well trained in using and accessing online learning resources, satisfaction is high (Lei & So, 2021).

Finally, although students reported a sense of connection with other students when engaging with the online community groups, students expressed that this was no reflection of the face-to-face interactions they had traditionally experienced in the educational setting. Students explained that their home environments lacked the formal education structure and thus impacted on the environmental cues and symbols that were needed to motivate peer-to-peer relationship development. In addition, students expressed feelings of physical and psychological distance. The physical closeness experienced in face-to-face environments allowed students to recognise non-verbal communication that aids in the establishment of relationships. It has been recommended that digital communities use virtual reality classrooms that mimic the face-to-face environment and allow students to identify non-verbal communication. Zou, Zhao and Siau (2020) identified that of the 14,000 undergraduate and graduate students surveyed, some stated that online lessons are not as effective as in person face-to-face lessons. The sudden switch from in-person to online teaching as a result of COVID-19 lockdown regulations has been associated with this negative perception (Lei & So, 2021).

References

Alemany-Arrebola, I., Rojas-Ruiz, G., Granda-Vera, J., & Mingorance-Estrada, Á. C. (2020). Influence of COVID-19 on the perception of academic self-efficacy, state anxiety, and trait anxiety in college students. *Frontiers in Psychology*, 11, 570017.

Allen, J., Robbins, S. B., Casillas, A., & Oh, I. (2008). Third-year college retention and transfer: Effects of academic performance, motivation, and social connectedness. *Research in Higher Education*, 49(7), 647–664.

Aristovnik, A., Keržič, D., Ravšelj, D., Tomaževič, N., & Umek, L. (2020). Impacts of the COVID-19 pandemic on life of higher education students: A global Perspective. *Sustainability*, 12(20), 8438.

Arslan, G. (2021). Loneliness, college belongingness, subjective vitality, and psychological adjustment during coronavirus pandemic: Development of the College Belongingness Questionnaire. *Journal of Positive School Psychology*, 5(1), 17–31.

Barbarick, D. (2013). *Connectedness: A Phenomenological Study of the Social Experiences of Adult Learners in an Online Course.* [Unpublished doctoral dissertation].

Barnard, L., Paton, V. O., & Rose, K. (2007). Perceptions of online course communications and collaboration. *Online Journal of Distance Learning Administration*, 10(4).

Beller, J., & Wagner, A. (2018). Loneliness, social isolation, their synergistic interaction, and mortality. *Health Psychology*, 37(9), 808–813.

Bridgstock, R., & Tippett, N. (2019). *Higher Education and the Future of Graduate Employability.* Edward Elgar Publishing: UK.

Brooman, S., & Darwent, S. (2014). Measuring the beginning: A quantitative study of the transition to higher education. *Studies in Higher Education*, 39(9), 1523–1541.

Cai, S., & Zhu, W. (2012). The impact of an online learning community project on university Chinese as a foreign language students' motivation. *Foreign Language Annals*, 45(3), 307–329.

Dewiyanti, S., Brand-Gruwel, S., Jochems, W., & Broers, N. J. (2007). Students' experiences with collaborative learning in asynchronous computer-supported collaborative learning environments. *Computers in Human Behavior*, 23(1), 496–514.

Doscher, S., Prior, C., & de Wit, H. (2022). *The Guide to COIL Virtual Exchange: Implementing, Growing, and Sustaining Collaborative Online International Learning.* Stylus Publishing, LLC.

Fink, J. E. (2014). Flourishing: Exploring predictors of mental health within the college environment. *Journal of American College Health,* 62(6), 380–388.

Flynn, D. (2014). Baccalaureate attainment of college students at 4-year institutions as a function of student engagement behaviors: Social and academic student engagement behaviors matter. *Research in Higher Education,* 55(5), 467–493.

Frisby, B. N., Hosek, A. M., & Beck, A. C. (2020). The role of classroom relationships as sources of academic resilience and hope. *Communication Quarterly,* 68(3), 289–305.

Gazica, M. W., Leto, G. D., & Irish, A. L. (2022). The effects of unexpected changes to content delivery on student learning outcomes: A psychological contract perspective during the COVID-19 era. *Psychology in the Schools,* 59, 1473–1491.

Goulas, S., Griselda, S., & Megalokonomou, R. (2021). Compulsory Class Attendance versus Autonomy. Available from: SSRN 4074761.

Huynh, J. Y. (2012). The Psychology of Volunteering: An In-Depth Examination of the Job Demands-Resources Model in the Volunteer Workforce. [Unpublished doctoral dissertation].

Jamison, T. E., & Bolliger, D. U. (2020). Student perceptions of connectedness in online graduate business programs. *Journal of Education for Business,* 95(5), 275–287.

Kiely, K. M., Sutherland, G., Butterworth, P., & Reavley, N. J. (2021). Age and gender differences in the reciprocal relationship between social connectedness and mental health. *Social Psychiatry and Psychiatric Epidemiology,* 56(6), 1069–1081.

Kramer, G. (2017). *Building Connectedness in the Classroom and on Campus: A Look at McGill University's Architecture and Infrastructure.* Available from: http://www.socialconnectedness.org.

Kuong, H. C. (2015). Enhancing online learning experience: From learners' perspective. *Procedia-Social and Behavioral Sciences,* 191, 1002–1005.

Kwan, J. (2022). Academic burnout, resilience level, and campus connectedness among undergraduate students during the Covid-19 pandemic: Evidence from Singapore. *Journal of Applied Learning and Teaching,* 5 (Sp. Iss. 1), 52–63.

Lambrinidis, G. (2014). Supporting online, non-traditional students through the introduction of effective e-learning tools in a pre-university tertiary enabling programme. *Journal of Higher Education Policy and Management*, 36(3), 257–267.

Laux, D., Luse, A., & Mennecke, B. E. (2016). Collaboration, connectedness, and community: An examination of the factors influencing student persistence in virtual communities. *Computers in Human Behavior*, 57, 452–464.

Lee, R. M., & Robbins, S. B. (1995). Measuring belongingness: The social connectedness and the social assurance scales. *Journal of Counseling Psychology*, 42(2), 232–241.

Lei, S. I., & So, A. S. I. (2021). Online teaching and learning experiences during the COVID-19 pandemic–A comparison of teacher and student perceptions. *Journal of Hospitality & Tourism Education*, 33(3), 148–162.

Lucas, R., & James, A. I. (2018). An evaluation of specialist mentoring for university students with autism spectrum disorders and mental health conditions. *Journal of Autism and Developmental Disorders*, 48(3), 694–707.

Ma, L., Bai, H., Dai, Q., & Wang, H. (2020). Practice and thinking of online teaching during epidemic period. In *2020 15th International Conference on Computer Science & Education (ICCSE)*, 568–571.

Maina, E. M., Wagacha, P. W., & Oboko, R. O. (2017). Enhancing active learning pedagogy through online collaborative learning. *Artificial Intelligence: Concepts, Methodologies, Tools, and Applications* (1031–1054). IGI Global.

Melkun, C. H. (2012). Nontraditional students online: Composition, collaboration, and community. *The Journal of Continuing Higher Education*, 60(1), 33–39.

O'Keeffe, P. (2020). The case for engaging online tutors for supporting learners in higher education in refugee contexts. *Research in Learning Technology*, 28, 2428.

Palloff, R. M., & Pratt, K. (2007). *Building Online Learning Communities: Effective Strategies for the Virtual Classroom*. John Wiley & Sons: San Francisco.

Peper, E., Wilson, V., Martin, M., Rosegard, E., & Harvey, R. (2021). Avoid Zoom fatigue, be present and learn. *NeuroRegulation*, 8(1), 47–56.

Rubin, J., & Guth, S. (eds.) (2022). *The Guide to COIL Virtual Exchange*. Virginia: Stylus Publishing.

Sahu, P. (2020). Closure of universities due to coronavirus disease 2019 (COVID-19): impact on education and mental health of students and academic staff. *Cureus*, 12(4): e7541.

Sole, G., Rose, A., Bennett, T., Jaques, K., Rippon, Z., & van der Meer, J. (2012). A student experience of peer assisted study sessions in physiotherapy. *Journal of Peer Learning*, 5(1), 42–51.

Sollitto, M., Johnson, Z. D., & Myers, S. A. (2013). Students' perceptions of college classroom connectedness, assimilation, and peer relationships. *Communication Education*, 62(3), 318–331.

Stahl, G. (2013). Theories of cognition in collaborative learning. *The International Handbook of Collaborative Learning*, 74–90.

Tadal, S., & Marino, M. (2022). MATCHING STUDENTS. *The Guide to COIL Virtual Exchange: Implementing, Growing, and Sustaining Collaborative Online International Learning*, 95.

Thomas, L., Orme, E., & Kerrigan, F. (2020). Student loneliness: The role of social media through life transitions. *Computers & Education*, 146, 103754.

Tinto, V. (1998). Colleges as communities: Taking research on student persistence seriously. *The Review of Higher Education*, 21(2), 167–177.

Tinto, V. (2005). *College Student Retention: Formula for Student Success*. Greenwood publishing group: USA.

Tinto, V. (2012). *Leaving College: Rethinking the Causes and Cures of Student Attrition*. USA: University of Chicago Press.

Van der Meer, J., & Scott, C. (2009). Students' experiences and perceptions of peer assisted study sessions: Towards ongoing improvement. *Journal of Peer Learning*, 2(1), 3–22.

Whitlock, J., Wyman, P. A., & Barreira, P. (2012). *Connectedness and Suicide Prevention in College Settings: Directions and Implications for Practice*. Ithaca, NY: Brofenbrenner Center for Translational Research, Cornell University, 1–34.

Wiederhold, B. K. (2020). Connecting through technology during the coronavirus disease 2019 pandemic: Avoiding "Zoom Fatigue". *Cyberpsychology, Behavior, and Social Networking*, 23(7), 437–438.

Zhao, L. (2002). Interactive television in distance education: Benefits and compromises. In *IEEE 2002 International Symposium on Technology and Society (ISTAS'02). Social Implications of Information and Communication Technology. Proceedings* (Cat. no. 02CH37293), 255–261.

Zou, C., Zhao, W., & Siau, K. (2020). COVID-19 pandemic: A usability study on platforms to support eLearning. In *International Conference on Human-Computer Interaction*, 333–340.

Compilation of References

Abusalim, N., Rayyan, M., Jarrah, M., & Sharab, M. (2020). Institutional adoption of blended learning on a budget. *International Journal of Educational Management*, 34(7), 1203–1220. https://doi.org/10.1108/IJEM-08-2019-0326

Aidoo, B., Macdonald, M. A., Vesterinen, V. M., Pétursdóttir, S., & Gísladóttir, B. (2022). Transforming Teaching with ICT Using the Flipped Classroom Approach: Dealing with COVID-19 Pandemic. *Education Sciences*, 12(6), 421.

Aitchison, C., Harper, R., Mirriahi, N., & Guerin, C. (2020). Tensions for educational developers in the digital university: Developing the person, developing the product. *Higher Education Research and Development*, 39(2), 171–184. https://doi.org/10.1080/07294360.2019.1663155

Al-Ani, W. T. (2013). Blended learning approach using moodle and student's achievement at Sultan Qaboos University in Oman. *Journal of Education and Learning*, 2(3), 96.

Al-Ayed, S. I., & Al-Tit, A. A. (2021). Factors affecting the adoption of blended learning strategy. *International Journal of Data and Network Science*, 5, 267–274. https://doi.org/10.5267/j.ijdns.2021.6.007Link

Al-Kumaim, N. H., Alhazmi, A. K., Mohammed, F., Gazem, N. A., Shabbir, M. S., & Fazea, Y. (2021). Exploring the impact of the COVID-19 pandemic on university students' learning life: An integrated conceptual motivational model for sustainable and healthy online learning. *Sustainability*, 13(5), 2546.

Alemany-Arrebola, I., Rojas-Ruiz, G., Granda-Vera, J., & Mingorance-Estrada, Á. C. (2020). Influence of COVID-19 on the perception of academic self-efficacy, state anxiety, and trait anxiety in college students. *Frontiers in Psychology*, 11, 570017.

Alexander, M. M. (2018). The flipped classroom: Engaging the student in active learning. *J. Legal Stud. Educ.*, 35, 277.

Ali, W. (2020). Online and remote learning in higher education institutes: A necessity in light of COVID-19 pandemic. *Higher education studies*, 10(3), 16–25.

Allen, J., Robbins, S. B., Casillas, A., & Oh, I. (2008). Third-year college retention and transfer: Effects of academic performance, motivation, and social connectedness. *Research in Higher Education*, 49(7), 647–664.

Almpanis, T., & Joseph-Richard, P. (2022). Lecturing from home: Exploring academics' experiences of remote teaching during a pandemic. *International Journal of Educational Research Open*, 3, 100133. https://doi.org/10.1016/j.ijedro.2022.100133

Angadi, N. B., Kavi, A., Shetty, K., & Hashilkar, N. K. (2019). Effectiveness of flipped classroom as a teaching–learning method among undergraduate medical students–An interventional study. *Journal of Education and Health Promotion*, 8.

Antunes, V. T., Armellini, A., & Howe, R. (2021). Academic staff perspectives on an institution-wide shift to active blended learning. *Italian Journal of Educational Technology*. https://doi.org/10.17471/2499-4324/1248

Arawi, T. (2010). Using medical drama to teach biomedical ethics to medical students. *Medical Teacher*, 32(5), e205-e210. Available from: https://doi.org/10.3109/01421591003697457

Aregbeyen, O. (2010). Students' perceptions of effective teaching and effective lecturer characteristics at the University of Ibadan, Nigeria. *Pakistan Journal of Social Sciences*, 7(2), 62–69.

Aristovnik, A., Keržič, D., Ravšelj, D., Tomaževič, N., & Umek, L. (2020). Impacts of the COVID-19 pandemic on life of higher education students: A global Perspective. *Sustainability*, 12(20), 8438.

Armstrong, P., & Freeston, M. (2006). Conceptualising and formulating cognitive therapy supervision. In N. Tarrier (ed.), *Case Formulation in Cognitive Behaviour Therapy* (349–371). London: Routledge.

Arora, S., Bhaukhandi, K., & Mishra, P. (2020). Coronavirus lockdown helped the environment to bounce back. *The Science of the Total Environment*, 742, 140573–140573.

Arslan, G. (2021). Loneliness, college belongingness, subjective vitality, and psychological adjustment during coronavirus pandemic: Development of the College Belongingness Questionnaire. *Journal of Positive School Psychology*, 5(1), 17–31.

Ashford-Rowe, K., Herrington, J., & Brown, C. (2014). Establishing the critical elements that determine authentic assessment. *Assessment & Evaluation in Higher Education*, 39(2), 205–222. doi:10.1080/02602938.2013.819566.

Ashwin, P. (2015). Seven myths of university teaching. *Times Higher Education* (26 February). Available from: https://www.timeshighereducation.com/comment/opinion/seven-myths-of-university-teaching/2018719.article [Accessed: 14 October 2022].

Aveyard, H. (2018). *Doing a literature review in health and social care: A practical guide.*

Bailey, D. R., & Lee, A. R. (2020). Learning from experience in the midst of COVID-19: Benefits, challenges, and strategies in online teaching. *Computer-Assisted Language Learning Electronic Journal*, 21(2), 178–198.

Bailey, J., Martin, N., Schneider, C., Vander Ark, T., Duty, L., Ellis, S., & Terman, A. (2013). Blended learning implementation guide 2.0. *Digital Shift.*

Balsam, J. S. (2019). Teaming up to Learn in the Doctrinal Classroom. *Journal of Legal Education*, 68(2), 261–283.

Barnard, L., Paton, V. O., & Rose, K. (2007). Perceptions of online course communications and collaboration. *Online Journal of Distance Learning Administration*, 10(4).

Baños, J., Lucena, M. I., Farré, M., & the Group for the Study of the Teaching Effectiveness of TV Series. (2019). The usefulness of TV medical dramas for teaching clinical pharmacology: A content analysis of house, M.D. *Educación Médica*, 20(5), 295–303. Available from: https://doi.org/10.1016/j.edumed.2018.07.011

Barbarick, D. (2013). *Connectedness: A Phenomenological Study of the Social Experiences of Adult Learners in an Online Course.* [Unpublished doctoral dissertation].

Beck, R. J. (2010). Teaching international law as a partially online course: The hybrid/blended approach to pedagogy. *International Studies Perspectives*, 11(3), 273–290.

Beller, J., & Wagner, A. (2018). Loneliness, social isolation, their synergistic interaction, and mortality. *Health Psychology*, 37(9), 808–813.

Bennett-Levy, J. (2006). Therapist skills: a cognitive model of their acquisition and refinement. *Behavioural and Cognitive Psychotherapy*, 34, 57–78.

Bennett-Levy, J., McManus, F., Westling, B. E., & Fennell, M. (2009a). Acquiring and refining CBT skills and competencies: Which training methods are perceived to be most effective? *Behavioural and Cognitive Psychotherapy*, 37(5), 571–583.

Bennett-Levy, J., Thwaites, R., Chaddock, A., & Davis, M. (2009b). Reflective Practice in Cognitive Behavioural Therapy: The Engine of Lifelong Learning. In R. Dallos & J. Stedmon (eds.), *Reflective Practice in Psychotherapy and Counselling* (115–135). New York: Open University Press.

Bennett-Levy, J., Hawkins, R., Perry, H., Cromarty, P., & Mills, J. (2012). Online cognitive behavioural therapy (CBT) training for therapists: outcomes, acceptability, and impact of support. *Australian Psychologist*, 47, 174–182.

Ben-Porat, A., & Itzhaky, H. (2011). The contribution of training and supervision to perceived role competence, secondary traumatization, and burnout among domestic violence therapists. *Clinical Supervisor*, 30(1), 95–108.

Bergmann, J., & Sams, A. (2012). Before you flip, consider this. *Phi Delta Kappan*, 94(2), 25–25.

Bernard, H. R., & Bernard, H. R. (2013). *Social research methods: Qualitative and quantitative approaches*. Sage.

Bernard, J. M., & Goodyear, R. K. (2013). *Fundamentals of Clinical Supervision* (5th ed.). Boston, MA: Pearson Education.

Bersin, J. (2004). *The blended learning book: Best practices, proven methodologies, and lessons learned*. John Wiley and Sons.

Biggs, J. (2014). Constructive alignment in university teaching. *HERDSA Review of Higher Education* (Vol. 1).

Birgili, B., & Demir, Ö. (2022). An explanatory sequential mixed-method research on the full-scale implementation of flipped learning in the first years of the world's first fully flipped university: Departmental differences. *Computers & Education*, 176, 104352.

Bliss, M. (1999). *William Osler: a life in medicine*. Toronto: University of Toronto Press.

Bloxham, S. (2015). Assessing Assessment: New Developments in Assessment Design, Feedback Practices and Marking in Higher Education. In H. Fry, S. Ketteridge & S. Marshall (eds.), *A Handbook for Teaching and Learning in Higher Education* (4th ed.; 107–122). Abingdon: Routledge.

Bohannon, R. L., & Bohannon, S. M. (2015). Mentoring: A decade of effort and personal impact. *Teacher Leadership in Nonsupervisory Roles*, 81(2), 31–36.

Bokolo, A., Kamaludin, A., Romli, A., Mat Raffei, A. F., A/L Eh Phon, D. N., Abdullah, A., Leong Ming, G., Shukor, N. A., Shukri Nordin, M., & Baba, S. (2020). A managerial perspective on institutions' administration readiness to diffuse blended learning in higher education: Concept and evidence. *Journal of Research on Technology in Education*, 52(1), 37–64. https://doi.org/10.1080/15391523.2019.1675203

Boote, D. N., & Beile, P. (2005). Scholars before researchers: On the centrality of the dissertation literature review in research preparation. *Educational Researcher*, 34(6), 3–15.

Boud, D., & Walker, D. (1990). Making the most of experience. *Studies in Continuing Education*, 12(2), 61–80.

Bowden, J., Hart, G., King, B., Trigwell, K., & Watts, O. (2000). *Generic capabilities of ATN university graduates*. Canberra: Australian Government Department of Education, Training and Youth Affairs.

Boyle, R. A. (2003). Employing active-learning techniques and metacognition in law school: Shifting energy from professor to student. *U. Det. Mercy L. Rev.*, 81, 1.

BPS (2022). https://www.bps.org.uk/news/psychology-staff-overworked-and-under-supported-light-covid-19-reveals-new-findings.

Bridgstock, R. (2009). The graduate attributes we've overlooked: Enhancing graduate employability through career management skills. *Higher Education Research & Development*, 28(1), 31–44.

Bridgstock, R., & Tippett, N. (2019). *Higher Education and the Future of Graduate Employability*. Edward Elgar Publishing: UK.

Brooman, S., & Darwent, S. (2014). Measuring the beginning: A quantitative study of the transition to higher education. *Studies in Higher Education*, 39(9), 1523–1541.

Brush, T., & Saye, J. (2008). The effects of multimedia-supported problem-based inquiry on student engagement, empathy, and assumptions about history. *Interdisciplinary Journal of Problem-Based Learning*, 2(1), 21–56.

Büchele, S. (2021). Evaluating the link between attendance and performance in higher education: The role of classroom engagement dimensions. *Assessment & Evaluation in Higher Education*, 46(1), 132–150.

Buhl-Wiggers, J., Kjærgaard, A., & Munk, K. (2022). A scoping review of experimental evidence on face-to-face components of blended learning in higher education. *Studies in Higher Education*, 1–23.

Bunce, L., Baird, A., & Jones, S. E. (2017). The student-as-consumer approach in higher education and its effects on academic performance. *Studies in Higher Education*, 42(11), 1958–1978.

Burns, K., Keyes, M., Wilson, T., & Stagg-Taylor, J. (2017). Active learning in law by flipping the classroom: An enquiry into effectiveness and engagement. *Legal Education Review*, 27(1), 6100.

Cabinet Office (2020). [Online]. Available from: https://www.gov.uk/government/organisations/cabinet-office [Accessed: 18 July 2020].

Cai, S., & Zhu, W. (2012). The impact of an online learning community project on university Chinese as a foreign language students' motivation. *Foreign Language Annals*, 45(3), 307–329.

Cameron-Standerford, A., Menard, K., Edge, C., Bergh, B., Shayter, A., Smith, K., & VandenAvond, L. (2020). The Phenomenon of Moving to Online/Distance Delivery as a Result of COVID-19: Exploring Initial Perceptions of Higher Education Faculty at a Rural Midwestern University. *Front. Educ.*, 5:583881. doi: 10.3389/feduc.2020.583881

Capranos, D., Dyers, L., & Magd, A. J. (2021). *Voice of the online learner 2021: Amplifying Student Voices in Extraordinary Times*. A Wiley Education services Project [Online]. Available from: https://universityservices.wiley.com/voice-of-the-online-learner-2021 [Accessed: 18 July 2022].

Carrillo, C., & Assunção Flores, M. (2020). COVID-19 and teacher education: a literature review of online teaching and learning practices. *European Journal of Teacher Education*, 43:4, 466–487 [Online]. Available from: DOI: 10.1080/02619768.2020.1821184 [Accessed: 18 July 2022].

Cevikbas, M., & Kaiser, G. (2020). Flipped classroom as a reform-oriented approach to teaching mathematics. *Zdm*, 1–15.

Chao, C. Y., Chen, Y. T., & Chuang, K. Y. (2015). Exploring students' learning attitude and achievement in flipped learning supported computer aided design curriculum: A study in high school engineering education. *Computer Applications in Engineering Education*, 23(4), 514–526.

Chen, Y., Wang, Y., & Chen, N. S. (2014). Is FLIP enough? Or should we use the FLIPPED model instead?. *Computers & Education*, 79, 16–27.

Choi, Y.-W., Tuel, A., & Eltahir, E. A. B. (2021). On the environmental determinants of COVID-19 seasonality. GeoHealth, 5, e2021GH000413 [Online]. Available from: https:// doi.org/10.1029/2021GH000413 [Accessed: 18 July 2021].

Christensen, C. M., Horn, M. B., & Staker, H. (2013). Is K-12 Blended Learning Disruptive? An Introduction to the Theory of Hybrids. *Clayton Christensen Institute for Disruptive Innovation*.

Cifuentes, L. (2021). Course designs for distance teaching and learning. In *A Guide to Administering Distance Learning* (174–205). Brill.

Cirillo, V. J. (2014). Arthur Conan Doyle (1859–1930): Physician during the typhoid epidemic in the Anglo-Boer war (1899–1902). *Journal of Medical Biography*, 22(1), 2.

Cordingley, P., Bell, M., Thomason, S., & Firth, A. (2005). The impact of collaborative continuing professional development (CPD) on classroom teaching and learning. Review: How do collaborative and sustained CPD and sustained but not collaborative CPD affect teaching and learning.

Crammer, S. (2006). Enhancing graduate employability: Best intentions and mixed outcomes. *Studies in Higher Education*, 31(2), 169–184.

Cromarty, P., Drummond, A., Francis, T., Watson, J., & Battersby, M. (2016). NewAccess for depression and anxiety: Adapting the UK Improving Access to Psychological Therapies Program across Australia. *Australasian Psychiatry*, 24(5), 489–492.

Cromarty, P., Gallagher, D., & Watson, J. (2020). Remote delivery of CBT training, clinical supervision and services: In times of crisis or business as usual. *The Cognitive Behaviour Therapist*, 13.

Dahms, K., Sharkova, Y., Heitland, P., Pankuweit, S., & Schaefer, J. R. (2014). Cobalt intoxication diagnosed with the help of Dr House. *Lancet*, 383(9916), 574. Available from: https://doi.org/10.1016/S0140-6736(14)60037-4

Davenport, N. C., Spath, M. L., & Blauvelt, M. J. (2009). A step-by-step approach to curriculum review. *Nurse Educator*, 34(4), 181–185.

Day, C. (2002). *Developing teachers: The challenges of lifelong learning*. Routledge.

Deci, E. L., & Ryan, R. M. (2012). Motivation, personality, and development within embedded social contexts: An overview of self-determination theory. In R. M. Ryan (ed.), *Oxford Handbook of Human Motivation* (85–107). Oxford, UK: Oxford University Press.

Deepwell, M., & O'Sullivan, H. (2020). *Learning Technology in the age of COVID-19: Key findings from the 2020 Annual Survey*. Association for Learning Technology (ALT) 2020 Survey. Available from: https://www.alt.ac.uk/news/all_news/key-findings-our-annual-survey-202021 [Accessed: 20 July 2022].

Dewiyanti, S., Brand-Gruwel, S., Jochems, W., & Broers, N. J. (2007). Students' experiences with collaborative learning in asynchronous computer-supported collaborative learning environments. *Computers in Human Behavior*, 23(1), 496–514.

DFE (2021). Covid Guidelines Coronavirus (COVID-19) DfE 2021 qualifications funding: form guidance [Online]. Available from: https://www.gov.uk/government/publications/dfe-exam-support-service-claiming-costs/coronavirus-covid-19-dfe-2021-qualifications-funding-form-guidance [Accessed: 18 July 2022].

DH (2012). Liberating the NHS: No decision about me, without me. Government response [Online]. Available from: http://data.parliament.uk/DepositedPapers/Files/DEP2012-1873/LiberatingtheNHS-Nodecisionaboutmewithoutme.pdf [Accessed: 22 September 2022].

DHSC (2022). Ockenden review: summary of findings, conclusions and essential actions [Online]. Available from: https://www.gov.uk/government/publications/final-report-of-the-ockenden-review/ockenden-review-summary-of-findings-conclusions-and-essential-actions [Accessed: 22 September 2022].

Divjak, B., Rienties, B., Iniesto, F., Vondra, P., & Žižak, M. (2022). Flipped classrooms in higher education during the COVID-19 pandemic: findings and future research recommendations. *International Journal of Educational Technology in Higher Education*, 19(1), 1–24.

Dochy, F., & McDowell, L. (1997). Assessment as a Tool for Learning. *Studies in Educational Evaluation*, 23(4), 279–298. doi:10.1016/S0191-491X(97)86211-6.

Doctor in the House (1954). Available from: https://www.imdb.com/title/tt0046921/ [Accessed: 12 September 2022].

Doscher, S., Prior, C., & de Wit, H. (2022). *The Guide to COIL Virtual Exchange: Implementing, Growing, and Sustaining Collaborative Online International Learning*. Stylus Publishing, LLC.

Dougall, I., Weick, M., & Vasiljevic, M. (2021). Inside UK Universities: Staff mental health and wellbeing during the coronavirus pandemic. Project Report. Durham University.

Dreyfus, H. L., & Dreyfus, S. E. (1986). *Mind over machine: The power of human intuition and expertise in the age of the computer.* Oxford, United Kingdom: Basil Blackwell Publishing. DOI, 10, 0377-2217.

EDEN Conference (2021). [Online]. Available from: https://eden-europe.eu/eden-2021-annual-conference [Accessed: 24 November 2022].

Elton, L. (1998). Dimensions of excellence in university teaching. *International Journal for Academic Development*, 3(1), 3–11.

Emery, C., Kramer, T., & Tian, R. (2001). Customers vs. products: Adopting an effective approach to business students. *Quality Assurance in Education*, 9(2): 110–115.

Erlam, G. D., Garrett, N., Gasteiger, N., Lau, K., Hoare, K., Agarwal, S., & Haxell, A. (2021). What really matters: Experiences of emergency remote teaching in university teaching and learning during the COVID-19 pandemic. *Frontiers in Education (Lausanne)*, 6. https://doi.org/10.3389/feduc.2021.639842

Espeland, W. N., Sauder, M., & Espeland, W. (2016). *Engines of Anxiety: Academic Rankings, Reputation, and Accountability.* Russell Sage Foundation.

Evans, G. (2021, 10 January). How I memorised everything in law school: Digestible notes. Available from: https://digestiblenotes.com/law/legal_guides/memorise_everything_law_school.php [Accessed: 12 October 2022].

Fancourt, D., Steptoe, A., & Bu, F. (2020). *Trajectories of anxiety and depressive symptoms during enforced isolation due to COVID-19 in England: a longitudinal observational study* [Online]. Available from: https://discovery.ucl.ac.uk/id/eprint/10117860/. [Accessed: 21 July 2022].

Faragher, E. B., Cass, M., & Cooper, C. (2005). The Relationship between Job Satisfaction and Health: A Meta-Analysis. Journal of Occupational Environmental Medicine, 62, 105–112 [Online]. Available from: http://dx.doi.org/10.1136/oem.2002.006734 [Accessed: 21 July 2022].

Fink, J. E. (2014). Flourishing: Exploring predictors of mental health within the college environment. *Journal of American College Health*, 62(6), 380–388.

Finlay, M. J., Simpson, T., & Tinnion, D. J. (2022). Association between attendance, online course activity time, and grades: Analysis of undergraduate sport science cohorts during the COVID-19 pandemic. *Journal of Hospitality, Leisure, Sport & Tourism Education*, 31, 100397.

Flynn, D. (2014). Baccalaureate attainment of college students at 4-year institutions as a function of student engagement behaviors: Social and academic student engagement behaviors matter. *Research in Higher Education*, 55(5), 467–493.

Fortin Lalonde, C. L. (2022). Educating for Meaningful Citizenship: A Critical Corpus Analysis of Public Education Policy in Canada (Doctoral dissertation, Carleton University).

Francis, R. (2013). Report of the Mid Staffordshire NHS Foundation Trust Public Inquiry [Online]. Available from: https://www.gov.uk/government/publications/report-of-the-mid-staffordshire-nhs-foundation-trust-public-inquiry [Accessed: 22 September 2022].

Frisby, B. N., Hosek, A. M., & Beck, A. C. (2020). The role of classroom relationships as sources of academic resilience and hope. *Communication Quarterly*, 68(3), 289–305.

Gadamer, H. G. (1976). *Hegel's Dialectic: Five Hermeneutical Studies*. Yale University Press.

Gazica, M. W., Leto, G. D., & Irish, A. L. (2022). The effects of unexpected changes to content delivery on student learning outcomes: A psychological contract perspective during the COVID-19 era. *Psychology in the Schools*, 59, 1473–1491.

Gersten, R., Morvant, M., & Brengelman, S. (1995). Close to the classroom is close to the bone: Coaching as a means to translate research into classroom practice. *Exceptional Children*, 62(1), 52–66.

Gibbs, G., Knapper, C., & Piccinin, S. (2009). *Departmental Leadership of Teaching in Research-Intensive Environments* (Ser. Research and Development Series). The Higher Education Academy.

Gladwin-Geoghegan, R., & Thompson, C. (2021). Legacy of Lockdown: Exploring the Opportunities for Development in Legal Education as a Consequence of the COVID-19 Pandemic. *Journal of Ethics and Legal Technologies*, 3(1).

Glesner, B. A. (1990). Fear and loathing in the law schools. *Conn. L. Rev.*, 23, 627.

Gough, L. A., Duffell, T., & Eustace, S. J. (2021). The impact of student attendance on assessment specific performance in sport degree programs. *Journal of Hospitality, Leisure, Sport & Tourism Education*, 29, Article 100323.

Goulas, S., Griselda, S., & Megalokonomou, R. (2021). Compulsory Class Attendance versus Autonomy. Available from: SSRN 4074761.

Gov.UK (2020). *Coronavirus Act 2020* [Online]. Available from: legislation.gov.uk [Accessed: 13 July 2022].

Gov.UK (2021). *Critical workers and vulnerable children who can access schools or educational settings – GOV.UK* [Online]. Available from: [Withdrawn] www.gov.uk [Accessed: 13 July 2022].

Graham, C. R., Allen, S., & Ure, D. (2003). Blended learning environments: A review of the research literature. *Unpublished manuscript, Provo, UT*.

Greatbatch, D., & Holland, J. (2016). *Teaching quality in higher education: Literature review and qualitative research*. Department for Business, Innovation and Skills.

Grey's Anatomy (n.d.). Available from: https://www.imdb.com/title/tt0413573/ [Accessed: 15 September 2022].

Grønlien, H. K., Christoffersen, T. E., Ringstad, Ø., Andreassen, M., & Lugo, R. G. (2021). A blended learning teaching strategy strengthens the nursing students' performance and self-reported learning outcome achievement in an anatomy, physiology and biochemistry course – A quasi-experimental study. *Nurse Education in Practice*, 52, 103046–103046. https://doi.org/10.1016/j.nepr.2021.103046

Gulikers, J. T., Bastiaens, T. J., & Kirschner, P. A. (2004). A five-dimensional framework for authentic assessment. *Educational technology research and development*, 52(3), 67–86.

Han, X., Wang, Y., & Jiang, L. (2019). Towards a framework for an institution-wide quantitative assessment of teachers' online participation in blended learning implementation. *The Internet and Higher Education*, 42, 1–12. https://doi.org/10.1016/j.iheduc.2019.03.003

Hartney, E., Melis, E., Taylor, D., Dickson, G., Tholl, B., Grimes, K., Chan, M., Van Aerde, J., & Horsley, T. (2022). Leading through the first wave of COVID: A Canadian action research study. *Leadership in Health Services*, 35(1), 30–45. https://doi.org/10.1108/LHS-05-2021-0042

Hegel, G. W. F. (1874). *The Logic of Hegel*. Clarendon Press.

Hegel, G. W. F. (1991). *Hegel: Elements of the Philosophy of Right*. Cambridge University Press.

Hegel, G. W. F., Burbidge, J., & Dickey, L. (1993). *The Cambridge Companion to Hegel*. Cambridge University Press.

Heinze, A. (2008). *Blended learning: An interpretive action research study*. University of Salford (United Kingdom).

Hess, G. F. (1999). Principle 3: Good practice encourages active learning. *Journal of Legal Education*, 49(3), 401–417.

Hewitt, A. (2015). Can you learn to lawyer online? A blended learning environment case study. *Law Teacher*, 49(1), 92–121.

Hirt, C., Wong, K., Erichsen, S., & White, J. S. (2013). Medical dramas on television: A brief guide for educators. *Medical Teacher*, 35(3), 237–242. Available from: https://doi.org/10.3109/0142159X.2012.737960

Hong, K. H., & Samimy, K. K. (2010). The influence of L2 teachers' use of CALL modes on language learners' reactions to blended learning. *Calico Journal*, 27(2), 328.

House (n.d.). Available from: https://www.imdb.com/title/tt0412142/ [Accessed: 12 September 2022].

House Trivia. (n.d.). Available from: https://www.imdb.com/title/tt0412142/trivia/ [Accessed: 12 September 2022].

Howard, J. (2010). The value of ethnic diversity in the teaching profession: A New Zealand case study. *International Journal of Education*, 2(1), 1.

Howell, R. A. (2021). Engaging students in education for sustainable development: The benefits of active learning, reflective practices and flipped classroom pedagogies. *Journal of Cleaner Production*, 325, 129318.

Hughes, C., & Barrie, S. (2010). Influences on the assessment of graduate attributes in higher education. *Assessment & Evaluation in Higher Education*, 35(3), 325–334.

Huynh, J. Y. (2012). The Psychology of Volunteering: An In-Depth Examination of the Job Demands-Resources Model in the Volunteer Workforce. [Unpublished doctoral dissertation].

Imperial War Museum (2022). Turing Enigma for an example [Online]. Available from: https://www.iwm.org.uk/history/how-alan-turing-cracked-the-enigma-code [Accessed: 22 September 2022].

Jafari, A. (2004). The 'sticky' ePortfolio system: Tackling challenges and identifying attribute. *EDUCAUSE Review*, 39(4), 38–49.

James, A. J., Chin, C. K., & Williams, B. R. (2014). Using the flipped classroom to improve student engagement and to prepare graduates to meet maritime industry requirements: a focus on maritime education. *WMU Journal of Maritime Affairs*, 13(2), 331–343.

James, N., & Thériault, V. (2020). Adult education in times of the COVID-19 pandemic: Inequalities, changes, and resilience. *Studies in the Education of Adults*, 52(2020): 129–133

[Online]. Available from: https://www.tandfonline.com/doi/full/10.1080/02660830.2020.1811474 [Accessed: 13 July 2022].

Jamison, T. E., & Bolliger, D. U. (2020). Student perceptions of connectedness in online graduate business programs. *Journal of Education for Business*, 95(5), 275–287.

Javier, C. (2020). The shift towards new teaching modality: Examining the attitude and technological competence among language teachers teaching Filipino. *Asian ESP*, 16(2.1), 210–244.

Jeffrey, L. M., Milne, J., Suddaby, G., & Higgins, A. (2014). Blended learning: How teachers balance the blend of online and classroom components. *Journal of Information Technology Education*, 13.

Jerrentrup, A., Mueller, T., Glowalla, U., Herder, M., Henrichs, N., Neubauer, A., & Schaefer, J. R. (2018). Teaching medicine with the help of 'Dr. House'. *PloS One*, 13(3), e0193972. Available from: https://doi.org/10.1371/journal.pone.0193972

Jia, C., Hew, K. F., Bai, S., & Huang, W. (2022). Adaptation of a conventional flipped course to an online flipped format during the Covid-19 pandemic: Student learning performance and engagement. *Journal of Research on Technology in Education*, 54(2), 281–301.

JISC. Learning and teaching reimagined. August 2020. https://www.jisc.ac.uk/learning-and-teaching-reimagined

Jones, A. (2009a). Generic attributes as espoused theory: The importance of context. *Higher Education*, 58(2), 175–191.

Jones, A. (2009b). Re-disciplining generic attributes: The disciplinary context in focus. *Studies in Higher Education*, 34(1), 85–100.

Jones, A. (2013). There is nothing generic about graduate attributes: unpacking the scope of context. *Journal of Further and Higher Education*, 37(5), 591–605.

Jones, K. A., & Ravishankar, S. (2021). *Higher Education 4.0: The Digital Transformation of Classroom Lectures to Blended Learning*. Springer Nature.

Jorre de St Jorre, T., & Oliver, B. (2018). Want students to engage? Contextualise graduate learning outcomes and assess for employability. *Higher Education Research & Development*, 37(1), 44–57.

Kafer, K. (2013). *The rise of K-12 blended learning in Colorado*. IP-5-2013). Denver, CO: Independence Institute.

Kaplarević-Mališić, A., Dimitrijević, S., Radojevic, I., & Kovačević, M. (2022). Developing Teaching Competencies for Implementing Blended Learning in Higher Education: Experiences of Faculty of Science, University of Kragujevac. In *Proceedings TIE 2022 9th International Scientific Conference Technics and Informatics in Education*. University of Kragujevac, Faculty of Technical Sciences, Čačak.

Kara, A. (2021). Covid-19 pandemic and possible trends into the future of higher education: A review. *Journal of Education and Educational Development*, 8(1). Available from: https://doi.org/10.22555/joeed.v8i1.183 [Accessed: 22 September 2022].

Kay, R., MacDonald, T., & DiGiuseppe, M. (2019). A comparison of lecture-based, active, and flipped classroom teaching approaches in higher education. *Journal of Computing in Higher Education*, 31(3), 449–471.

Kennedy, A. (2005). Models of continuing professional development: A framework for analysis. *Journal of In-service Education*, 31(2), 235–250.

Kerns, B. R. (2019). A case study of a flipped curriculum using collaborative and active learning with an adaptive learning system (Doctoral dissertation, Indiana State University).

Keyes, M., & Johnstone, R. (2004). Changing legal education: rhetoric, realty, and prospects for the future. *Sydney L. Rev.*, 26, 537.

Khayat, D., & Osama, S. (2022). The impact of using flipped mobile learning in continuing professional development to develop electronic lecture skills among female university teachers in the kingdom of Saudi Arabia (Doctoral dissertation, University of Southampton).

Kiely, K. M., Sutherland, G., Butterworth, P., & Reavley, N. J. (2021). Age and gender differences in the reciprocal relationship between social connectedness and mental health. *Social Psychiatry and Psychiatric Epidemiology*, 56(6), 1069–1081.

Kim, L. E., & Asbury, K. (2020). 'Like a rug had been pulled from under you': The impact of COVID-19 on teachers in England during the first six weeks of the UK lockdown. *British Journal of Educational Psychology*, 90(4), 1062–1083. https://doi.org/10.1111/bjep.12381 [Accessed: 11 June 2022].

Kim, L. E., Oxley, L., & Asbury, K. (2021). 'My brain feels like a browser with 100 tabs open': A longitudinal study of teachers' mental health and well-being during the COVID-19 pandemic. *Br J Educ Psychol*, 92(1), 299–318. doi: 10.1111/bjep.12450. Epub 2021 Aug 1. PMID: 34337737; PMCID: PMC8420299 [Accessed: 11 June 2022].

Kirpalani, A., Grimmer, J., & Peebles, E. R. (2020). A Blended Model of Case-Based Learning in a Paediatric Clerkship Program. *Medical Science Educator*, 30(1), 23–24.

Kitchenham, A. (2005). Adult-Learning Principles, Technology and Elementary Teachers and their Students: the perfect blend? *Education, Communication and Information*, 5(3), 285–302.

Kliger, D., & Pfeiffer, E. (2011). Engaging students in blended courses through increased technology. *Journal of Physical Therapy Education*, 25(1), 11–14.

Knight, P., & Page, A. (2007). The assessment of 'wicked' competences: A report to the practice-based professional learning centre for excellence in teaching and learning in the Open University. Available from: http://www.open.ac.uk/cetl-workspace/cetlcontent/documents/460d21bd645f8.pdf [Accessed: 22 February 2009].

Koivu, A., Saarinen, P. I., & Hyrkas, K. (2012). Who benefits from clinical supervision and how? The association between clinical supervision and the work-related well-being of female hospital nurses. *Journal of Clinical Nursing*, 21(17–18), 2567–2578.

Kolb, D. A. (1984). *Experiential Learning: Experience as the Source of Learning and Development*. Englewood Cliffs, NJ: Prentice Hall.

Kop, R., & Hill, A. (2008). Connectivism: Learning theory of the future or vestige of the past? *International Review of Research in Open and Distance Learning*, 9(3).

Kramer, G. (2017). *Building Connectedness in the Classroom and on Campus: A Look at McGill University's Architecture and Infrastructure*. Available from: http://www.socialconnectedness.org.

Kuong, H. C. (2015). Enhancing online learning experience: From learners' perspective. *Procedia-Social and Behavioral Sciences*, 191, 1002–1005.

Kuyken, W., Padesky, C. A., & Dudley, R. (2009). *Collaborative Case Conceptualization: Working Effectively with Clients in Cognitive-Behavioral Therapy*. New York: Guilford.

Kwan, A. (2009). Problem-based learning. In *The Routledge International Handbook of Higher Education* (91–107).

Kwan, J. (2022). Academic burnout, resilience level, and campus connectedness among undergraduate students during the Covid-19 pandemic: Evidence from Singapore. *Journal of Applied Learning and Teaching*, 5 (Sp. Iss. 1), 52–63.

Kwong, K. (2013). TV medical dramas: pure entertainment or a useful teaching tool? *Healthydebate*. Available from: https://healthydebate.ca/2013/11/about-healthy-debate/opinions-about-healthy-debate/tv-medical-dramas-useful-teaching-tool/ [Accessed: 15 September 2022

Lambrinidis, G. (2014). Supporting online, non-traditional students through the introduction of effective e-learning tools in a pre-university tertiary enabling programme. *Journal of Higher Education Policy and Management*, 36(3), 257–267.

Lane, S. (2015). Information Age to Interaction Age in Legal Education: How Far Have We Progressed?. *American Journal of Educational Research*, 3(12), 1511–1518.

Laux, D., Luse, A., & Mennecke, B. E. (2016). Collaboration, connectedness, and community: An examination of the factors influencing student persistence in virtual communities. *Computers in Human Behavior*, 57, 452–464.

Law Vicissitudes. (2013). Ten things I wish I'd known before becoming a law student. *Guardian* (25 July).

Lee, R. M., & Robbins, S. B. (1995). Measuring belongingness: The social connectedness and the social assurance scales. *Journal of Counseling Psychology*, 42(2), 232–241.

Lei, S. I., & So, A. S. I. (2021). Online teaching and learning experiences during the COVID-19 pandemic–A comparison of teacher and student perceptions. *Journal of Hospitality & Tourism Education*, 33(3), 148–162.

Lewis, E. G., & Cardwell, J. M. (2019). A comparative study of mental health and wellbeing among UK students on professional degree programmes. *Journal of Further and Higher Education*, 43(9), 1226–1238. DOI: 10.1080/0309877X.2018.1471125.

Li, Q., Li, Z., & Han, J. (2021). A hybrid learning pedagogy for surmounting the challenges of the COVID-19 pandemic in the performing arts education. *Education and Information Technologies*, 26(6), 7635–7655.

Liu, W. C., Wang, C. K. J., Kee, Y. H., Koh, C., Lim, B. S. C., & Chua, L. L. (2014). College students' motivation and learning strategies profiles and academic achievement: a self-determination theory approach. *Educational Psychology*, 34(3), 338–353.

Lo, V. I. (2014). A Transnational Law Subject in the Australian Law Curriculum. *Bond L. Rev.*, 26, 53.

Low, M. C., Lee, C. K., Sidhu, M. S., Lim, S. P., Hasan, Z., & Lim, S. C. (2021). Blended learning to enhanced engineering education using flipped classroom approach: An overview. *Electronic Journal of Computer Science and Information Technology*, 7(1).

Lucas, R., & James, A. I. (2018). An evaluation of specialist mentoring for university students with autism spectrum disorders and mental health conditions. *Journal of Autism and Developmental Disorders*, 48(3), 694–707.

Lukas, B. A., & Yunus, M. M. (2021). ESL Teachers' Challenges in Implementing E-learning during COVID-19. *International Journal of Learning, Teaching and Educational Research*, 20(2), 330–348.

Ma, L., & Lee, C. S. (2021). Evaluating the effectiveness of blended learning using the ARCS model. *Journal of Computer Assisted Learning*, 37(5), 1397–1408.

Ma, L., Bai, H., Dai, Q., & Wang, H. (2020). Practice and thinking of online teaching during epidemic period. In *2020 15th International Conference on Computer Science & Education (ICCSE)*, 568–571.

MacDonald, J. (2008). *Blended learning and online tutoring: Planning learner support and activity design*. Gower Publishing, Ltd.

Mahavongtrakul, M. (2020, March 5). *Implementing Flipped Classrooms into Law School Pedagogy*. Available from: https://dtei.uci.edu/2020/03/05/implementing-flipped-classrooms-into-law-school-pedagogy/ [Accessed: 13 October 2022].

Maina, E. M., Wagacha, P. W., & Oboko, R. O. (2017). Enhancing active learning pedagogy through online collaborative learning. *Artificial Intelligence: Concepts, Methodologies, Tools, and Applications* (1031–1054). IGI Global.

Mali, D., & Lim, H. (2021). How do students perceive face-to-face/blended learning as a result of the Covid-19 pandemic?. *International Journal of Management Education*, 19(3), 100552.

Mani, N., Slevin, N., & Hudson, A. (2011). What three wise men have to say about diagnosis. *BMJ*, 343(7837), d7769. Available from: https://doi.org/10.1136/bmj.d7769

Mannix, K. (2017). *With the End in Mind: Dying, Death and Wisdom in an Age of Denial*. Glasgow: William Collins.

Marsh, H. (2014). *Do No Harm: Stories of Life, Death, and Brain Surgery*. London: Orion.

McFadyen, J., & Rankin, J. (2016). The Role of Gatekeepers in Research: Learning from Reflexivity and Reflection. *GSTF Journal of Nursing and Health Care*, 4(1), 82–88 [Online]. Available from: http://dl6.globalstf.org/index.php/jnhc/article/view/1745 [Accessed: 12 November 2022].

McGhee, P. (2020) The University of Bolton on Opening its Campuses and Protecting Quality and Standards. June. https://www.qaa.ac.uk/news-events/blog/university-of-bolton-opening-campuses-and-protecting-quality-and-standards

McGhee, P. (2022) 'Campus Plus' – An institutional model for success after Covid. April. https://www.qaa.ac.uk/en/news-events/blog/campus-plus-institutional-model-for-success

Means, B., Toyama, Y., Murphy, R., Bakia, M., & Jones, K. (2009). Evaluation of evidence-based practices in online learning: A meta-analysis and review of online learning studies.

Megahed, N., & Hassan, A. (2022). A blended learning strategy: Reimagining the post-Covid-19 architectural education. *Archnet-Ijar*, 16(1), 184–202. https://doi.org/10.1108/ARCH-04-2021-0081Link

Melkun, C. H. (2012). Nontraditional students online: Composition, collaboration, and community. *The Journal of Continuing Higher Education*, 60(1), 33–39.

Mielkov, Y., Bakhov, I., Bilyakovska, O., Kostenko, L., & Nych, T. (2021). Higher education strategies for the 21st century: philosophical foundations and the humanist approach. *Revista Tempos e Espaços em Educação*, 14(33), e15524. Available from: http://dx.doi.org/10.20952/revtee.v14i33.15524.

Mihai, A., Questier, F., & Zhu, C. (2021). The institutionalisation of online and blended learning initiatives in politics and international relations at European universities. *European Political Science*, 20(2), 359–377. https://doi.org/10.1057/s41304-020-00307-5

Milakovich, M. E., & Wise, J. M. (2019). Overcoming the digital divide: Achieving access, quality, and equality. In *Digital Learning*. Edward Elgar Publishing.

Milne, D. (2009). *Evidence-based Clinical Supervision: Principles and Practice* (1st ed.). Oxford: Blackwell.

Mirriahi, N., Alonzo, D., McIntyre, S., Kligyte, G., & Fox, B. (2015). Blended learning innovations: Leadership and change in one Australian institution. *International Journal of Education and Development using ICT*, 11(1).

Mishra, L., Gupta, T., & Shree, A. (2020). Online teaching-learning in higher education during lockdown period of COVID-19 pandemic. *International Journal of Educational Research Open*, 1, 100012.

MOD UK (2022). Phoenix damage repair instructional unit [Online]. Available from: https://www.royalnavy.mod.uk/our-organisation/bases-and-stations/training-establishments/hms-excellent/phoenix-damage-repair-instructional-unit

Moore, A. (2020). Evaluating factors for student success in a flipped classroom approach. *EAI Endorsed Transactions on e-learning*, 18(3), 1–11. Available from: https://doi.org/10.4108/eai.3-12-2020.167293.

Muhuro, P., & Kang'ethe, S. M. (2021). Prospects and pitfalls associated with implementing blended learning in rural-based higher education institutions in southern Africa. *Perspectives in Education*, 39(1), 427–441. https://doi.org/10.18820/2519593X/pie.v39.i1.26Link

Murray, I., Cianfrini, M., Clements, J., & Wilson-Rogers, N. (2019). Taxation, innovation and education: Reflections on a flipped lecture room. *J. Australasian Tax Tchrs. Ass'n*, 14, 122.

Neumeier, P. (2005). A closer look at blended learning—parameters for designing a blended learning environment for language teaching and learning. *ReCALL*, 17(2), 163–178.

NHS (2017). *Multi-professional framework for advanced clinical practice in England*. England: NHS. Available from: https://advanced-practice.hee.nhs.uk/multi-professional-framework-for-advanced-clinical-practice-in-england/ [Accessed: 15 September 2022].

NHS England (2022). Provisional publication of Never Events reported as occurring between 1 April and 31 July 2022. Published 8 September 2022 [Online]. Available from: https://www.england.nhs.uk/wp-content/uploads/2022 September Provisional-publication-NE-1-April-31-July-2022.pdf [Accessed: 22 September 2022].

NHS UK (2022). Anaphylaxis [Online]. Available from: https://www.nhs.uk/conditions/anaphylaxis/ [Accessed: 22 September 2022].

Nicol, D., Thomson, A., & Breslin, C. (2014). Rethinking Feedback Practices in Higher Education: A Peer Review Perspective. *Assessment & Evaluation in Higher Education*, 39(1): 102–122. doi:10.1080/02602938.2013.795518.

Nikitaki, S., Papadima-Sophocleous, S., & Nicolaou, A. (2022). From Face-to-face to Online Foreign Language Teaching: Capitalising on Lessons Learned During COVID-19. In *English as a Foreign Language in a New-Found Post-Pandemic World* (1–28). IGI Global.

Nižetić, S. (2020). Impact of coronavirus (COVID-19) pandemic on air transport mobility, energy, and environment: A case study. *International Journal of Energy Research*, 44(13), 10953–10961.

Nudzor, H. P. (2013). The big question: Why do change initiatives in education often fail to yield desired results. *Educational Futures*, 6(1), 79–94.

Nurwakhidah, A., & Suganda, A. D. (2022). Capacity Building in an Effort of Improving Blended Learning-Based Teacher Competence during Covid-19 Pandemic. *Tarbawi: Jurnal Keilmuan Manajemen Pendidikan*, 8(01), 121–128.

Oakes, J., Battersby, M., Pols, R., & Cromarty, P. (2007). Exposure therapy for problem gambling via videoconferencing. *Journal of Gambling Studies*, 24, 107–118.

O'Keeffe, P. (2020). The case for engaging online tutors for supporting learners in higher education in refugee contexts. *Research in Learning Technology*, 28, 2428.

Oliveira, G., Grenha Teixeira, J., Torres, A., & Morais, C. (2021). An exploratory study on the emergency remote education experience of higher education students and teachers during the COVID-19 pandemic. *British Journal of Educational Technology*, 52(4), 1357–1376.

Oliver, B. (2011). *Assuring graduate outcomes good practice report*. Sydney: Australian Learning and Teaching Council.

Oliver, B. (2015). *Assuring graduate capabilities: Evidencing levels of achievement for graduate employability*. Sydney: Office for Learning and Teaching.

Oliver, B., & Jorre de St Jorre, T. (2018). Graduate attributes for 2020 and beyond: recommendations for Australian higher education providers. *Higher Education Research & Development*, 1–16.

Olivier, J. (2011). *Accommodating and promoting multilingualism through blended learning* (Doctoral dissertation, North-West University).

Olokooba, I. N. (2015). Availability and Use of Computer-Based Instructional Materials (CIM) by Upper Basic Social Studies Teachers in Ilorin, Nigeria. *Nigeria Journal of Educational Foundations*, 14(1), 16–28.

Ololube, N. P., Ubogu, A. E., & Egbezor, D. E. (2007). ICT and distance education programs in a sub-Saharan African country: a theoretical perspective. *Journal of Information Technology Impact*, 7(3), 181–194.

Ololube, N. P. (ed.) (2015). *Handbook of Research on Enhancing Teacher Education with Advanced Instructional Technologies*. IGI Global.

Osguthorpe, R. T., & Graham, C. R. (2003). Blended learning environments: Definitions and directions. *Quarterly review of distance education*, 4(3), 227–233.

Padlet (2022). It's a beautiful day. Make something beautiful [Online]. Available from: www.padlet.com [Accessed: 22 September 2022].

Palloff, R. M., & Pratt, K. (2007). *Building Online Learning Communities: Effective Strategies for the Virtual Classroom*. John Wiley & Sons: San Francisco.

Palmer, R. E. (2008). *Ultimate leadership: winning execution strategies for your situation*. Pearson Prentice Hall.

Pardo, A., Gašević, D., Jovanovic, J., Dawson, S., & Mirriahi, N. (2018). Exploring student interactions with preparation activities in a flipped classroom experience. *IEEE Transactions on Learning Technologies*, 12(3), 333–346.

Parsons, D. (ed.) (2016). *Mobile and Blended Learning Innovations for Improved Learning Outcomes*. IGI Global.

Peper, E., Wilson, V., Martin, M., Rosegard, E., & Harvey, R. (2021). Avoid Zoom fatigue, be present and learn. *NeuroRegulation*, 8(1), 47–56.

Peterson, S. J., & Smith, G. T. (2019). Impulsigenic personality: Is urgency an example of the jangle fallacy? *Psychological Assessment*, 31(9), 1135–1144 [Online]. Available from: https://doi.org/10.1037/pas0000740 [Accessed: 2 November 2022].

Pokhrel, S., & Chhetri, R. (2021). A literature review on impact of COVID-19 pandemic on teaching and learning. *Higher Education for the Future*, 8(1), 133–141.

Pollock, L. (2021). *The Book About Getting Older*. UK: Penguin Random House.

Poon, J. (2013). Blended learning: An institutional approach for enhancing students' learning experiences. *Journal of Online Learning and Teaching*, 9(2), 271–288.

Price, D., Wagstaff, C. R., & Thelwell, R. C. (2022). Opportunities and considerations of new media and technology in sport psychology service delivery. *Journal of Sport Psychology in Action*, 13(1), 4–15.

Pritchard, A. (2007). *Effective teaching with internet technologies: Pedagogy and practice*. SAGE.

Pulido, M. L. (2012). The ripple effect: Lessons learned about secondary traumatic stress among clinicians responding to the September 11th terrorist attacks. *Clinical Social Work Journal*, 40(3), 307–315.

QAA in June 2020. Building a Taxonomy for Digital Learning. https://www.qaa.ac.uk/docs/qaa/guidance/building-a-taxonomy-for-digital-learning.pdf

Rabinowitz, F. E., Heppner, P. P., & Roehlke, H. J. (1986). Descriptive study of process and outcome variables of supervision over time. *Journal of Counselling Psychology*, 33(3), 292–300.

Radloff, A., de la Harpe, B., Scoufis, M., Dalton, H., Thomas, J., Lawson, A., … Girardi, A. (2009). *The B factor project: Understanding academic staff beliefs about graduate attributes*. Melbourne: ALTC.

Ramos-Sánchez, L., Esnil, E., Goodwin, A., Riggs, S., Touster, L. O., Wright, L. K., & Rodolfa, E. (2002). Negative supervisory events: Effects on supervision satisfaction and supervisory alliance. *Professional Psychology: Research and Practice*, 33(2), 197–202.

Rapanta, C., Botturi, L., Goodyear, P., Guàrdia, L., & Koole, M. (2021). Balancing technology, pedagogy and the new normal: Post-pandemic challenges for higher education. *Postdigital Science and Education*, 3(3), 715–742.

Rasheed, R. A., Kamsin, A., & Abdullah, N. A. (2020). Challenges in the online component of blended learning: A systematic review. *Computers and Education*, 144, 103701. https://doi.org/10.1016/j.compedu.2019.103701

Ravenscroft, B., Luhanga, U. (2018). Enhancing student engagement through an institutional blended learning initiative: A case study. *Teaching and Learning Inquiry*, 6(2), 97–114. https://doi.org/10.20343/teachlearninqu.6.2.8

Ravitz, P., & Silver, I. (2004). Advances in psychotherapy education. *Canadian Journal of Psychiatry*, 49(4), 230–237.

Raymond, J., Homer, C., Smith, R., & Gray, J. (2013). Learning through Authentic Assessment. An Evaluation of a New Development in the Undergraduate Midwifery Curriculum. *Nurse Education in Practice*, 13(5): 471–476. doi:10.1016/j.nepr.2012.10.006.

Reel, J. J. (2020). Leading During a Pandemic: Lessons Gleaned from Sport Psychology. *Journal of Clinical Sport Psychology*, 14(4), 325–329.

Reeve, J. (2009). Why teachers adopt a controlling motivating style toward students and how they can become more autonomy supportive. *Educational Psychology*, 44, 159–178.

Rehman, U., & Lakhan, M. A. S. A. (2021). A review on state of the art in flipped classroom technology a blended e-learning. *Int. J*, 9.

Reynolds, D. (2006). Teachers' continuing professional development: A new approach. In 20th Annual World International Congress for Effectiveness and Improvement.

Robinson, C., & Sebba, J. (2004). *A review of research and evaluation to inform the development of the new postgraduate professional development programme*. TTA/University of Sussex.

Roehling, P. V. (2017). *Flipping the College Classroom: An Evidence-based Guide*. Springer.

Rubin, E. (2007). What's Wrong with Langdell's Method, and What to Do About It. *Vand. L. Rev.*, 60, 609.

Rubin, J., & Guth, S. (eds.) (2022). *The Guide to COIL Virtual Exchange*. Virginia: Stylus Publishing.

Rudder, D. (1993). Dedication (A Praise Song) [Audio song]. Available from: https://open.spotify.com/track/5HzWV5eFVhjfuonmi8lpJC [Accessed: 15 September 2022].

Ryan, M. (2018). The Complicated Mind of Sherlock Holmes. *Line by Line: A Journal of Beginning Student Writing*, 4(2), article 4. Available from: https://ecommons.udayton.edu/lxl/vol4/iss2/4 [Accessed: 14 September 2022].

Ryan, R. M., & Deci, E. L. (2000). Self-determination theory and the facilitation of intrinsic motivation, social development and wellbeing. *American Psychologist*, 55(1), 68–78.

Şahin, M., & Kurban, C. F. (2019). *The New University Model: Flipped, Adaptive, Digital and Active Learning (FADAL)*. FL Global Publishing.

Sahu, P. (2020). Closure of universities due to coronavirus disease 2019 (COVID-19): impact on education and mental health of students and academic staff. *Cureus*, 12(4): e7541.

Salvador, R., Limon, M., Borromeo, C. M., Parinas, M. A., Manrique, L., de la Cruz, L., & Dalere, J. M. (2022). Exploring Technical-Vocational Education Teachers' Challenges and Adaptation Strategies in Teaching Courses Outside their Specializations. *Journal of Technical Education and Training*, 14(2), 34–48.

Sambell, K., McDowell, L., & Montgomery, C. (2013). *Assessment for Learning in Higher Education*. London: Routledge.

Sannicandro, K., De Santis, A., Bellini, C., & Minerva, T. (2021). Blended learning design for teaching innovation: University teachers' perceptions. *REM: Research on Education and Media*, 13(2), 36–45. https://doi.org/10.2478/rem-2021-0011

Santos, J., Figueiredo, A. S., and Vieira, M. (2019). Innovative pedagogical practices in higher education: An integrative literature review. *Nurse Education Today*, 72: 12–17.

Schinke, R., Papaioannou, A., Henriksen, K., Si, G., Zhang, L., & Haberl, P. (2020a). Sport psychology services to high performance athletes during COVID-19. *International Journal of Sport and Exercise Psychology*, 18(3), 269–272.

Schinke, R., Papaioannou, A., Maher, C., Parham, W. D., Larsen, C. H., Gordin, R., & Cotterill, S. (2020b). Sport psychology services to professional athletes: working through COVID-19. *International Journal of Sport and Exercise Psychology*, 18(4), 409–413.

Schön, D. (1983). *The Reflective Practitioner: How Professionals Think in Action*. New York: Basic Books.

Schraw, G., Brownlee, J. L., Olafson, L., & Brye, M. V. V. (2017). *Teachers' personal epistemologies evolving models for informing practice*. IAP, Information Age Publishing, Inc.

Scott, C. L. (2015). THE FUTURES of LEARNING 3: What kind of pedagogies for the 21st century? UNESCO Education Research and Foresight, Paris. [ERF Working Papers Series, No. 15].

Senekal, J. S., & Smith, M. R. (2022). Assessing the employability and employment destinations of professional psychology alumni. *South African Journal of Psychology*, 52(1), 11–22.

Serrano, D. R., Dea-Ayuela, M. A., Gonzalez-Burgos, E., Serrano-Gil, A., & Lalatsa, A. (2019). Technology-enhanced learning in higher education: How to enhance student engagement through blended learning. *European Journal of Education*, 54(2), 273–286.

Serrone, R. O., Weinberg, J. A., Goslar, P. W., Wilkinson, E. P., Thompson, T. M., Dameworth, J. L., Dempsey, S. R., & Petersen, S. R. (2018). Grey's Anatomy effect: television portrayal of patients with trauma may cultivate unrealistic patient and family expectations after injury. *Trauma Surgery & Acute Care Open*, 3(1), e000137. Available from: https://doi.org/10.1136/tsaco-2017-000137

Sharpe, R., Benfield, G., Roberts, G., & Francis, R. (2006). The undergraduate experience of blended e-learning: a review of UK literature and practice. *The higher education academy*, 1–103.

Shem, S. (1978). *The House of God*. New York: Richard Marek Publishers.

Silver, C., & Ballakrishnen, S. S. (2022). Where Do We Go from Here? International Students, Post-Pandemic Law Schools, and the Possibilities of Universal Design. *Can. J. Comp. & Contemp. L.*, 8, 313.

Singh, J., Steele, K., & Singh, L. (2021). Combining the Best of Online and Face-to-Face Learning: Hybrid and Blended Learning Approach for COVID-19, Post Vaccine, & Post-Pandemic World. *Journal of Educational Technology Systems*, 50(2), 140–171.

Singh, P., Thambusamy, R., & Ramly, M. (2014). Fit or Unfit? Perspectives of Employers and University Instructors of Graduates' Generic Skills. *Social and Behavioral Sciences*, 123, 315–324. Doi:10.1016/j.sbspro.2014.01.1429.

Slido (2022). Your go-to interaction app for hybrid meetings [Online]. Available from: https://www.slido.com/ [Accessed: 22 September 2022].

Sloman, M. (2007). Making sense of blended learning. *Industrial and commercial training*, 39(6), 315–318.

Slomanson, W. R. (2014). Blended learning: A flipped classroom experiment. *J. Legal Educ.*, 64, 93.

Smith, M. (2020). Integrating technology in contemporary legal education. *Law Teacher*, 54(2), 209–221.

Sole, G., Rose, A., Bennett, T., Jaques, K., Rippon, Z., & van der Meer, J. (2012). A student experience of peer assisted study sessions in physiotherapy. *Journal of Peer Learning*, 5(1), 42–51.

Sollitto, M., Johnson, Z. D., & Myers, S. A. (2013). Students' perceptions of college classroom connectedness, assimilation, and peer relationships. *Communication Education*, 62(3), 318–331.

Spencer, A. B. (2012). The law school critique in historical perspective. *Wash. & Lee L. Rev.*, 69, 1949.

Spurgeon, D. (2002). TV dramas may raise false hope of surviving heart attack. *BMJ*, 325(7361), 408. Available from: https://doi.org/10.1136/bmj.325.7361.408/f

Stahl, G. (2013). Theories of cognition in collaborative learning. *The International Handbook of Collaborative Learning*, 74–90.

Staker, H., & Horn, M. B. (2012). Classifying K-12 blended learning. *Innosight Institute.*

Stone, A. (2008). The holistic model for blended learning: A new model for K-12 district-level cyber schools. *International Journal of Information and Communication Technology Education (IJICTE),* 4(1), 56–71.

Sturm, S., & Guinier, L. (2007). The law school matrix: Reforming legal education in a culture of competition and conformity. *Vand. L. Rev.,* 60, 515.

Sudak, D. M., Codd, R. T., III, Ludgate, J., Sokol, L., Fox, M. G., Reiser, R., & Milne, D. L. (2016). *Teaching and supervising cognitive behavioral therapy.* Hoboken, NJ: John Wiley & Sons.

Sullivan, S. E., & Baruch, Y. (2009). Advances in career theory and research: A critical review and agenda for future exploration. *Journal of Management,* 35(6), 1542–1571.

Tabassum, A. (2021). A Comparative Analysis of Traditional Flipping Versus Virtual Flipping. *Journal of English Language Teaching and Applied Linguistics,* 3(4), 57–62.

Tadal, S., & Marino, M. (2022). MATCHING STUDENTS. *The Guide to COIL Virtual Exchange: Implementing, Growing, and Sustaining Collaborative Online International Learning,* 95.

Tashiro, J., & Hebeler, A. (2019, July). An adaptive blended learning health education model for families of a parent with serious medical problems. In *International Conference on Blended Learning* (59–71). Springer, Cham.

Tett, L. (2020). A response to Vol. 11, supplementary issue, 2020. *Concept,* 11(2), 1–3 [Online]. Available from: http://concept.lib.ed.ac.uk/article/view/4459/6043 [Google Scholar] [Accessed: 22 November 2022].

Thistlethwaite, J. E., Davies, D., Ekeocha, S., Kidd, J. M., MacDougall, C., Matthews, P., Purkis, J., & Clay, D. (2012). The effectiveness of case-based learning in health professional education. A BEME systematic review: BEME guide no. 23. *Medical Teacher,* 34(6), e421–e444. Available from: https://doi.org/10.3109/0142159X.2012.680939

Thomas, L., Orme, E., & Kerrigan, F. (2020). Student loneliness: The role of social media through life transitions. *Computers & Education,* 146, 103754.

Tinto, V. (1998). Colleges as communities: Taking research on student persistence seriously. *The Review of Higher Education,* 21(2), 167–177.

Tinto, V. (2005). *College Student Retention: Formula for Student Success*. Greenwood publishing group: USA.

Tinto, V. (2012). *Leaving College: Rethinking the Causes and Cures of Student Attrition*. USA: University of Chicago Press.

Tomas, L., Evans, N. S., Doyle, T., & Skamp, K. (2019). Are first year students ready for a flipped classroom? A case for a flipped learning continuum. *International Journal of Educational Technology in Higher Education*, 16(1), 1–22.

Törnquist, A., Rakovshik, S., Carlsson, J., & Norberg, J. (2018). How supervisees on a foundation course in CBT perceive a supervision session and what they bring forward to the next therapy session. *Behavioural and Cognitive Psychotherapy*, 46(3), 302.

Towfigh, E. V., Keesen, J., & Ulrich, J. (2022). Blended Learning und Flipped Classroom in der grundständigen Lehre. *ZDRW Zeitschrift für Didaktik der Rechtswissenschaft*, 9(2), 87–111.

Treleaven, L., & Voola, R. (2008). Integrating the development of graduate attributes through constructive alignment. *Journal of Marketing Education*, 30(2), 160–173.

Tucker, C. R. (2012). *Blended Learning in Grades 4–12: Leveraging the Power of Technology to create Student-centered Classrooms*. Corwin Press.

Turnbull, D., Chugh, R., & Luck, J. (2021). Transitioning to E-Learning during the COVID-19 Pandemic: How Have Higher Education Institutions Responded to the Challenge?. *Education and Information Technologies*, 26(5), 6401–6419.

Turpin, G., & Wheeler, S. (2011). *Supervision Guidance*. Department of Health: London.

University of Bolton. (2018). TIRI Conference 2018. University of Bolton. Available from: https://www.bolton.ac.uk/events/tiri [Accessed: 14 September 2020].

University of Bolton (2020). Coronavirus [Online]. Available from: https://www.bolton.ac.uk/coronavirus/ [Accessed: 24 November 2022].

University of Bolton Access and Participation Plan (2022). [Online]. Available from: Access and Participation | University of Bolton [Accessed: 12 June 2022].

University of Victoria (2022). [Online]. Available from: https://www.uvic.ca [Accessed: 13 June 2022].

Valantinaitė, I., & Sederevičiūtė-Pačiauskienė, Ž. (2020). The change in students' attitude towards favourable and unfavourable factors of online learning environments. *Sustainability (Basel, Switzerland), 12*(19), 7960. https://doi.org/10.3390/su12197960

Valenti, M., La Malfa, G., Tomassini, A., Masedu, F., Tiberti, S., & Sorge, G. (2014). Burnout among therapists working with persons with autism after the 2009 earthquake in L'aquila, Italy: A longitudinal comparative study. *Journal of Psychiatric and Mental Health Nursing, 21*(3), 234–240.

Valz, J. (2022). *An Examination of Pandemic Challenges Faced by Professors at Two Universities and the Need for Improved Technology Integration in Pre-service Teacher Preparation Programs* (Doctoral dissertation, Texas Wesleyan University).

van Caenegem, W. A., & Mundy, T. (2021). Special Report on Online Legal Education in Australia. Available from: SSRN 3951659.

Van Den Berg, H. A. (2018). Occam's razor: From Ockham's *via moderna* to modern data science. *Science Progress, 101*(3), 261–272. doi.org/10.3184/003685018X15295002645082

Van der Meer, J., & Scott, C. (2009). Students' experiences and perceptions of peer assisted study sessions: Towards ongoing improvement. *Journal of Peer Learning, 2*(1), 3–22.

Van der Werf, W. M., Slot, P. L., Kenis, P. N., & Leseman, P. P. M. (2021). Inclusive practice and quality of education and care in the Dutch hybrid early childhood education and care system. *International Journal of Child Care and Education Policy, 15*(1), 1–29.

van Klink, B., & de Vries, U. (eds.) (2016). *Academic Learning in Law: Theoretical Positions, Teaching Experiments and Learning Experiences*. Edward Elgar Publishing.

Vanaki, Z., & Memarian, R. (2009). Professional Ethics: Beyond the Clinical Competency. *Journal of Professional Nursing, 25*, 285–291. doi:10.1016/j.profnurs.2009.01.009.

Vargiu, P. (2022). Downsizing Teaching: The Case for Seminars as the Backbone of Law Degrees. *Asian Journal of Legal Education, 9*(1), 114–123.

Vaughan, N. (2014). Student engagement and blended learning: Making the assessment connection. *Education Sciences, 4*(4), 247–264.

Verghese, A. (2011). A doctor's touch [TED Talk]. Available from: https://www.ted.com/talks/abraham_verghese_a_doctor_s_touch?language=en [Accessed: 12 September 2022].

Vermeulen, F. (2017) Many Strategies Fail Because They're Not Actually Strategies. *Harvard Business Review*. November. https://hbr.org/2017/11/many-strategies-fail-because-theyre-not-actually-strategies

Villarroel, V., Bloxham, S., Bruna, D., Bruna, C., & Herrera-Seda, C. (2018). Authentic assessment: creating a blueprint for course design. *Assessment & Evaluation in Higher Education*, 43(5), 840–854.

Wallace, D. P., & van Fleet, C. J. (2012). Knowledge into action: Research and evaluation in library and information science: Research and evaluation in library and information science. ABC-CLIO.

Wang, A. K. J. (2017). The joy of learning: what is it and how to achieve it. *Exchange*, 1, 7–11.

Watson, J. (2008). Blended Learning: The Convergence of Online and Face-to-Face Education. Promising Practices in Online Learning. North American Council for Online Learning.

Watson, J., Murin, A., Vashaw, L., Gemin, B., & Rapp, C. (2013). Keeping Pace with K-12 Online and Blended Learning: An Annual Review of Policy and Practice. 10 Year Anniversary Issue. *Evergreen Education Group*.

Wehling, J., Volkenstein, S., Dazert, S., Wrobel, C., van Ackeren, K., Johannsen, K., & Dombrowski, T. (2021). Fast-track flipping: flipped classroom framework development with open-source H5P interactive tools. *BMC Medical Education*, 21(1), 1–10.

Wetchler, J. L., Trepper, T. S., McCollum, E. E., & Nelson, T. S. (1993). Videotape supervision via long-distance telephone. *American Journal of Family Therapy*, 21(3), 242–247.

White, T. L., & McBurney, D. H. (2012). *Research methods*. Cengage Learning.

Whitlock, J., Wyman, P. A., & Barreira, P. (2012). *Connectedness and Suicide Prevention in College Settings: Directions and Implications for Practice*. Ithaca, NY: Brofenbrenner Center for Translational Research, Cornell University, 1–34.

Wicclair, M. R. (2008). The pedagogical value of house, M.D. – can a fictional unethical physician be used to teach ethics? *American Journal of Bioethics*, 8(12), 16–17. Available from: https://doi.org/10.1080/15265160802478503

Wiederhold, B. K. (2020). Connecting through technology during the coronavirus disease 2019 pandemic: Avoiding "Zoom Fatigue". *Cyberpsychology, Behavior, and Social Networking*, 23(7), 437–438.

Wikipedia (2022). Fort Boyard game show [Online]. Available from: https://en.wikipedia.org/wiki/Fort_Boyard_(game_show) [Accessed: 22 September 2022].

Williams, R., Evans, L., & Alshareef, N. T. (2015). Using TV dramas in medical education. *Education for Primary Care*, 26(1), 48–49. Available from: https://doi.org/10.1080/14739879.2015.11494308

Williams, S. N., Armitage, C. J., Tampe, T., & Dienes, K. (2020). Public perceptions and experiences of social distancing and social isolation during the COVID-19 pandemic: a UK-based focus group study. *BMJ Open*, 10(7): e039334. doi: 10.1136/bmjopen-2020-039334. PMID: 32690752; PMCID: PMC7387310. Available from: https://pubmed.ncbi.nlm.nih.gov/32690752/ [Accessed: 13 June 2022].

Williamson, B. (2018). Three stages of student engagement in a flipped classroom environment. *Journal of Learning and Student Experience*, 1: 2.

Wind, J., & Rangaswamy, A. (2001). Customerization: The next revolution in mass customization. *Journal of Interactive Marketing*, 15(1), 13–32.

Wise, J. (2014). TV show House helped doctors spot cobalt poisoning. *BMJ* [Online], 348(feb06 9), g1424. Available from: https://doi.org/10.1136/bmj.g1424

Wolff, L. C., & Chan, J. (2016). *Flipped Classrooms for Legal Education* (Vol. 13). New York: Springer.

Yeigh, T., Sell, K., Lynch, D., Willis, R., Smith, R., Provost, S., & Turner, D. (2017). *Towards a Strategic Blend in Education: A review of the blended learning literature.* Lulu. com.

Yilmaz, Y., Durak, H. I., & Yildirim, S. (2022). Enablers and Barriers of Blended Learning in Faculty Development. *Cureus*, 14(3).

Yorke, M., & Knight, P. T. (2006). *Embedding Employability into the Curriculum.* Heslington, York: The Higher Education Academy.

Zain, F. M., & Sailin, S. N. (2020). Students' experience with flipped learning approach in higher education. *Universal Journal of Educational Research*, 8(10), 4946–4958.

Zainuddin, Z., Habiburrahim, H., Muluk, S., & Keumala, C. M. (2019). How do students become self-directed learners in the EFL flipped-class pedagogy? A study in higher education. *Indonesian Journal of Applied Linguistics*, 8(3), 678–690.

Zawilinski, L., Shattuck, J., & Hansen, D. (2020). Professional development to promote active learning in the flipped classroom: A faculty perspective. *College Teaching*, 68(2), 87–102.

Zhampeiis, K., Assanova, G., Toishybaeva, G., Saparbaeva, A., Orazbaeva, A., & Manapova, G. (2022). Academic Lectures: Communicative Approaches to Interactive Lectures in Today's Classroom. *Journal of Positive School Psychology*, 7545–7555.

Zhao, L. (2002). Interactive television in distance education: Benefits and compromises. In *IEEE 2002 International Symposium on Technology and Society (ISTAS'02). Social Implications of Information and Communication Technology. Proceedings* (Cat. no. 02CH37293), 255–261.

Zheng, W., Ma, Y. Y., & Lin, H. L. (2021). Research on blended learning in physical education during the covid-19 pandemic: A case study of Chinese students. *SAGE Open*, 11(4), 21582440211058196.

Zou, C., Zhao, W., & Siau, K. (2020). COVID-19 pandemic: A usability study on platforms to support eLearning. In *International Conference on Human-Computer Interaction*, 333–340.

www.ingramcontent.com/pod-product-compliance
Lightning Source LLC
Chambersburg PA
CBHW041137110526
44590CB00027B/4044